Workplace Skills

Locating Information

Career Readiness Preparation

Mc Graw Hill **Contemporary**

The **McGraw-Hill** Companies

www.mhcontemporary.com

 **Contemporary**

Send all inquiries to:
McGraw-Hill/Contemporary
130 East Randolph, Suite 400
Chicago, IL 60601

ISBN 978-0-07-657482-7
MHID 0-07-657482-2

4 5 6 7 8 9 QDB 16 15 14 13 12 11

Contents ▪ ▪

Introduction ▪ ▪ ▪

Today's employers want to know if you have the skills and knowledge needed to be productive in the 21ˢᵗ Century workplace. *Workplace Skills* is designed to help you to certify the career readiness skills that you already have and to help you to improve your skill levels for greater career success and mobility. By completing this series, you will be better prepared to take a career readiness test and receive a Career Readiness Certificate.

The *Workplace Skills* series provides instruction and practice in three skill areas identified by employers as holding the key to your success in more than 85 percent of current and emerging careers. These areas are: Applied Mathematics, Reading for Information, and Locating Information. The questions you are asked in each of these areas are taken from actual workplace situations. They are designed to help you to identify, understand, and solve problems that you may encounter on the job.

Each book contains lessons that include a step-by-step example to introduce the skill and *On Your Own* problems to practice the skill. The lessons in the book will guide you through progressively higher skill levels, from those needed for entry-level employment to those required in higher-level jobs. Foundational skills are listed in the *Remember!* notes included in each lesson. *Performance Assessment* problems with answers and explanations at the end of each skill level allow you to review and assess your mastery of the skills at that level. In each of the three subject areas, employers have determined the skill level required for a job, and you may ask for that information from your instructor.

Workplace Skills: Locating Information ▪ ■ ▪

In today's workplace, a great deal of information is presented through graphic formats such as tables, graphs, form letters, and invoices. In many instances you must be able use multiple graphics, such as flowcharts and diagrams, to determine how to perform your job functions. Employers need to know that employees have the skills needed to locate, understand, synthesize, and use job-related information when it is presented in various graphic formats.

Workplace Skills: Locating Information contains lessons that will help you develop and practice skills in understanding information presented graphically in realistic workplace scenarios.

Two-Step Approach ▪ ■ ▪

Knowing how to approach Locating Information problems will give you confidence when solving them. Though different problems require application of different skills, the problem-solving process can be summarized in two essential steps.

 Step 1 **Understand the Problem** ▪ ■ ▪

Before approaching any problem, you must be sure you understand what you are being asked to do. You can use the *Plan for Successful Solving* to help you organize the information presented in a problem and then plan how to solve it. The plan includes five questions:

Plan for Successful Solving	
What am I asked to do?	Determine what information you are being asked to find. This is usually found in the question posed at the end of the problem.
What are the facts?	Identify what information is shown in the graphic(s). Knowing how the information is organized will help you determine the graphic's purpose.
How do I find the answer?	Determine where within the graphic the answer can be found. Titles and labels often provide important clues.
Is there any unnecessary information?	Review the information from the problem and decide if any of it is not needed. Having a clear focus of what to look for can help.
What prior knowledge will help me?	Think about personal background knowledge and experience you have that might help you better understand the question and what steps are needed to find an answer.

Think and Ask Questions About Graphics

Solving a problem that requires you to locate information from graphics can be like decoding a message or solving a puzzle. You must determine what information is needed to answer the question. Below are four skills that you should use when reading documents that contain information presented graphically. For each skill, there are questions that will help you better understand information communicated through graphics.

Skill	Key Questions
Locate information from graphics	· What information does the graphic show? Does it communicate data, instructions, local information, or measurement readings? · How is the information organized? Are there titles, labels, or keys (legends) that help me understand what is being shown?
Identify trends from graphics	· Are there recognizable patterns that are shown in the graphic? · If the graphic is a graph, does it show an increasing or decreasing trend?
Draw conclusions from graphics	· What general assumptions can be made based on the graphic? · What comparisons can be made based on the data? · How should I interpret the graphic?
Apply information from graphics	· What information do I need from this graphic? How will I use it? · How does the information in this graphic or form help inform my decision-making in future situations?

 Step 2 Find and Check Your Answer ▪ ▪ ▪

Sometimes finding the right answer may require you to adjust your initial plan. It is important to review all answer choices to be sure that the answer you have selected is the best option. Once you have identified the best answer choice, it is a good idea to review the original question to be sure your understanding of what you are being asked to do is correct and that your answer makes sense. If you determine that your answer may be incorrect, you should look back at your plan and revise it. Then perform the steps needed to arrive at and check your revised answer.

The two-step approach to problem solving is an easy-to-follow model for you to use as you develop the confidence needed to successfully approach problems you will encounter both in the workplace and on a Career Readiness Certificate test. *Do not worry yet about memorizing the steps.* With practice, you will naturally learn and remember this extremely useful approach. Over time, learning this model and using it carefully in your preparation for the test will provide you with a reliable approach to problem solving.

Remember!

If necessary, revise your *Plan for Successful Solving.*
· Determine and apply your solution approach.
· Select the correct option.
· Check your answer.

Level 3 Introduction ▪ ▪ ▪

The lesson and practice pages that follow will give you the opportunity to develop and practice the reading and interpretation skills needed to answer work-related questions at a Level 3 rating of difficulty. The *On Your Own* practice problems provide review and practice of key skills needed for locating information from graphical sources in the workplace. These skills are applied through effective problem-solving approaches. The *Performance Assessment* provides problems similar to those you will encounter on a Career Readiness Certificate test. By completing the Level 3 *On Your Own* and *Performance Assessment* questions, you will gain the ability to confidently approach workplace scenarios that require understanding and application of the skills featured in the following lessons:

Lesson 1: Find Information in Graphics

Lesson 2: Add Missing Information to Graphics

These skills are intended to help you successfully use workplace graphics such as charts, tables, graphs, floor plans, flowcharts, instrument gauges, and forms. Finding or completing information in these types of graphics often requires the ability to:

- determine what information is being requested,
- identify where information is located within the graphic.

Through answering document-related questions at this level, you will begin to develop problem-solving approaches and strategies that will help you determine the correct answer in real-world and test-taking situations.

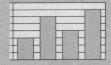
Lesson 1 ■ ■ ■
Find Information in Graphics

Skill: Find one or two pieces of information in a graphic

When you are on the job, you sometimes need to know how to locate and understand information that is presented in graphic forms, such as charts, tables, and graphs. What is the temperature indicated on a thermometer? Where in a job manual can you find information about a certain topic? This lesson will help you practice finding one or two pieces of information in different kinds of simple graphics.

Skill Example

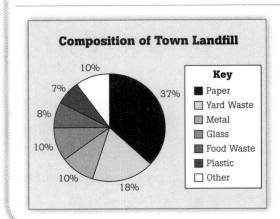

Composition of Town Landfill

Locate data within a circle, bar, or line graph.

A graph is a useful tool for taking a set of data and displaying it in a simple, easy-to-understand visual format. Most graphs have a title that tells what information is being shown. For circle graphs, a key often identifies the different categories of information being shown. Using the key on the graph to the left, you can see that paper is the largest waste in this town's landfill, more than double that of yard waste.

Regional Sales Managers		
Region	Contact	States
Northeast	Sandra Vasquez	CT, DC, DE, ME, MD, MA, NH, NJ, NY, PA, RI, VT
Southeast	Jane Park	AL, FL, GA, KY, LA, MS, NC, SC, TN, VA, WV
Midwest	Sal Gundy	IL, IN, IA, KS, MI, MN, MO, NE, ND, OH, SD, WI
Southwest	Colvin Taylor	AR, AZ, CO, NM, NV, OK, TX, UT
West	Mackenzie Carter	AK, CA, HI, ID, MT, OR, WA, WY

Skill Practice

Use the table to the left to answer the following questions.

1. You are a customer service representative. A customer in New Hampshire (NH) is interested in having her employees trained on your product. To which regional sales manager should you refer the customer?

   A. Sandra Vasquez

   B. Jane Park

   C. Sal Gundy

   D. Colvin Taylor

   E. Mackenzie Carter

2. As a warehouse manager, you have a question about a shipment being sent to customers in Nevada (NV). Which regional sales manager should you contact?

   F. Sandra Vasquez

   G. Jane Park

   H. Sal Gundy

   J. Colvin Taylor

   K. Mackenzie Carter

Try It Out! ■ ■ ■

You are an appliance installer delivering a stove to a studio apartment. Where in the apartment do you install the stove?

A. beside the TV

D. beside the dresser

B. between the dishwasher and the refrigerator

E. across from the kitchen door

C. beside the sink

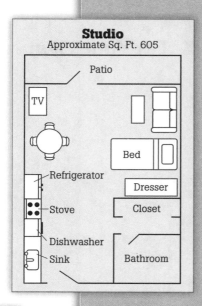

Studio
Approximate Sq. Ft. 605

Patio
TV
Bed
Refrigerator
Dresser
Stove
Closet
Dishwasher
Sink
Bathroom

Step 1 ## Understand the Problem ■ ■ ■

Complete the *Plan for Successful Solving*.

Plan for Successful Solving

What am I asked to do?	What are the facts?	How do I find the answer?	Is there any unnecessary information?	What prior knowledge will help me?
Locate where the stove should be installed.	In the diagram, all appliances are labeled. I can use this information to locate where the stove should be installed.	Look for the stove symbol or label on the floor plan.	Information about pieces of furniture and other appliances that are not near the stove; the fact that it is a studio apartment.	I know I should locate the kitchen first.

Step 2 ## Find and Check Your Answer ■ ■ ■

- Confirm your understanding of the question and revise your plan as needed.

- Based on your plan, determine your solution approach: *The first step is to find where the stove is on the diagram. I know that the stove should be in the kitchen. The next step is to look at where the other things in the kitchen are in relation to the stove. The stove is against the kitchen wall. It is between the dishwasher and the refrigerator.*

- Check your answer: Refer to the floor plan. Gather facts by determining where the stove is on the drawing. It is between the dishwasher and the refrigerator.

- **Select the correct answer:** **B.** between the dishwasher and the refrigerator. Using prior knowledge of where a stove should be located helps you find where to look on the diagram. Using the diagram labels helps you locate exactly where the stove should be installed.

On Your Own ▪ ▪ ▪

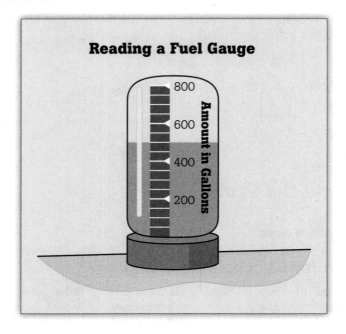

Reading a Fuel Gauge

1. As a furnace repair technician, you must drain oil from a heating system before you can repair it. How many total gallons of oil are currently in the tank?

   A.   200 gallons

   B.   350 gallons

   C.   400 gallons

   D.   450 gallons

   E.   500 gallons

2. Approximately how many gallons of oil does the tank hold altogether?

   F.   200 gallons

   G.   400 gallons

   H.   600 gallons

   J.   700 gallons

   K.   800 gallons

Chain Sling Capacity (pounds)

Chain Size (inch)	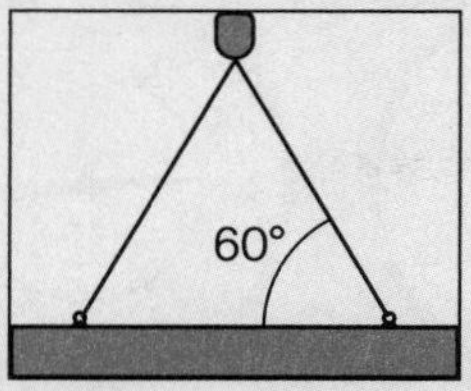	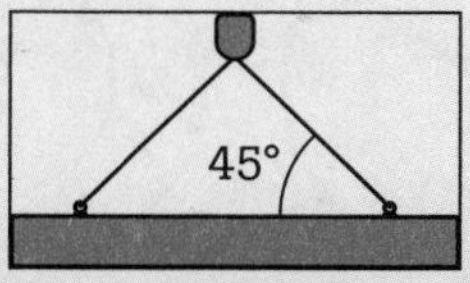	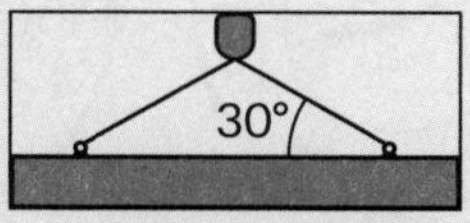
	60°	45°	30°
CHAIN GR-8 DESIGN FACTOR 4/1	60-DEGREE SLING ANGLE	45-DEGREE SLING ANGLE	30-DEGREE SLING ANGLE
	Maximum Weight Capacities		
$\frac{1}{2}$	20,750	16,950	12,000
$\frac{5}{8}$	31,350	26,500	16,100
$\frac{3}{4}$	49,000	40,000	20,300
$\frac{7}{8}$	59,200	48,350	34,200
1	82,500	67,450	47,700

3. You are a crane operator. You have a $\frac{1}{2}$-inch and a $\frac{3}{4}$-inch chain. You want to move a load of 48,000 pounds. Which chain size and sling angle should you use?

A. $\frac{1}{2}$-inch chain, 45° sling angle

B. $\frac{1}{2}$-inch chain, 60° sling angle

C. $\frac{3}{4}$-inch chain, 30° sling angle

D. $\frac{3}{4}$-inch chain, 45° sling angle

E. $\frac{3}{4}$-inch chain, 60° sling angle

4. For an upcoming job, you will need to move loads that range from 10,000 to 25,000 pounds. Which of the following chain sizes will you *not* be able to use for weights in this range?

F. $\frac{1}{2}$ inch

G. $\frac{5}{8}$ inch

H. $\frac{3}{4}$ inch

J. $\frac{7}{8}$ inch

K. 1 inch

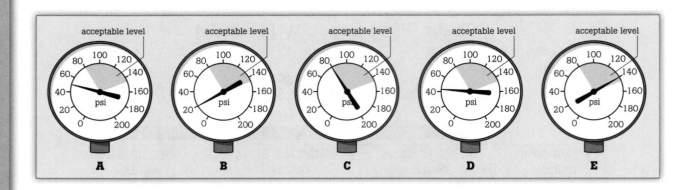

5. One of your responsibilities as a water pump installer is to check the pressure level on residential water pumps. Which pressure gauge reads 41 psi?

    A. A

    B. B

    C. C

    D. D

    E. E

6. The grey area on the gage indicates the range of acceptable pressure levels. Which gauges show pressures at levels that are acceptable?

    F. A and C

    G. B and E

    H. A and D

    J. B and D

    K. C and E

Chapter 15: Railroad Regulations

15.001	Street Crossings, Stop Regulations, and Exceptions
15.005	Whistle and Bell Regulations
15.010	Persons Getting On or Off Moving Trains
15.015	Gates at Street Crossings
15.020	Failure to Erect Gates
15.025	Gates Erected and Maintained at Cost of Company
15.030	Cab Stands
15.035	Cab Stand Regulations
15.040	Rules for Owners of Cabs
15.045	Passenger Rules/Standards of Conduct
15.050	Prohibited Operations
15.060	Ditches, Drains, etc.
15.065	Railroad Crossings
15.070	Head and Rear Light Requirements
15.080	Railroad Trains and Street Cars not to Block Streets
15.999	Penalty

7. As an engineer for a commuter train, you are looking for information about the regulations for blowing the train's whistle. Which section of the above chapter should you read?

A. 15.005

B. 15.015

C. 15.040

D. 15.065

E. 15.080

8. One of your passengers reports that a man on the train is talking loudly and disturbing other passengers. Which section should you read to locate regulations regarding passenger behavior?

F. 15.020

G. 15.045

H. 15.060

J. 15.070

K. 15.999

RN	Samuels, Meg	LPN		NA	Jansen, Pam
			(your name)		

Patient	Room #
Adams, Thomas B.	355
deVecchio, Angelina M.	362
Lichens, Marie L.	368
Mundorf, Donald J.	350
Sheehan, Evan A.	352

9. You are a licensed practical nurse (LPN) working in a busy hospital. Your nursing supervisor gives you the above assignment sheet. Who is your nursing assistant (NA)?

    A. Pam Jansen

    B. Meg Samuels

    C. Angelina deVecchio

    D. Marie Lichens

    E. Evan Sheehan

10. The doctor asks you to check on the patient in room 355. You like to address new patients formally by using their last name. How will you address the patient?

    F. Mr. Adams

    G. Ms. deVecchio

    H. Ms. Lichens

    J. Mr. Mundorf

    K. Mr. Sheehan

Federal Shipping Regulations

PART 125-EXPORTS 1

Sec. 125.1	How to affix stamps and marking products for export.
125.2	Information on export certificates; instructions concerning insurance.
125.3	How to transfer products for export.
125.4	Information on clearance of vessels and transportation without certificate prohibited; exceptions.
125.5	Non-inspected tallow, stearin, oleo oil, etc., not to be exported unless certified as prescribed.

11. You are a ship loader. Your supervisor has asked you to oversee the transfer of oleo oil for export. Which section(s) of the federal regulations on exports will you read to learn about specific regulations regarding the export of oleo oil?

    A.   section 125.1

    B.   sections 125.2 and 125.3

    C.   section 125.3

    D.   sections 125.3 and 125.5

    E.   section 125.5

12. What are the topics of sections 125.1 and 125.5?

    F.   how to mark products for export and restrictions on exporting oils

    G.   what kind of postage needs to be put on exported goods

    H.   how to ship exported products

    J.   how to get export documents and get clearance

    K.   marking and transferring products for export

FEATURES	BRENNAN Model TX-33	MONDO VAK Model 0101
Weight/portability	15 pounds	15 pounds
Adjust to different heights?	Yes	No
Various handle positions	3	2
Dust capacity	No	Yes
Cord length and release	25 ft.	35 ft.
Metal brushes	1	2
Filter systems	Hypo-Allergenic Filtration	Hypo-Allergenic Filtration
Edge cleaning	Bristled Edge Cleaning System	None
Optional tools	Nylon Bristle 2 Straight Wands	Horsehair Bristle Telescoping Wand
Headlight	None	Twin LED
Other	1. Sound Dampening Technology 2. Cord Guard 3. Non-marring Wheels	1. Long lasting drive belts 2. Easy Load Bag Dock 3. Carpet and Rug Industry Approved

13. As part of your duties as a school janitorial supervisor, you are asked to compare two vacuum cleaners, the Brennan Model TX-33 and the Mondo Vak Model 0101. Which of the following are features only of the Brennan?

    A. 3 handle positions, 2 metal brushes

    B. 2 handle positions, hypo–allergenic filtration

    C. horsehair bristle, 25-foot cord

    D. nylon bristle, sound–dampening technology

    E. long-lasting drive belts, can adjust to different heights

14. Which of the following are features only of the Mondo Vak?

    F. dust capacity, horsehair bristle

    G. 15 pounds, bristled edge cleaning

    H. telescoping wand, can adjust to different heights

    J. 3 handle positions, 15 pounds

    K. hypo-allergenic filtration, 25-foot cord

Cholesterol Readings for Sanchez, R.		
	Patient Score (mg/dl)	Reference Range (mg/dl)
Total Cholesterol	142	125–200
HDL Cholesterol	58	≥ 40
Cholesterol/HDL Ratio	2.4	≤ 5.0
LDL Cholesterol, Calculated	70	< 130

15. You are a home health aide. You are reviewing cholesterol readings for one of your patients. Based on the chart above, what is the patient's cholesterol/HDL ratio?

A. 2.4

B. ≤ 5.0

C. 70

D. 142

E. 125–200

16. What is the reference range for LDL cholesterol?

F. ≤ 40

G. ≥ 40

H. ≤ 50

J. < 130

K. 125–200

Table 105.01

Diameter of Rope	Number of Clips Required	Space Between Clips
$1\frac{1}{2}$ inch	8	10 inches
$1\frac{3}{8}$ inch	7	9 inches
$1\frac{1}{4}$ inch	6	8 inches
$1\frac{1}{8}$ inch	5	7 inches
1 inch	5	6 inches
$\frac{7}{8}$ inch	5	$5\frac{1}{4}$ inches
$\frac{3}{4}$ inch	5	$4\frac{1}{2}$ inches
$\frac{3}{8}$ to $\frac{5}{8}$ inch	4	3 inches

17. You are a crane operator placing rope clips on a $\frac{7}{8}$-inch rope. According to Table 105.01, how many clips do you need, and how far apart should they be?

- **A.** 5 clips, $4\frac{1}{2}$ inches
- **B.** 5 clips, $5\frac{1}{4}$ inches
- **C.** 5 clips, 6 inches
- **D.** 6 clips, 5 inches
- **E.** 7 clips, 9 inches

18. You have a $1\frac{3}{8}$-inch rope. How far apart should the clips be placed?

- **F.** $4\frac{1}{2}$ inches
- **G.** 5 inches
- **H.** 7 inches
- **J.** 9 inches
- **K.** 10 inches

FISH AND SEAFOOD NUTRITIONAL INFORMATION

Species	Calories	Protein (grams)	Fat (grams)	Cholesterol (milligrams)
Snails	75	14.40	1.90	N/A
Snapper	100	20.51	1.34	37
Sole	91	18.84	1.19	48
Squid	92	15.58	1.38	233
Striped Bass	97	17.73	2.33	80
Swordfish	121	19.80	4.01	39
Trout (Rainbow)	118	20.55	3.36	57
Tuna (Bluefin)	144	23.33	4.90	38
Tuna (Skipjack)	103	22.00	1.01	47
Tuna (Yellowfin)	108	23.38	0.95	45

19. You are a nutritionist at an assisted living facility looking for healthy seafood selections for the residents. What is the cholesterol level for sole?

    A.   37 milligrams

    B.   39 milligrams

    C.   48 milligrams

    D.   57 milligrams

    E.   92 milligrams

20. What species contains the highest amount of calories?

    F.   snails

    G.   squid

    H.   tuna (bluefin)

    J.   tuna (skipjack)

    K.   swordfish

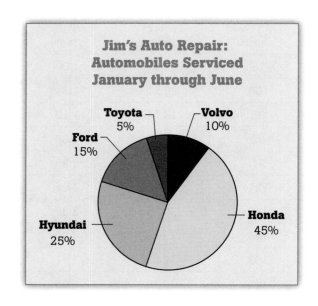

Jim's Auto Repair:
Automobiles Serviced
January through June

Toyota 5%
Volvo 10%
Ford 15%
Hyundai 25%
Honda 45%

21. You are the manager of Jim's Auto Repair. According to the circle graph, what percentage of the cars that you have serviced have been Fords?

    A.   5%

    B.   10%

    C.   15%

    D.   25%

    E.   45%

22. Which make of cars have you serviced the most?

    F.   Volvo

    G.   Honda

    H.   Hyundai

    J.   Ford

    K.   Toyota

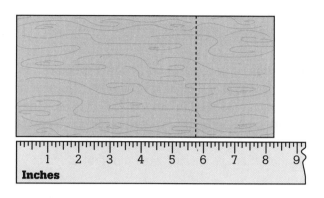

23. You are a hand cutter for a furniture maker. What is the length shown by the line on the board?

    A. $4\frac{3}{4}$ inches

    B. $5\frac{1}{4}$ inches

    C. $5\frac{1}{2}$ inches

    D. $5\frac{3}{4}$ inches

    E. 6 inches

24. What is the length of the entire board?

    F. 7 inches

    G. $7\frac{1}{4}$ inches

    H. $7\frac{1}{2}$ inches

    J. $7\frac{3}{4}$ inches

    K. $8\frac{1}{4}$ inches

Answers are on page 245.

Lesson 2 ■ ■ ■
Add Missing Information to Graphics

Skill: Fill in one or two pieces of information that are missing from a graphic

Some workplace documents and graphics require you to add information. In particular, forms that include graphics such as tables and charts often need to have information added in order to be complete. These forms are used to keep track of information such as order details, work completed, and budgets. The goal of this lesson is to give you the opportunity to practice filling in multiple pieces of information that are missing from different kinds of workplace graphics.

Skill Example

Day	Date	Circle Shift Worked	Time In	Time Out	Total Hours
Mon.	6/7	① 2 3	7:45 A.M.		
Tues.		1 2 3			
Wed.		1 2 3			
Thurs.		1 2 3			
Fri.		1 2 3			
Sat.		1 2 3			
Sun.		1 2 3			

Add missing information to tables.

Tables are useful graphics for keeping information organized. The timesheet to the left is an example of a table. The employee has written in information for "Date" and "Time In," and he has circled the shift worked. At the end of the day, the employee will write the time he leaves work in the "Time Out" column and will write the number of hours worked that day in the "Total Hours" column.

Skill Practice

Receipt of Revision

Acknowledgement is hereby made of receipt of the following issued during the billing period:

Revision No. ___26A___
Dated _____
☐ Bid revised per receipt of revision

Revision No. ___26B___
Dated _____
☐ Bid revised per receipt of revision

Revision No. ___26B1___
Dated _____
☐ Bid revised per receipt of revision

Use the form to the left to answer the following questions.

1. You are bidding on a construction contract. The client sends you revisions to the bid. You receive revision 26A on 9/14. You receive revision 26B on 9/18. You receive revision 26B1 on 9/23. What date do you record by Revision No. 26B?

   A. 9/14
   B. 9/15
   C. 9/18
   D. 9/23
   E. 9/28

2. So far, the bid has only been revised based on the requests made in the first two revisions. For which revision(s) should the "Bid Revised" box be checked?

   F. 26A and 26B
   G. 26A and 26B1
   H. 26B and 26B1
   J. 26B1
   K. 26A, 26B, and 26B1

Try It Out! ■ ■ ■

You are a maintenance worker who has fixed a garage door. On the invoice you record that you used 3, 10-millimeter bearings and the cost per bearing was $9.42. What should the last line of the "Parts and Items" section look like now?

Installation Maintenance and Repair

Part & Items

Item Description	Qty	Price	Total
9-Volt Battery	1	$2.47	$2.47
Battery Transmitter	2	$2.26	$4.52
10-millimeter Bearing			

A. 10-millimeter Bearing   1 $9.42 $9.42

B. 30-millimeter Bearing   1 $9.42 $28.26

C. 10-millimeter Bearing   3 $9.42 $28.26

D. 10-millimeter Bearing $28.62 $9.42   3

E. 10-millimeter Bearing $28.62 $9.42   1

Step 1   Understand the Problem ■ ■ ■

Complete the *Plan for Successful Solving.*

Plan for Successful Solving

What am I asked to do?	What are the facts?	How do I find the answer?	Is there any unnecessary information?	What prior knowledge will help me?
Fill in the invoice with the missing information.	I used 3, 10-millimeter bearings that cost $9.42 each.	Identify the answer that correctly lists the new information.	No.	Qty. is an abbreviation for quantity.

Step 2   Find and Check Your Answer ■ ■ ■

- Confirm your understanding of the question and revise your plan as needed.

- Based on your plan, determine your solution approach: *The instructions indicate that I used 3, 10-millimeter bearings. The number 3 belongs in the "Qty" column. The cost per bearing is $9.42. This goes in the "Price" column. The total cost is $28.26. This belongs in the "Total" column.*

- Check your answer. Based on the column titles and how previous items have been entered in, the information should be in this order: item description, quantity, price, and total.

- **Select the correct answer:**   C. 10-millimeter Bearing   3 $9.42 $28.26 This answer records the information in the correct order.

Problem Solving Tip

When using workplace forms, it can be helpful to see how previous forms have been completed. In this problem, information for the use of a 9-volt battery and for transmitter batteries has been entered on the form. By studying how the item description, quantity, price, and total columns were completed for these items, you can determine how to enter the information for the 10-millimeter bearings.

Remember!

An invoice is a workplace document that provides a written record of goods or services provided and the amount charged for them. When more than one of the same item is ordered, the price for one item is usually listed as well as the number of items ordered. To calculate the total, you multiply the price of the item by the number of items ordered.

Inspector Record

VEHICLE IDENTIFICATION

_____   _____
              Make   Serial Number

_____   _____
              Year   Unit Number

          Date   **Inspected**

_____   1. Make a visual check for body damage

_____   2. Check lights and reflectors

_____   3. Check turn signals

_____   4. Check wheel lugs

_____   5. Check mud flaps

_____   6. Check lubricant in wheels

_____   7. Check brake linings & drum condition

_____   8. Bleed air tanks

                              Date: _____

                         Signature: _____

1. You are a government trailer inspector. You complete your inspection of a trailer on July 17. Where should you write *July 17* on the above record?

   A. on the line that says "Unit Number"

   B. beside lines 4 and 5 in the list

   C. on the line at the bottom by the word "Date"

   D. beside lines 1 and 2 in the list

   E. beside lines 5 and 6 in the list

2. In the list, where do you record that you have inspected the mud flaps?

   F. line 2

   G. line 3

   H. line 4

   J. line 5

   K. line 6

SAFEGUARDING REGULATION CHECKLIST	Yes	No	N/A
1. All hazardous moving parts have safeguards.	☐	☐	☐
2. Safeguards prevent body parts from touching moving parts.	☐	☐	☐
3. Fixed safeguards require tools for removal.	☐	☐	☐
4. Safeguards ensure no objects fall into moving parts.	☐	☐	☐
5. Machines can be maintained without removing safeguards.	☐	☐	☐
6. Safeguards have not been tampered with, altered, or removed.	☐	☐	☐
7. Dust-generating tools and machinery have controls to minimize dust.	☐	☐	☐

3. As part of your job as a government health inspector, you are inspecting a machine shop for safety issues. You need to fill out the above Safeguarding Regulation Checklist. You find that all hazardous moving parts have safeguards. How do you show this on the form?

    A. Check the Yes box in line 1.

    B. Check the No box in line 2.

    C. Check the Yes box in line 3.

    D. Check the N/A box in line 4.

    E. Check the No box in line 6.

4. There are no tools or machinery that produce dust. How do you show this on the form?

    F. Check the Yes box in line 5.

    G. Check the No box in line 5.

    H. Check the Yes box in line 7.

    J. Check the No box in line 7.

    K. Check the N/A box in line 7.

Closing Form

Manuela Santos	07/28
Employee Name	Date
35	8
Employee Number	Register Number

INTAKE	DOLLAR AMOUNT
Coins	
Pennies	1.57
Nickels	6.85
Dimes	4.20
Quarters	9.50
Currency	
Ones	18.00
Fives	35.00
Tens	70.00
Twenties	40.00
Fifties	400.00
Hundreds	0.00
Checks	411.12
Credit Card	
Store Charge	657.85
Vista Gold	428.88
Americard	942.02
First Bank	244.89
Total	3,269.88

5. You are a cashier at a department store. You are closing your register and counting your drawer. What was the dollar amount of purchases made on the store credit card?

A. $244.89

B. $428.88

C. $657.85

D. $942.02

E $3,269.88

6. What was the total dollar amount for the day?

F. $400.00

G. $411.12

H. $657.85

J. $942.02

K. $3,269.88

AUTO BODY REPAIR
CUSTOMER SERVICE EVALUATION FORM

Name: _____ Date: _____

Address: _____

City: _____ State: _____ Zip: _____

Telephone Number: Work: _____ Home: _____

Date of Contact/ Service: _____ Employee(s) contacted (if known): _____

How was the contact made? ☐ by phone ☐ by email ☐ in person

This is a (please check appropriate box): ☐ Complaint ☐ Comment

Descriprion of situation (please use additional pages if needed):

Has the problem been resolved? ☐ Yes ☐ No ☐ N/A

If not, what resolution are you requesting?

Thank You!

---

7. You work as the receptionist at an auto body repair shop. A customer comes into the office to leave a comment. You fill out a customer service evaluation form. How do you report the way in which the customer reported the situation to you?

   A. Write *walk in* beside "Date of Contact/ Service."

   B. Check the "in person" box.

   C. Write *walk in* under "Description of situation."

   D. Check the "by phone" box.

   E. Check the "by email" box.

8. During the customer's visit, he tells you that Peter Collins did a very good job of fixing the dent in the trunk of his car. What other information should you add?

   F. Check the "Comment" box.

   G. Check the "No" box by "Has the problem been resolved?"

   H. Write the customer's name in the "Employee(s) contacted" line.

   J. Write Peter Collins on the "Name" line.

   K. Record Peter Collins's work number on the work telephone number line.

Green Thumb Floral Shoppe

ORDER FORM
Order Date: _____ 7 / 30 _____   Delivery Date: _____ 8 / 1 _____

INFORMATION OF RECIPIENT
Name: _____ Mr. Ryan James _____
Address: _____ 265 E. Main Street _____
_____ York, PA _____
Telephone: _____ 717-555-1234 _____

REQUEST FOR:
- ☐ Opening Flower Basket
- ☐ Flower Bouquet
- ☐ Fruit Basket / Hamper
- ☐ Funeral Flower Basket
- ☒ Flower Arrangement
- ☐ Orchid Plant Arrangement
- ☐ Other: _____

Budget: _____ Special instructions: _____ daisies, zinnias, mums _____

Message: _____ Dear Ryan, Best wishes for a Happy Birthday. _____

INFORMATION OF SENDER:
Name: _____ Ms. Jennie Lynn _____
Mobile: _____ 708-321-0000 _____
Address: _____

PAYMENT METHOD: ☒ Vista ☐ First Bank ☐ Americard
Expire Date: _____ 07/10 _____
Cardholder: _____ Jennie Lynn _____
Card Number: _____ 426-111-1111 _____
Bank of Issue: _____
Signature: _____ JLyn _____

Green Thumb Floral Shoppe

---

9. You are a florist in the Green Thumb Floral Shoppe. Jennie Lynn faxes in an order for a flower arrangement. She wants daisies, mums, and zinnias. The arrangement will be delivered to her cousin Ryan James at 265 E. Main Street, York, PA. Her budget is $75.00. The message should read "Dear Ryan, Best wishes for a Happy Birthday." Ms. Lynn's cell phone is 708-321-0000, and she paid using a Vista. What information is missing from the order?

A. Mr. James' delivery address

B. Ms. Lynn's credit card number

C. the message

D. the budget

E. the kinds of flowers

10. Ms. Lynn calls in to add some details to her order. She wants the flowers in fall colors and would like a small teddy bear placed at the center. Where should you write this?

F. beside "Message"

G. beside "Special instructions"

H. beside "Other"

J. beside "Mobile"

K. beside "Address" under "Information of Sender"

Harvey's Rentals

PRE-RENTAL INSPECTION

Car No. _____ #524 _____

License No. _____

Space _____ 30 _____ Color _____ blue _____

Model _____ Stylus _____

Mileage _____ 15,091 _____

Scratch

Front
(hood)   Back
                                           (trunk)

Driver   Passenger

Damage _Scratch passenger side on_
trunk. Ding on driver's side door. Chip
on passenger side windshield.

Service Technician _____ Jerry _____

Customer _____ Gino _____

11. You work as a service technician at Harvey's Rentals, a rental car company. You verify the condition of the cars with the customer before renting them. What information is missing from the top of the Pre–Rental Inspection slip?

    A. the make of the car

    B. the license number

    C. the mileage

    D. the space

    E. the car color

12. The customer made some notes in the "Damage" section. He did not mark all the damages on the drawing of the car. What needs to be added to the drawing?

    F. a scratch on the driver's side door and a ding on the trunk

    G. a flat tire and a scratch on the driver's side door

    H. a ding on the driver's side door and a flat tire

    J. a chipped windshield and a flat tire

    K. a ding on the driver's side door and a chipped windshield

Referral Scheduling

Name: _____

Daytime Phone Number _____
☐ Okay to leave message

Appointment Preference
☐ AM
☐ PM

Unavailable Times_____

Urgency of Appointment _____

---

13. You work as a receptionist at a doctor's office. A patient calls in at 4:30 P.M. on June 8 to schedule an appointment. She would like to come in within the next 3 days, but cannot come in on Tuesday after 3 P.M. What do you write beside "Urgency of Appointment?"

    A. *4:30 P.M. on June 8*

    B. *Tuesday after 3 P.M.*

    C. *No afternoon appointments*

    D. *Yes*

    E. *by June 11*

14. The patient states she does not want morning appointments. How do you show that?

    F. Mark the P.M. box under "Appointment Preference."

    G. Write *no mornings* beside "Urgency of Appointment."

    H. Write *mornings only* beside "Appointment Preference."

    J. Mark the A.M. box under "Appointment Preference."

    K. Write *afternoon* beside "Unavailable Times."

Cropping History of Little Acres Farm

Field Name	Zone	Management Unit	3 Years Ago	2 Years Ago	Last Year	This Year
A	I	1	corn	soybean	oats/spelt	_____
B	I	3	soybean	oats/spelt	spelt/hay	_____
C	I	4	soybean	oats/spelt	spelt/hay	_____
D	II	5	soybean	oats/spelt	spelt/hay	_____
E	II	6	oats/spelt	spelt/hay	hay	_____
F	II	7	oats/spelt	spelt/hay	hay	_____
G	II	8	oats/spelt	spelt/hay	hay	_____

15. You are a farm worker on Little Acres. Your supervisor asks you to look at the crop rotation table. Every three years crops must be rotated. In Field F Zone II, what crop should be planted this year?

   A. corn

   B. hay

   C. soybean

   D. oats/spelt

   E. spelt/hay

16. Soybeans can be planted only every three years. Which field cannot have soybeans planted in it this year?

   F. Field C, Zone I, Management Unit 4

   G. Field A, Zone I, Management Unit 1

   H. Field B, Zone I, Management Unit 3

   J. Field E, Zone II, Management Unit 6

   K. Field G, Zone II, Management Unit 8

JULY

Sun	Mon	Tue	Wed	Thur	Fri	Sat
			1	2	3	4
5	6	7	8	9	10	11
12	13	14	15	16	17	18
19	20	21	22	23	24	25
26	27	28	29	30	31	

17. You are a housekeeping supervisor. You keep a calendar in your office for your housekeepers' reference. Paydays are the first and third Friday of each month. You mark paydays with a *P*. Which dates should have a *P*?

    A.   July 3 and 10

    B.   July 3 and 17

    C.   July 10 and 17

    D.   July 10 and 24

    E.   July 11 and 25

18. The Fourth of July is a national holiday. Since the holiday is on a Saturday this year, the employees get the first Monday after the Fourth of July off. You mark holidays with an *H*. Which date should have an *H*?

    F.   July 3

    G.   July 6

    H.   July 11

    J.   July 13

    K.   July 20

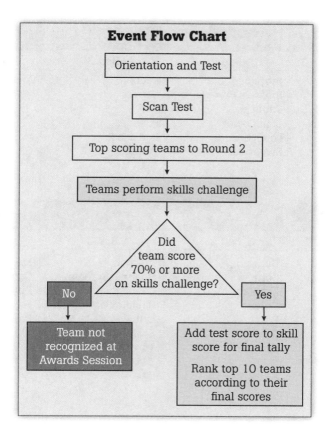

Event Flow Chart

Orientation and Test

↓

Scan Test

↓

Top scoring teams to Round 2

↓

Teams perform skills challenge

↓

Did team score 70% or more on skills challenge?

No → Team not recognized at Awards Session

Yes → Add test score to skill score for final tally

Rank top 10 teams according to their final scores

---

19. You are an administrative support worker. You are planning a competition for an office training event. The flow chart shows what will happen at the event. When do the competitors perform the skills challenge?

A. directly after orientation

B. directly after the tests are scanned

C. directly before the tests are scanned

D. directly after the top-scoring teams go to Round 2

E. directly before the top-scoring teams go to Round 2

20. What happens if a team scores 50% on the skills challenge?

F. The tests are scanned.

G. The team is in the top 10.

H. The teams perform the skills.

J. The team's test score is added to the skill score.

K. The team is not recognized at the awards session.

Current Year			
Bed 1	**Bed 2**	**Bed 3**	**Bed 4**
Garlic Celery Corn Eggplant Onions Peas Peppers Squash Tomatoes	Broccoli Brussels Sprouts Cabbage Cauliflower Lettuce Sweet Basil	Beets Carrots Dill Potatoes Radishes Turnips	Cover Crop

Next Year			
Bed 1	**Bed 2**	**Bed 3**	**Bed 4**
Cover Crop	Garlic Corn Eggplant Onions Peas Squash Tomatoes	Broccoli Brussels Sprouts Cabbage Cauliflower Lettuce Sweet Basil Turnips	Beets Carrots Dill Potatoes Radishes

21. As the manager of a small farm, you need to plan your crop rotation for the next two years. Each year you rotate beds and always plant the same crops together. This means the crops in Bed 1 for the current year will be planted in Bed 2 next year. As you check your plan to make sure it is correct, what crops must you add to Bed 2 for next year?

A. celery, peppers

B. celery, broccoli

C. radishes, beets

D. peppers, carrots

E. cabbage, corn

22. You realize that you have listed next year's turnip crop in the wrong bed. In which bed should it be listed?

F. Bed 1

G. Bed 2

H. Bed 3

J. Bed 4

K. Beds 3 and 4

HOME HEALTH AIDE INSTRUCTION SHEET

Client:	Marie Paul			Day/Date:	August 18

✓	Bath	
✓	Grooming	
	Dressing	
	Mobility	
	ROM	
✓	Catheter	*Empty urinary drainage unit.*
✓	Temperature	☐ Oral ☐ Tympanic ☐ Rectal
	Pulse	☐ Apical ☐ Radial
	Respiration	
	Blood Pressure	

Other Instructions:	
	Housekeeping
	Meals

Additional Instructions:	
✓	*Get help to move client up in bed using a drawsheet as needed.*

RN Signature:	L. Painter R.N.	**Date:**	8/18

23. You are a home health aide supervisor. You are sending a home health aide out to care for Marie Paul. You would like the aide to brush and style Marie's hair. Where do you record this on the instruction sheet?

    A. by "Dressing"

    B. by "Mobility"

    C. by "Bath"

    D. by "Grooming"

    E. by "Housekeeping"

24. Marie's daughter calls in and says that Marie prefers to have her temperature taken orally, not tympanically. How do you show this on the sheet?

    F. Mark the "Oral" box by "Temperature."

    G. Write *Take temperature orally* by "Respiration."

    H. Mark the "Tympanic" box by "Temperature."

    J. Write *Take temperature tympanically* by "Blood pressure."

    K. Mark the "Tympanic" and "Rectal" boxes by "Temperature."

Answers are on page 245.

Level 3 Performance Assessment

The following problems will test your ability to answer questions at a Level 3 rating of difficulty. These problems are similar to those that appear on a Career Readiness Certificate test. For each question, you can refer to the answer key for answer justifications. The answer justifications provide an explanation of why each answer option is either correct or incorrect and indicate the skill lesson that should be referred to if further review of a particular skill is needed.

From: March 25
To: March 31

Name: Rhonda Kimmel

		In	Out	In	Out	Daily Total
Monday	3/25	8:00	12:00	1:00	5:00	8
Tuesday	3/26	8:30	12:00	1:00	5:00	$7\frac{1}{2}$
Wednesday	3/27	9:00	12:00	1:00	7:00	9
Thursday	3/28	7:30	12:30	1:45	5:00	$8\frac{1}{4}$
Friday	3/29					
Saturday	3/30					
Sunday	3/31	10:00	1:00	2:15	5:30	$6\frac{1}{4}$
				Weekly Total		

Employee's Signature _____

Supervisor's Signature _____

1. As a mechanic for the city transit authority, you must submit your timesheet for the week. What is the total number of hours that you worked on Wednesday, 3/27?

   A. $6\frac{1}{4}$

   B. $7\frac{1}{2}$

   C. 8

   D. $8\frac{1}{4}$

   E. 9

2. On which two days did you not work?

   F. Monday and Tuesday

   G. Wednesday and Thursday

   H. Thursday and Friday

   J. Friday and Saturday

   K. Saturday and Sunday

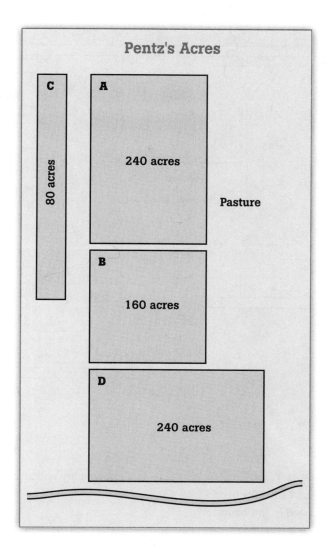

Pentz's Acres

C — 80 acres

A — 240 acres

Pasture

B — 160 acres

D — 240 acres

3. You are a farm worker on Pentz's Acres. The farm manager assigns you to plow the smallest field on the farm. Which field do you plow?

   A. Field A

   B. Field B

   C. Field C

   D. Field D

   E. the pasture

4. The manager needs you to plant 240 acres of soybeans and 240 acres of wheat. In which fields can you plant these two crops?

   F. Fields A and B

   G. Fields A and C

   H. Fields A and D

   J. Fields C and D

   K. Fields B and C

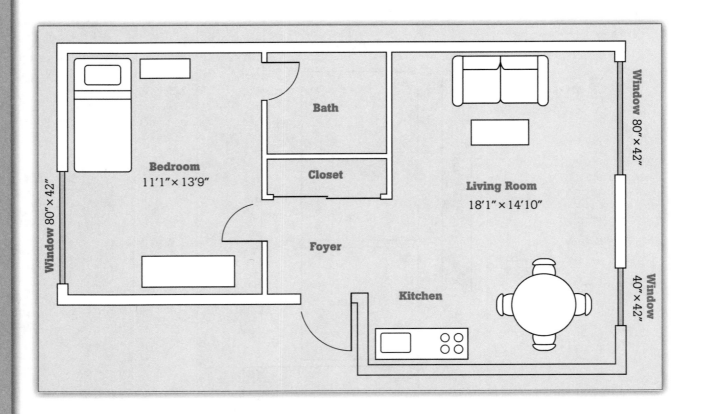

Window 80" × 42"

Bath

Bedroom
11'1" × 13'9"

Closet

Living Room
18'1" × 14'10"

Window 80" × 42"

Window 80" × 42"

Foyer

Kitchen

Window 40" × 42"

5. You work as a window installer. You are installing windows in a condo with the above floorplan. What size window do you need in the bedroom?

    A. 40" x 42"

    B. 42" x 80"

    C. 80" x 42"

    D. 11' 1" x 13' 9"

    E. 18'1" x 14'10"

6. How many windows total are in the condo?

    F. 0

    G. 1

    H. 2

    J. 3

    K. 4

Permissible (Allowed) and Non-Permissible Activities

HOME HEALTH AIDE (HHA) SERVICES

Functions/Tasks	Activities	Permissible HHA	Permissible Under Special Circumstances HHA	Non-Permissible HHA
Performing simple measurements and tests to routinely monitor the patient's medical condition				
– vital signs	1. assemble necessary equipment.	x		
	2. position patient for task.	x		
	3. take blood pressure:			
	a. arm;	x		
	b. other sites.			x
	4. take temperature:			
	a. oral;	x		
	b. axillary;	x		
	c. rectal.	x		
	5. take pulse:			
	a. radial	x		
	b. apical.		x	
	6. count respirations.	x		
	7. dispose of used supplies.	x		

7. You are a home health aide who is learning what you can and cannot do to aid your client. What are you not allowed to do to measure the patient's vital signs?

    A. Take temperature orally.

    B. Take blood pressure using the arm.

    C. Move the patient so you can take the vital signs.

    D. Take blood pressure using sites other than the arm.

    E. Throw away supplies you use to take the vital signs.

8. Which activity could you do under special circumstances?

    F. Count breaths.

    G. Take the pulse radially.

    H. Take the pulse apically.

    J. Take the axillary temperature.

    K. Assemble the equipment you need.

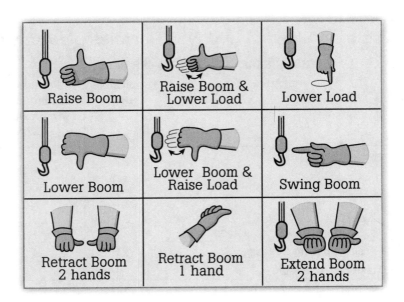

9. You are a crane operator. You are learning the hand signals that will be used by the person supervising the lift. Which hand signal means lower load?

    A. thumb pointing upward

    B. index finger pointing toward the boom

    C. hands closed, thumbs pointing at each other

    D. index finger pointing downward, making circles

    E. thumb pointing downward, hand moving from right to left

10. The signalman closes both fists and points the thumbs at each other. What does this signal mean?

    F. Raise the boom.

    G. Lower the boom.

    H. Swing the boom.

    J. Retract the boom.

    K. Extend the boom.

Tool Rental Order Form

	Tool	Number	Rate	Days
1	Tool bucket, with hand cutter	3–4		○
2	Tool bucket, without hand cutter	2		○
3	Small wet saw	5	17,50	3
4	Large wet saw	2–3	35⁰⁰	3

11. You work as a contractor and you need to rent equipment to install tile. You need to rent 2 tool buckets without hand cutters, 3 tool buckets with hand cutters, 5 small wet saws, and 2 large wet saws. You need the saws for three days. Large saws are $35 per day. Small saws are $17.50 per day. What do you write under "Rate" and "Days" on line 3 of the order form?

    A. Rate: $0, Days: 3

    B. Rate: $17.50, Days: 2

    C. Rate: $17.50, Days: 3

    D. Rate: $17.50, Days: 5

    E. Rate: $35.00, Days: 3

12. You call the tool rental company to tell them that you will need one more tool bucket with hand cutters and one more large saw. They ask you to fill out a new rental order form. Which two lines change?

    F. lines 1 and 2

    G. lines 1 and 4

    H. lines 2 and 3

    J. lines 2 and 4

    K. lines 3 and 4

P&R
PRINTING

Miller Mall
244 Main Street
Littletown, AL 36123
(205) 555-1212
FAX (205) 555-0230

Date _____   Number of Copies ___47___

SERVICE	QUANTITY	UNIT PRICE	TOTAL
FAX			
Phone Time			
$8\frac{1}{2} \times 11$	47	.08	$3.76
$8\frac{1}{2} \times 14$			
Other			
Collate			
Supplies			
SUBTOTAL			
TAX			.30
TOTAL			$4.06

WORLD'S LARGEST PRINTING CHAIN

13. You work as a teacher's aid at a day care center, and the director has asked you to pick up flyers that have been printed for an upcoming open house. What is the total amount that you have to pay for the job?

    A. $0.08

    B. $0.30

    C. $3.76

    D. $4.06

    E. $47.00

14. The number listed under "Quantity" matches what other item listed on the form?

    F.   Unit Price

    G.   Tax

    H.   Number of Copies

    J.   Total

    K.   Subtotal

Home Health Aide Charting Sheet
Speciality Care

Employee Name:

	Task	SAT	SUN	MON	TUES	WEDS	THURS	FRI
Begin a **NEW** worksheet every week. Report any changes/observations to your supervisor as soon as possible.	Date	9/17	9/18	9/19	9/20	9/21	9/22	9/23
	Time In	4pm	4pm	9Am		9Am		9am
	Time Out	12mn	mn	6p		6p		6pm
	Total Time							
	Tasks Completed	m bk	m	B m		B m		B m

15. As a home health aide caring for a patient, you have to fill out a charting sheet. This week you worked from 9 A.M. to 6 P.M. on Monday, Wednesday, and Friday. You worked from 4 P.M. until midnight on Saturday and Sunday. What times do you write in the "Time In" lines for 9/19 and 9/22?

    A.   9 A.M. and 4 P.M.

    B.   6 P.M. and 4 P.M.

    C.   nothing and 6 P.M.

    (D.) 9 A.M. and nothing

    E.   6 P.M. and nothing

16. You bathed the patient on Monday, Wednesday, and Friday. You prepared meals every day you worked this week. On Saturday you did some housekeeping. Which task(s) should be written under "Tasks Completed" for 9/17?

    F.   bath

    G.   meal preparation

    H.   bath, housekeeping

    (J.) meal preparation, housekeeping

    K.   meal preparation, bath, housekeeping

COMBINATION BOILERS ONLY

1	Is the installation in a hard water area (above 200ppm)?	Yes ☑		No ☐
2	If yes, has a water scale reducer been fitted? ⌄		Yes ☐	No ☐
3	What type of scale reducer has been fitted? *aqua dial scale reducer*			

DOMESTIC HOT WATER MODE Measure and Record

4	Gas Rate	☐ m³/hr OR		☐ ft³/hr
5	Burner Operating Pressure (at maximum rate)	☐ mbar OR	Gas Inlet Pressure (at maximum rate) ☐	mbar
6	Cold Water Inlet Temperature		☐	°C
7	Hot water has been checked at all outlets	Yes ☑ Temperature	*50°* ☐	°C
8	Water Flow Rate		☐	t/min

17. You work as a boiler commissioner and you are filling out a checklist for a new combination system. The system has been installed in an area where the calcium hardness is 220 ppm, and an Aqua Dial scale reducer has been added. What do you record on line 1?

A. 50°C

B. Aqua Dial

C. 220 ppm

D. Check the "No" box.

E. Check the "Yes" box.

18. You have completed your inspection, during which you have checked the hot water at all outlets. The hot water outlet temperature you have recorded is 50°C. On what line do you record this information, and what do you record?

F. Line 6, write *50°C*

G. Lines 2 and 3, check the "Yes" box and write *Aqua Dial*

H. Line 1, write *220 ppm*

J. Line 7, check the "No" box and write *50°C*

K. Line 7, check the "Yes" box and write *50°C*

Bidder's Checklist

The following documents must be submitted with your bid:

- [x] Proposal Form – completed, signed and notarized.
- [ ] Receipt of Addendum Form – completed, signed and notarized.
- [x] Identical Tie Bids Statement – completed, signed and notarized.
- [ ] Public Entity Crimes Sworn Statement – completed, signed and notarized.
- [ ] Affidavit of Compliance with Minority Business Participation Construction – completed, signed and notarized.
- [x] Copy of Current Florida Occupational License.
- [ ] References and Qualifications, if requested.

19. You are a construction contractor and are using a bid checklist to put together a bid. You have completed, signed, and notarized the proposal form but are waiting for the addendum form to arrive. You have completed the identical tie bids statement, and you have a copy of your current Florida occupational license. Which checklist items can you mark as being completed?

   A. "Proposal Form" and "Receipt of Addendum"

   B. "Identical Tie Bids Statement" and "Proposal Form"

   C. "Identical Tie Bids Statement" and "Florida Occupational License"

   D. "Florida Occupational License" and "Receipt of Addendum"

   E. "Proposal Form" and "Florida Occupational License"

20. Today you completed and signed the public entity crimes sworn statement. According to the checklist, what do you still need to do before you can check the public entity crimes sworn statement as being completed?

   F. Sign it.

   G. Notarize it.

   H. Complete it.

   J. Make a copy of it.

   K. Complete and sign it.

SHIPPING FORM

1 Ship to:

1A Address:

1B Phone: *recipients*

2 Package contents:

2A Weight: *7lb 7ounces*

2B Dimensions: ___l (in.) x ___w (in.) ___h (in.)

2C Value of contents:

3 Account Number:

4 Shipping Method (overnight, 2nd day, etc.):

5 Sender:

5A Address:

5B Phone:

---

21. You are an office worker in Texas. Part of your job is to fill out shipping requests. You have to fill out a shipping request for a package that needs to be delivered to Michigan the following day. What information do you enter under "Shipping Method?"

    A. 2nd day

    B. international

    C. overnight

    D. courier

    E. certified mail

22. The package you are sending is 20 pounds, 7 ounces. The recipient's phone number is 313-686-2255 and his fax number is 313-686-2200. Your phone number is 281-857-5000 and your company's account number is 25-687-6341. What information do you enter for "Phone" on line 1B?

    F. 20 pounds, 7 ounces

    G. 25-687-6341

    H. 281-857-5000

    J. 313-686-2200

    K. 313-686-2255

Answers are on page 245.

Level 4 Introduction ▪ ▪ ▪

The lesson and practice pages that follow will give you the opportunity to develop and practice the reading and interpretation skills needed to answer work-related questions at a Level 4 rating of difficulty. The *On Your Own* practice problems provide review and practice of key skills needed for locating information from graphical sources in the workplace. These skills are applied through effective problem-solving approaches. The *Performance Assessment* provides problems similar to those you will encounter on a Career Readiness Certificate test. By completing the Level 4 *On Your Own* and *Performance Assessment* questions, you will gain the ability to confidently approach workplace scenarios that require understanding and application of the skills featured in the following lessons:

Lesson 3: Find Information from One or Two Graphics

Lesson 4: Understand How Graphics Relate

Lesson 5: Summarize Information from One or Two Graphics

Lesson 6: Identify Trends

Lesson 7: Compare Information and Trends in Graphics

These skills are intended to help you successfully read and understand workplace documents and forms such as summary reports, work orders, and invoices that communicate information through graphics. It is important to be able to locate, understand, and apply the information within these graphics so it can be used to perform workplace tasks effectively. Reading and understanding documents that communicate information through graphics often requires the ability to:

- identify several pieces of information in graphics,
- use multiple graphics at the same time,
- determine the relationship among the data presented in multiple graphics,
- summarize information and trends from graphics.

Through answering document- and graphic-related questions at this level, you will continue to develop problem-solving approaches and strategies that will help you determine the correct answer in real-world and test-taking situations.

Lesson 3 ■ ■ ■
Find Information from One or Two Graphics

Skill: Find several pieces of information in one or two graphics

When looking at work-related graphics such as blueprints, price estimates, and floor plans, you need to be able to find information. Which parts need to be ordered to complete a job? What are the important deadlines for a key project? Knowing how to find the important facts quickly, as well as how to ignore unnecessary information, will help you work efficiently.

Skill Example

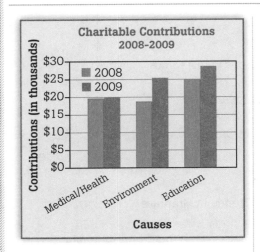

Find information in two graphics.

Different graphical formats can display the same information. The two graphics show the charitable contributions of a small company. The table shows the exact dollar amount donated to each cause. The bar graph helps you quickly identify data such as to which cause the company contributed the most money each year.

Charitable Causes	2008	2009
Medical/Health	$19,500	$20,000
Environment	$18,000	$25,550
Education	$25,150	$28,500
Total	$62,650	$74,050

Maintenance Check List

Maintenance as Required
Check Inflation Pressure
Adjust Brakes

Clean Cab Air Filter
Tighten Loose Nuts or Bolts
Repair Worn or Damaged Parts
Adjust Headlights
Remove Grease, Chaff and Soil

10 Hours (Daily)
Check Air Cleaner/ Pre-cleaner
Check Crankcase Oil Level
Check Cooling System Level
Lubricate Grease Fittings
Check Fuel Sediment Bowl
Check for Loose or Damaged Parts
Check for Leaks
Check for Drive Belts and Hoses

50 Hours (Weekly)
Check Battery Electrolyte Level
Check Hydraulic System Fluid Level
Check Transmission Oil Level
Clean Dry-Element Air Cleaner
Check Inflation Pressure
Perform 10-Hour Maintenance

100 Hours (Every 2 Weeks)
Change Crankcase Oil and Filter
Perform 10 and 50-Hour Maintenance

250 Hours (Monthly)
Clean Battery
Check Belt Tension
Check and Adjust Brakes
Perform 10 and 50-Hour Maintenance

500 Hours (Every 2 Months)
Replace Fuel Filter
Perform 10, 50, 100 and 250-Hour Maintenance

1000 Hours (Yearly)
Drain and Refill Transmission Maintenance and Hydraulic System
Adjust Engine Governor if Recommended by Manufacturer
Clean and Repack Front Wheel
Drain, Clean, and Refill Cooling System
Check Air Conditioning Components
Perform 10, 50, 100, 250, and 500-Hour Maintenance

Skill Practice

Use the document to the left to answer the following questions.

1. As an industrial machinery mechanic, a customer brings in a tractor for yearly maintenance. Which of the following is done only for the 1,000-hour maintenance?

 A. Check Inflation Pressure

 B. Check Cooling System Level

 C. Clean and Repack Front Wheel

 D. Check Hydraulic System Fluid Level

 E. Replace Fuel Filter

2. When you do the monthly (250-hour) maintenance, you should also perform what other maintenance?

 F. 10-Hour and 100-Hour

 G. 10-Hour and 50-Hour

 H. 50-Hour and 100-Hour

 J. only 250-Hour

 K. 100-Hour and 500-Hour

Try It Out! ■ ■ ■

You are a mechanical engineering technician. Your supervisor gives you an Internal Labor form. She sees that several tasks took 9 hours to complete. She asks you to list the labor dates on which the nine-hour tasks were performed. Which of the following lists of dates is correct?

A. 3/14, 3/15, 3/1, 3/20

B. 1/26, 2/02, 3/11, 3/13, 3/14

C. 1/26, 3/14, 3/15, 3/18, 3/20

D. 1/26, 3/14, 3/18, 3/20

E. 1/26, 3/13, 3/15, 3/18, 3/21

Internal Labor

Date	Task ID		Hours	Cost
1/26	690-501	Assembly – Complete (Headquarters shop)	9.00	$328.50
2/02	699-501	Equipment Transport or Tow	1.50	$ 54.75
3/11	690-501	Assembly – Complete (Headquarters shop)	4.00	$219.00
3/13	690-501	Assembly – Complete (Headquarters shop)	5.00	$182.50
3/14	690-501	Assembly – Complete (Headquarters shop)	9.00	$328.50
3/15	690-501	Assembly – Complete (Headquarters shop)	9.00	$328.50
3/16	690-501	Assembly – Complete (Headquarters shop)	4.00	$146.00
3/17	690-501	Assembly – Complete (Headquarters shop)	7.00	$255.50
3/17	690-503	Paint – Complete (Headquarters shop)	3.00	$109.50
3/18	690-501	Assembly – Complete (Headquarters shop)	9.00	$492.75
3/20	690-501	Assembly – Complete (Headquarters shop)	9.00	$328.50
3/21	690-501	Assembly – Complete (Headquarters shop)	5.00	$182.50
3/21	690-501	Assembly – Complete (Headquarters shop)	2.00	$ 73.00
3/22	690-503	Paint – Complete (Headquarters shop)	1.00	$ 36.50
3/23	690-604	Certification – Soft Accessory and Final	5.00	$182.50
3/24	690-604	Certification – Soft Accessory and Final	5.00	$273.75

 Step 1 ## Understand the Problem ■ ■ ■

Complete the *Plan for Successful Solving*.

Plan for Successful Solving

What am I asked to do?	What are the facts?	How do I find the answer?	Is there any unnecessary information?	What prior knowledge will help me?
List the dates on which there were tasks that took nine hours to complete.	The graphic has columns for hours and labor dates.	Find tasks that took nine hours in the hours column. For each 9-hour task, look in date column.	The columns do not list hours or labor date, the tasks that are less or more than nine hours	A column in a table shows the same information for every task. A row has all the information for one task.

 Step 2 ## Find and Check Your Answer ■ ■ ■

- Confirm your understanding of the question and revise your plan as needed.

- Based on your plan, determine your solution approach: *First, I will scan the "Hours" column and find all of the tasks that took nine hours. For those tasks, I will find the "Labor Date", which indicates the date the task took place.*

- Check your answer: Refer to the form. Mark all of the nines in the *Hours* column. Mark the corresponding labor dates within each row, double-checking to see that the answer option you have chosen includes all of these dates.

- **Select the correct answer:** C. 1/26, 3/14, 3/15, 3/18, 3/20
  By scanning the "Hours" column for the number *9*, you can quickly determine the dates on which nine-hour tasks were performed.

Problem Solving Tip

When the problem does not tell you how many answers you have to find, be sure to check every part of the graphic to find all the needed information.

To help eliminate answers, check each answer as you work. In the *Try It Out* example, once you identify that 1/26 is one of the dates, you can immediately eliminate option A as a possible answer because that date is not listed. By finding that 3/14 is the next date on which a nine-hour task took place, you can eliminate options B and E as well, leaving just two possible correct answers.

Remember!

Information in a table is listed in columns and rows. All the data in one column is of the same type. The same is true for the data in one row.

On Your Own ▪ ▪ ▪

Ortega and Sons Construction Company Estimate Town of Mason, Lot B

Cost of a 66-space parking lot

Item	Unit Cost	Project Cost
Grading	$1,000 site	$ 1,000
Paving	$76/ton	$ 6,500
Curbing & Gutter	$36/linear ft.	$ 14,400
Striping	$150 entire lot	$ 150
Plant Materials	$17.50 every 4 ft. on center	$ 1,050
Irrigation	$2.25/sq. ft.	$ 4,500
Signage	$500 ea.	$ 1,000
Lighting	$5,000 ea.	$ 20,000
Trees	$250 ea.	$ 5,500
Project Total		$ 54,100
Approximate Cost Per Parking Space		$ 820

Annual Improvement & Override Budget Town of Mason

Department	Item	Budget
Landscaping	New trees High School entrance	$ 55,000
Landscaping	New trees Town Office entrance	$ 75,000
Landscaping	New trees Parking Lots A, B, & C	$ 45,000
Landscaping	Plant Materials, new, Parking Lots A, B, & C	$ 3,000
Landscaping	Irrigation, Parking Lots A, B, & C	$ 13,500
Parking	Grading, Lot A	$ 3,500
Parking	Grading, Lot B	$ 1,250
Parking	Paving, Lot A	$ 5,700
Parking	Paving, Lot B	$ 6,000
Parking	Paving, Lot C	$ 5,000
Parking	Curbing and Gutter, Lot B	$ 15,000
Parking	Striping, Lots B & C	$ 350
Parking	Signage, Lots B & C	$ 2,500
Lighting	Street, new and repairs	$ 335,000
Lighting	Parking, Lots A, B, & C	$ 110,000
Maintenance	Snow Removal	$ 350,000
Maintenance	Sand & Salt	$ 150,000
	Total:	$ 1,175,800

1. You are a contractor's assistant. You are helping to complete a bid estimate for a project to be contracted through the town of Mason. For which item as part of your bid have you estimated higher than the town's budgeted amount?

   A. Grading

   B. Paving

   C. Striping

   D. Irrigation

   E. Lighting

2. For which items would it help to know the town's budgeted costs of items for lot A in order to form a more accurate estimate?

   F. Paving, striping, signage, and trees

   G. Striping, plant materials, irrigation, and lighting

   H. Plant materials, lighting, irrigation, and trees

   J. Grading, plant materials, irrigation, and trees

   K. Plant materials, signage, lighting, and trees

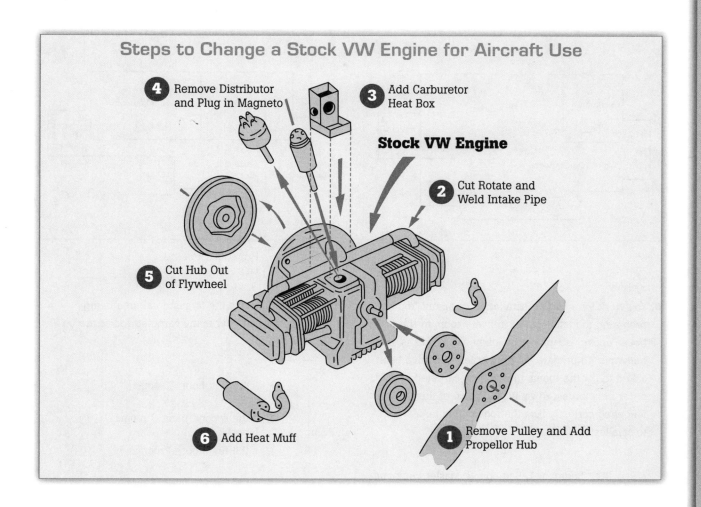

Steps to Change a Stock VW Engine for Aircraft Use

4 Remove Distributor and Plug in Magneto

3 Add Carburetor Heat Box

Stock VW Engine

2 Cut Rotate and Weld Intake Pipe

5 Cut Hub Out of Flywheel

6 Add Heat Muff

1 Remove Pulley and Add Propellor Hub

3. You are an aircraft mechanic. Your supervisor puts you in charge of making changes to a stock VW engine so that it can be put into an airplane. According to the graphic, which parts do you remove?

    A.   Pulley, Heat Muff, and Intake Pipe

    B.   Pulley and Distributor

    C.   Carburetor Heat Box and Distributor

    D.   Distributor, Fly Wheel Hub, and Propellor Hub

    E.   Pulley, Distributor, and Heat Muff

4. If your supervisor asks you to complete the needed changes, which parts do you add or plug in?

    F.   Propellor Hub, Carburetor Heat Box, and Intake Pipe

    G.   Propellor Hub, Carburetor Heat Box, Heat Muff, and Magneto

    H.   Propellor Hub, Heat Muff, and Distributor

    J.   Carburetor Heat Box, Magneto, and Fly Wheel Hub

    K.   Heat Muff, Carburetor Heat Box, and Pulley

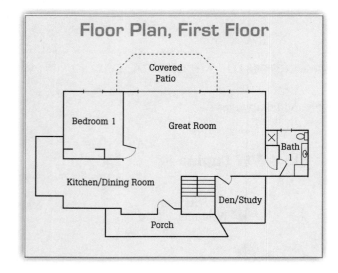

Floor Plan, First Floor

Covered Patio

Bedroom 1

Great Room

Bath 1

Kitchen/Dining Room

Den/Study

Porch

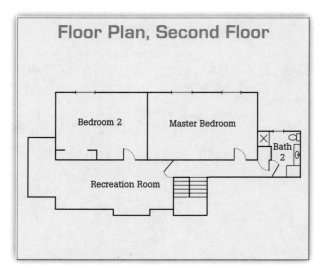

Floor Plan, Second Floor

Bedroom 2

Master Bedroom

Bath 2

Recreation Room

5. You work for a carpet installation company. You are preparing to install carpet in every room in the house above except for the kitchen, bathrooms, and hallways. To prepare a carpet order, you have been asked to list the rooms that will be carpeted in order from largest to smallest. Which of the following correctly lists the rooms from largest to smallest?

    A. Bedroom 1, Bedroom 2, Master Bedroom, Recreation Room, and Great Room

    B. Great Room, Kitchen/Dining Room, Bedroom 1, Den/Study, and Bath 1

    C. Great Room, Kitchen/Dining Room, Recreation Room, Master Bedroom, and Bedroom 2

    D. Bedroom 2, Master Bedroom, Recreation Room, Kitchen/Dining Room, and Great Room

    E. Great Room, Recreation Room, Master Bedroom, Bedroom 2, Bedroom 1, and Den/Study

6. Which floor has the largest total area being carpeted and how many carpeted rooms are on that floor?

    F. the first floor; 7 rooms

    G. the second floor; 3 rooms

    H. the first floor; 3 rooms

    J. the second floor; 2 rooms

    K. the first floor; 3 rooms

List of Drill Bits Available

Drill Bit ID Number	Diameter
101–857	12 millimeters
672–861	16 millimeters
507–796	25 millimeters
312–804	30 millimeters
152–367	32 millimeters

Barrow Tool Supply

Item No.	Quick Reference Number	No. of Hole Sizes per Bit	Size Range (Hole Diameter)	Pilot Hole Required	Electric Drill Size	Depth Penetration for Each Step	Weight (lbs.)
59021	1-M	9 in 1 mm increments	4 mm to 12 mm	no	1/4" and larger	5 mm	.05
59022	20-M	6 in 2 mm increments	14 mm to 24 mm	yes, 12 mm or larger	1/2" and larger	5 mm	.25
59023	3-M	7 in 2 mm increments	6 mm to 18 mm	no	3/8" and larger	5 mm	.10
59024	21-M	8 in 2 mm increments	20 mm to 34 mm	yes, 18 mm or larger	1/2" and larger	5 mm	.45
59025	2-M	5 in 2 mm increments	4 mm to 12 mm	no	1/4" and larger	11 mm	.05

7. As a machinist, you are ordering drill bits. You have a chart that tells you your company's drill bit ID numbers. You also have a catalog from Barrow Tool Supply that lists the item numbers of drill bits that are available to order. If you need to order drill bit 312–804, which item number should you order?

- **A.** 59021
- **B.** 59022
- **C.** 59023
- **D.** 59024
- **E.** 59025

8. For your next job, your boss tells you that you should use drill bit number 672–861. You will need to order new drill bits from the catalog for this job. Which items from Barrow Tool Supply can you order for this project?

- **F.** Item Numbers 59021 and 59023
- **G.** Item Numbers 59022 and 59023
- **H.** Item Numbers 59023 and 59025
- **J.** Item Numbers 59021 and 59024
- **K.** Item Numbers 59021 and 59025

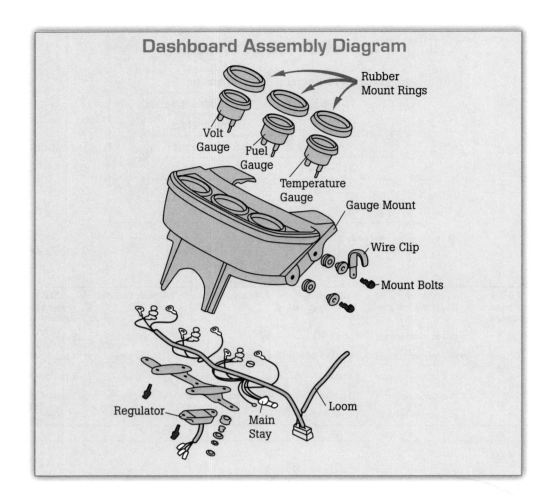

Dashboard Assembly Diagram

Rubber Mount Rings

Volt Gauge

Fuel Gauge

Temperature Gauge

Gauge Mount

Wire Clip

Mount Bolts

Regulator

Main Stay

Loom

9. As an automotive technician, you must pull three gauges from inventory in order to put them into a dashboard assembly. Based on the diagram, what are the three gauges?

    A.   Volt, Fuel, Temperature

    B.   Volt, Fuel, Oil

    C.   Loom, Fuel, Temperature

    D.   Oil, Volt, Temperature

    E.   Volt, Loom, Oil

10. Which set of parts is not listed in the diagram?

    F.   Regulator, Main Stay, Loom

    G.   Wire Harness, Metal Screws, Capacitor

    H.   Rubber Mount Rings, Gauge Mount, Main Stay

    J.   Wire Clip, Mount Bolts, Volt Gauge

    K.   Fuel Gauge, Gauge Mount, Loom

Marina Han
Sales Representative

direct 555-212-6200
mhan@publishinggroup.com

Tel 555-212-1000 Fax 555-212-8080
100 5th Ave. New York, NY 10011
www.publishinggroup.com

Publishing Group is a full-service editorial, art, and design production house specializing in professional books, science and technology books, engineering books, computer books, and corporate, professional, and technical documentation. Since 1999, we have used top-notch writers, designers, and editors to produce the best materials for all of our clients, large and small.

Contacts

Gregory Hennesy
28 years experience
President & CEO
555-212-6100

Anita Slovinsky
25 years experience
Managing Editor
555-212-6300

Glen Hopkins
14 years experience
Head of Art & Design
555-212-6400

Jillian Baker
8 years experience
Science Editor
555-212-6500

Marcus Fowler
5 years experience
Technology Editor
555-212-6600

Jason Wu
6 years experience
Engineering Editor
555-212-6700

---

11. You are a managing editor at a science and technology publishing company. You receive the above business card and flyer from a company that you think may be able to help you with your latest project. A note on the back of the business card said you should feel free to contact anyone on the staff with questions. You decide to e-mail the technology editor with some questions about the company's technology experience. Who do you e-mail and what is his/her e-mail address?

    A. Marina Han;
mhan@publishinggroup.com

    B. Marcus Fowler;
mfowler@publishinggroup.com

    C. Jason Wu;
jason_wu@publishinggroup.com

    D. Marcus Fowler;
technology@publishinggroup.com

    E. Jason Wu; jwu@publishinggroup.com

12. You hire Publishing Group to work on your project and need to fax an agreement to the President & CEO. To whose attention do you send the fax and what number do you use?

    F. Gregory Hennesy; 555-212-6100

    G. Marina Han; 555-212-6200

    H. Gregory Hennesy; 555-212-8080

    J. Marina Han; 555-212-1000

    K. Anita Slovinsky; 555-212-1000

Errors Report Database

Robot Number	Errors per Thousand Welds				
	M	T	W	Th	F
1	0.8	1.03	1.05	1.5	1.3
2	1.8	2.14	2.0	2.1	2.5
3	1.5	1.65	1.8	1.6	1.4
4	1.0	1.9	2.8	2.0	2.3
5	4.0	2.74	3.5	4.5	5.0

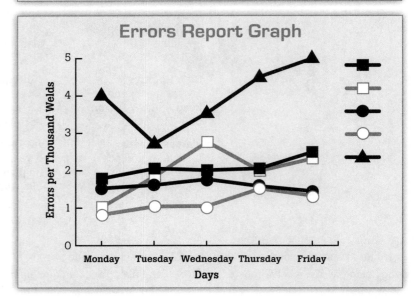

Errors Report Graph

13. As an industrial engineering technician, your job is to check the quality of the work of five robots that weld parts on an automobile assembly line. Your boss asks you to create a graph based on the table that shows the errors for the week. You create the graph above and need to add a key. Which robot has the best quality, or lowest error rate, and which line on the graph corresponds to that robot?

A. Robot 1; gold line with circles

B. Robot 1; black line with circles

C. Robot 3; gold line with circles

D. Robot 3; black line with circles

E. Robot 4; black line with triangles

14. You also want to tell your boss which robot consistently had the lowest quality performance. Which robot is this, which line corresponds to this robot, and what was its highest errors per thousand welds in one day?

F. Robot 1; black line with triangles; 5.0

G. Robot 4; gold line with circles; 5.0

H. Robot 4; gold line with squares; 2.8

J. Robot 5; gold line with squares; 5.0

K. Robot 5; black line with triangles; 5.0

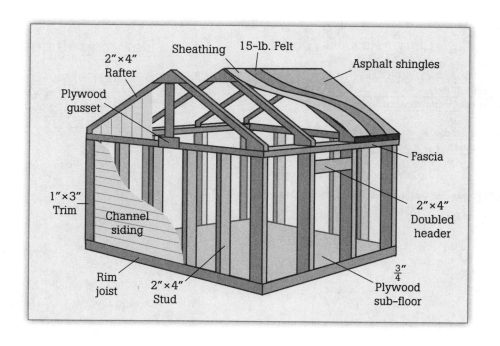

15. You work as an installation specialist for a major home supply store. Your job today is to put a roof on a shed. According to the graphic, what are the three items you must put on top of the rafters?

    A.   Sheathing, 15-lb. felt, Asphalt shingles

    B.   Sheathing, 15-lb. felt, 2"×4" Rafters

    C.   Sheathing, Plywood gusset, Asphalt shingles

    D.   Channel siding, 15-lb. Felt, Asphalt shingles

    E.   2"×4" stud, 1"×3" trim, Rim joist

16. Which parts of the shed require 2"×4" boards?

    F.   Rafter, Stud, Plywood sub-floor

    G.   Fascia, Plywood gusset, Sheathing

    H.   Rafter, Trim, Doubled header

    J.   Rim joist, Stud, Doubled header

    K.   Rafter, Stud, Doubled header

Copy Center Request Form

Today's Date/Time: Oct. 12/2:30 p.m.
Requested by: J. Brown
Department/Cost Center Number: Operations

Date/Time Required: Oct. 13/9:30 a.m.
Telephone Number: 555-123-7023

Job Description

Number of Pages per Original: 65   Number of Copies/Sets: 3

Standard Copies:

☐ Covers

☐ 8.5 × 11   Front _3_   Back _3_

☐ 8.5 × 14   Black ____   White ____

☑ 11 × 17   Clear ____   Special ____

☐ Other:

Finishing Services

☑ Tape Binding

Black ___   White ✓

☐ Wire Binding

☐ GBC Binding

Special Request/Services: Please ship one set to Janet Fry and deliver two sets to Operations

---

Shipping Request Form

TO: Janet Fry, Marketing Manager
        20217 S. Sudbury Ave.
        Linoden, OH 79800
        (555)-820-1837

FROM: John Brown
DEPARTMENT:
COST CENTER:

EXPRESS	
First Overnight	☑
Priority Overnight	☐
Standard Overnight	☐
Second Day	☐
Other	☐

OPTIONS	
Saturday Delivery	☐
Signature Release	☑
International	☐

Bill Third Party
74500231 MKTG-03

SPECIAL INSTRUCTIONS: Please bill shipping cost to Marketing Department c/o Janet Fry, with third party billing code.

---

17. You are an administrative coordinator working in the shipping and copying department of a large insurance company. Based on the forms, how many copies need to be shipped, and to where do they need to be shipped?

   A.   Three sets need to be shipped to Ohio.

   B.   One set needs to be shipped to Ohio.

   C.   Two sets need to be shipped to Operations.

   D.   Two sets need to be shipped to Ohio.

   E.   Three sets need to be shipped to Operations.

18. Based on the forms, which department requested shipping and who should be charged for shipping costs?

   F.   Janet Fry requested shipping. Operations should be charged.

   G.   Operations requested shipping. John Brown should be charged.

   H.   Operations requested shipping, and it should be charged.

   J.   Janet Fry requested shipping, and she should be charged.

   K.   Operations requested shipping and Marketing should be charged.

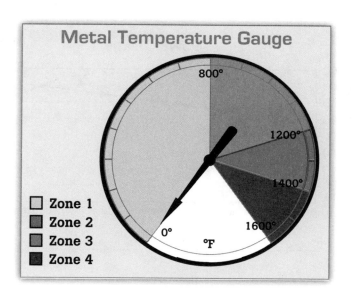

Metal Temperature Gauge

800°
1200°
1400°
0°
1600°
°F

☐ **Zone 1**
◻ **Zone 2**
◻ **Zone 3**
■ **Zone 4**

19. As a molding and casting worker, you must monitor the temperature of the metal that is being poured into the mold. The temperature is shown on the gauge above. To make a good cast, the temperature should be in Zone 2. What is the lowest temperature at which the metal can be in Zone 2?

    A. 0°

    B. 800°

    C. 1200°

    D. 1400°

    E. 1600°

20. Reaching Zone 4 means that the temperature has reached a dangerous level. What temperature indicates that the metal has just entered Zone 4?

    F. 0°

    G. 800°

    H. 1200°

    J. 1400°

    K. 1600°

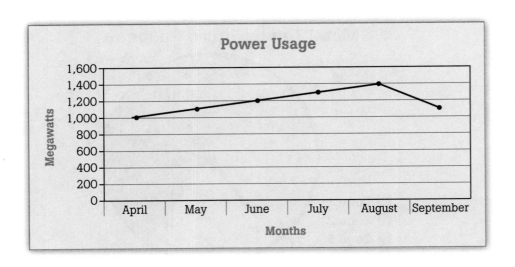

Power Usage

21. You are an operator at a power generating plant. Your assignment is to plan for how much power will be needed next spring and summer. You begin by looking at how much power was used last year, as shown in the chart above. How many megawatts of power were used in June of last year?

    A. 1,100

    B. 1,200

    C. 1,300

    D. 1,400

    E. 1,500

22. Which month on the chart required the most power?

    F. April

    G. May

    H. June

    J. August

    K. September

Project Database

Project Price			Project Cost			Project Profit		
Labor	$920.00		Labor	$350.00		Labor	$570.00	
Overtime	$320.00		Overtime	$200.00		Overtime	$120.00	
Travel	$400.00		Travel	$400.00		Travel	$0.00	
Materials	$2,640.00		Materials	$1,260.00		Materials	$1,380.00	
Services	$300.00		Services	$150.00		Services	$150.00	
Other Charges	$400.00		Other Charges	$260.00		Other Charges	$140.00	
Subtotal	$4,980.00		Subtotal	$2,620.00		Subtotal	$2,360.00	
Discount	−$250.00		Discount	N/A		Discount	−$250.00	
Total	$4,730.00		Total	$2,620.00		Total	$2,110.00	

23. As an accounting manager, you are responsible for reporting project financial reports to management. The vice president of your company asks you to list all of the line items for a recent project that had a profit greater than $200. Based on the Project Database, which of the following lists is correct?

A. Labor, Overtime

B. Labor, Materials

C. Travel, Materials

D. Labor, Services

E. Materials, Tip Charge

24. Which factor played a role in reducing the total profits for the project?

F. Labor

G. Overtime

H. Materials

J. Discount

K. Other Charges

Answers are on page 248.

When information in
one graphic relates to
information in another
graphic, it is helpful to
first understand the
content of each graphic.
In the *Try It Out!*
example, you can
scan the graphics to
determine that the
same machines are
listed in both tables.
This helps you
understand that each
table likely lists
different information
about the machines.
By examining the
tables more closely,
you are able to see that
the information
presented in both
tables is related to
machine maintenance.

Lesson 4 ■ ■ ■
Understand How Graphics Relate

Skill: Understand how graphics are related to each other

There are times at the workplace when you need to get information from
multiple graphics or documents before making decisions. Before a work order
can be filled, an inventory or supplies list must be checked to see if the
materials needed to make the repair are available. Managers must compare
shift schedules to employee days off requests when scheduling weekly shifts.
Workplace decision-making is often dependent on understanding and using
information from multiple graphics.

Skill Example

Routine Maintenance Schedule

Lathe	Weekly
Milling Machine	Monthly
Shaper	Monthly
Grinder	Daily
Drill Press	Weekly

Machine Maintenance Log

Machine	Last Maintenance Done
Lathe	August 27
Milling Machine	August 1
Shaper	September 1
Grinder	September 1
Drill Press	September 1

Understand how graphics relate to
each other

When scheduling machine
maintenance, a machinist must
know how often each machine
should have routine maintenance
performed, and when the last
maintenance was performed. The
first table is a schedule that lists
how often maintenance should be
performed on each machine. The
second table is a log used to keep
track of when the maintenance of
each machine was last performed.
By using the log and the
maintenance schedule, you can
determine when the next
maintenance for each machine
should take place.

Skill Practice

Use the tables above to answer the following questions.

1. Today is September 2. Which of the
   machines that needs monthly
   maintenance should have its
   maintenance done today?

   A. lathe

   B. milling machine

   C. shaper

   D. grinder

   E. drill press

2. Which of the machines that needs
   weekly maintenance should have its
   maintenance done today?

   F. milling machine

   G. lathe

   H. shaper

   J. grinder

   K. drill press

Try It Out! ■ ■ ■

As a boat builder, you have to know about the kinds of materials used to build boats. The first graphic shows you the specifications for the hull and deck of a new boat. The second graphic describes boat building supply dealers who provide materials used to build boats. Which dealer or dealers would you call to get the materials you would need for the new boat?

A. Brooklyn Boats & Materials and Massachusetts Marine Supplies

B. Valley Forge

C. Brooklyn Boats & Materials

D. Massachusetts Marine Supplies and Valley Forge

E. Massachusetts Marine Supplies

Boston Boat Builders
Boston, MA

Customer: ___S. Johnson___

Date: ___3/30/2010___

Construction Specifications	
Product	20-foot pleasure boat
Hull	Monolithic polyester with floater foam addition; fiberglass
Deck	Polyester resin sandwich; core in high density foam
Other Information	

Boat Building Supply Dealers

Name of Dealer	Dealer Phone	Type of Dealer	Types of Materials
Valley Forge	(215) 555-0573	Metal	Stainless steel, aluminum
Brooklyn Boats & Materials	(347) 555-1358	Plastic/ Fiberglass	Polyester, floater foam, high-density foam
Massachusetts Marine Supplies	(617) 555-7199	Wood	Marine plywood, cypress, white oak

Step 1 Understand the Problem ■ ■ ■

Complete the *Plan for Successful Solving*.

Plan for Successful Solving

What am I asked to do?	What are the facts?	How do I find the answer?	Is there any unnecessary information?	What prior knowledge will help me?
Determine which dealer to contact for boat materials.	The specs indicate that the boat hull and deck will be made of polyester, fiberglass, and foam.	Look through the table of dealers to find who specializes in polyester, fiberglass, and foam.	The types of metal and wood used to build boats.	Specifications, or "Specs," list all materials needed. The information I need is based on these specs.

Step 2 Find and Check Your Answer ■ ■ ■

- Confirm your understanding of the question and revise your plan as needed.

- Based on your plan, determine your solution approach: *I will first identify what materials are needed by looking at the construction specifications. Then I will use the table to match the materials that are needed based on the specs to those listed for each dealer in the "Types of Materials" column. This will help me determine which dealer specializes in the materials I need.*

- Check your answer. Review all answers to determine if the answer you have selected is the best possible answer.

- **Select the correct answer:** **C.** Brooklyn Boats & Materials
  The construction specifications list floater foam, polyester, high-density foam, and fiberglass as the materials needed to build the boat. The supply dealers table shows that Brooklyn Boats & Materials carries all of these materials.

On Your Own ▪ ■ ▪

Title: Laboratory Assistant

Req Number: bd-4782

Job Type: Regular Full-time

Location: Cleveland, OH

The position will reside in the Cleveland, OH offices. Day-to-day responsibilities include, but are not limited to:

1. Set up laboratory and field equipment to help science research workers.

2. Clean laboratory, field equipment, and work areas.

3. Plant seeds and count the categories of plants that grow.

4. Examine animals for diseases.

5. Record data.

R. Donovan
555 Maple Street
Apartment 5
Cleveland, Ohio 44102

Experience

Houston Science Laboratory, Houston, TX, 5 years

Skills

(a) Use science to solve problems.

(b) Use math to solve problems.

(c) Determine when something is wrong.

(d) Choose the right equipment needed to do a job.

(e) Control operation of equipment.

(f) Put information into categories.

Education

Houston Metro Community College, biology major

---

1. As a human resources specialist, you are reviewing applications for an open biology laboratory assistant position. The job ad above shows the tasks required for the job and the résumé shows one applicant's skills. Which of the skills listed on the résumé show that the applicant can successfully perform task 1?

    A.   (a), (b), (e)

    B.   (b), (d), (e)

    C.   (a), (d), (e)

    D.   (a), (b), (f)

    E.   (a), (d), (f)

2. Which skill shows that the applicant can successfully perform task 3?

    F.   (e)

    G.   (f)

    H.   (c)

    J.   (b)

    K.   (d)

www.123CarCare.com
Preventive Maintenance Checklist

Vehicle System or Component	Check Monthly	Check When Changing Oil	Service Notes
Engine Air Filter in Engine Compartment		✓	• Replace if dirty as needed, or replace every 15,000 to 30,000 miles
Cabin Air Filter in Car Behind Glovebox or at Windshield Base		✓	• Replace odor filters yearly • Replace dust filters 30,000
Engine Coolant (Antifreeze)	✓		• Check level, add specified coolant if low • Replace green antifreeze 2-3 years • Replace orange/yellow antifreeze 5 Years or 15,000 miles
Battery & Cables		✓	• Check battery posts for corrosion • Check for loose/damaged cables
Belts	✓		• Inspect belts for cracks or glazing, replace if worn or noisy • Check belt tension
Brake Fluid	✓		• Check fluid level in master brake cylinder resevoir • Add specified fluid if low

Engine Oil & Filter		✓	• Check oil level with engine off if level below ADD mark on dipstick, add 1 quart
			• Change oil & filter
			  – Every 3,000 miles (severe driving)
			  – Every 5,000 miles (normal driving)
			• Use recommended oil viscosity

Customer List

Customer Name	Work Required
Maria Ramirez	oil change
Samuel Davis	oil change
Joseph Yanos	oil change
Katie Palmisano	monthly maintenance
Eddie Iwasaki	oil change
Angila Cooley	monthly maintenance

3. As an automotive master mechanic, you need to tell your specialty technicians what work to do for each customer. What systems or components should be checked or replaced for Maria Ramirez, Samuel Davis, Joseph Yanos, and Eddie Iwasaki?

    A. engine air filter, engine coolant, battery & cables

    B. brake fluid, cabin air filter, battery & cables

    C. engine air filter, cabin air filter, belts

    D. engine air filter, cabin air filter, battery & cables, engine oil & filter

    E. engine coolant, belts, brake fluid

4. What systems or components should be checked or replaced for Katie Palmisano and Angila Cooley?

    F. engine coolant, engine air filter, brake fluid

    G. engine coolant, belts, brake fluid

    H. engine coolant, belts, battery & cables

    J. cabin air filter, belts, brake fluid

    K. engine air filter, cabin air filter, battery & cables

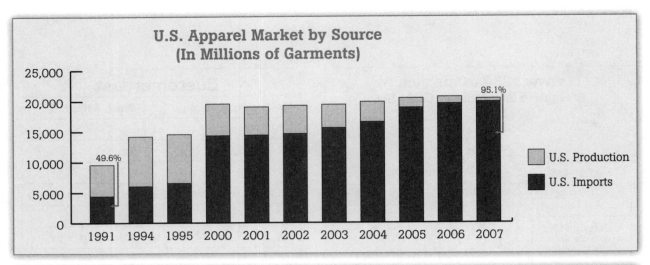

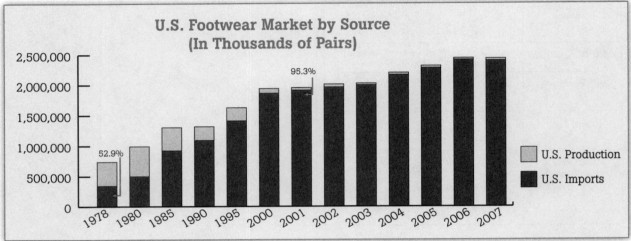

5. You are an assistant to the vice president of business operations for a company that produces apparel and footwear. You are responsible for creating graphics for a presentation on production trends since the late 1970s. According to the graphics

    A. imports have come to supply nearly 100% of the market for footwear only.

    B. imports have come to supply nearly 50% of the market for apparel and footwear.

    C. imports have come to supply nearly 50% of the market for footwear only.

    D. imports have come to supply nearly 100% of the market for both apparel and footwear.

    E. imports have come to supply nearly 100% of the market for apparel only.

6. Based on the U.S. production numbers for apparel and footwear, you could state that the period of time in which the market went from about 50% supplied by US production to over 95% imports

    F. was shorter for apparel (16 years) than it was for footwear (29 years).

    G. was longer for apparel (23 years) than it was for footwear (16 years).

    H. was the same for apparel (23 years) as it was for footwear (23 years).

    J. was shorter for apparel (16 years) than it was for footwear (23 years).

    K. was the same for footwear (29 years) as it was for footwear (29 years).

Font Specifications

Font	Characters per Pica
Arial	2.4
Bookman Old Style	2.2
Garamond	2.7
Souvenir	2.6
Times New Roman	2.6

Booklet Specifications

Booklet	Characters	Picas Available	Minimum Characters per Pica
1	42,997	20,475	2.1
2	43,325	18,837	2.3
3	34,398	17,199	2.0
4	51,187	20,475	2.5
5	54,463	20,475	2.7

7. As a graphic designer, you choose the fonts that are used for projects. You are working on five booklets. The second table above lists the minimum number of characters per pica needed for the font that you choose for each booklet. Using this information, which font or fonts could you use for booklet #3?

    A. Arial, Garamond, Souvenir, Times New Roman

    B. Garamond

    C. Arial, Bookman Old Style, Souvenir, Times New Roman

    D. Garamond, Souvenir, Times New Roman

    E. Arial, Bookman Old Style, Garamond, Souvenir, Times New Roman

8. Which font or fonts could you use for booklet #5?

    F. Arial, Bookman Old Style, Souvenir, Times New Roman

    G. Bookman Old Style

    H. Arial, Garamond, Souvenir, Times New Roman

    J. Garamond

    K. Garamond, Souvenir, Times New Roman

Types of Pipe for Gas Lines

Steel	expensive installation, many couplings and fittings required, heavy, rigid, available in pre-threaded lengths, better for short lines
Corrugated stainless steel tubing	flexible, requires professional installation, cannot be in contact with ground, safest material, better for long lines
Galvanized steel	expensive installation, many couplings and fittings required, heavy, rigid, available in pre-threaded lengths, better for short lines
Soft copper tubing	flexible, fewer fittings required, better for long lines, not available in pre-threaded lengths

Repair Job Schedule

123. Replace natural gas line to water heater	meet safety codes, long line, flexible material required
124. Fix leak in line to gas barbecue	short line, contact with ground, pre-threaded lengths must be used

9. You are a gas appliance repairer. When you look at your repair job schedule, you must choose what kind of pipe to use. Based on the above tables, what type(s) of pipe do you need for job 123?

    A.   steel

    B.   galvanized steel

    C.   corrugated stainless steel tubing or steel

    D.   corrugated stainless steel tubing or soft copper tubing

    E.   galvanized steel or steel

10. What type(s) of pipe do you need for job 124?

    F.   steel or corrugated stainless steel tubing

    G.   steel or galvanized steel

    H.   soft copper tubing

    J.   corrugated stainless steel tubing

    K.   soft copper tubing or galvanized steel

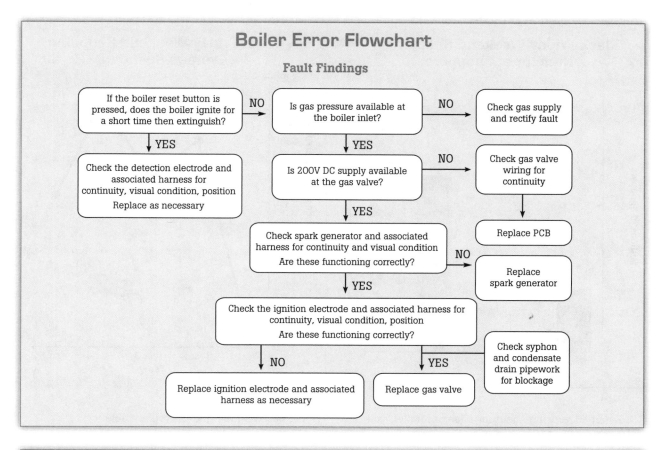

Boiler Error Flowchart

Fault Findings

If the boiler reset button is pressed, does the boiler ignite for a short time then extinguish?

NO → Is gas pressure available at the boiler inlet?

NO → Check gas supply and rectify fault

YES ↓ Check the detection electrode and associated harness for continuity, visual condition, position
Replace as necessary

YES ↓ Is 200V DC supply available at the gas valve?

NO → Check gas valve wiring for continuity

↓ Replace PCB

YES ↓ Check spark generator and associated harness for continuity and visual condition
Are these functioning correctly?

NO → Replace spark generator

YES ↓ Check the ignition electrode and associated harness for continuity, visual condition, position
Are these functioning correctly?

NO → Replace ignition electrode and associated harness as necessary

YES → Replace gas valve

Check syphon and condensate drain pipework for blockage

Boiler Flame Error Report

Basement boiler	boiler stays lit after pushing reset button, gas pressure available at inlet, 200V DC is not available at gas valve
First-floor boiler	boiler stays lit after pushing reset button, gas pressure available at inlet, 200V DC is available at gas valve, spark generator functioning, ignition electrode functioning

11. As a boilermaker, you have received an e-mail with the above error report. To determine what is needed to fix each boiler, you refer to the flowchart. What is required to fix the basement boiler?

    A.   Check gas supply and rectify fault

    B.   Replace spark generator

    C.   Replace PCB

    D.   Replace ignition electrode

    E.   Replace gas valve

12. What is required to fix the first-floor boiler?

    F.   Replace ignition electrode

    G.   Replace gas valve

    H.   Replace PCB

    J.   Replace spark generator

    K.   Check gas supply and rectify fault

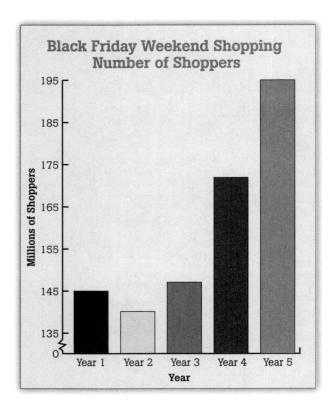

**Black Friday Weekend Shopping
Number of Shoppers**

Millions of Shoppers / Year

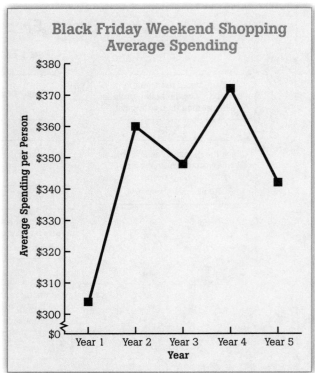

**Black Friday Weekend Shopping
Average Spending**

Average Spending per Person / Year

13. As an advertising agent for a major retailer, you are in charge of analyzing shopping trends to determine the advertising needs based on sales from previous years. Based on the graphs, how is the average spending per person on Black Friday weekend related to the number of shoppers that weekend?

    A. As the number of shoppers increases, so does the average amount of spending per person.

    B. As the number of shoppers decreases, so does the average amount of spending per person.

    C. As the average number of shoppers increases, the average amount of spending per person decreases.

    D. The average number of shoppers increases or decreases at the same rate as the average amount of spending per person.

    E. There is no clear relationship between the average amount of shoppers and the average amount of spending per person.

14. Based on the graphs, you are able to determine that

    F. the number of shoppers decreases each year, so you need more advertising to attract more shoppers.

    G. despite an increase in shoppers, average spending per person decreased in Year 5; more advertising and lower pricing could increase sales.

    H. average spending per person has increased every year, so you do not need to increase advertising.

    J. average spending per person has decreased every year, so you need to increase advertising.

    K. the number of shoppers increases each year, so you do not need to increase advertising.

Printing Jobs Scheduled for Today

Job Number	Number of Colors	Number of Copies
A745	2	10,000
A862	2	45,000
A3345	4	50,000

List of Presses

Press Number	Number of Ink Wells	Number of Copies per Hour
101	1	5,000
201	2	10,000
301	4	10,000
401	2	20,000
501	4	30,000

15. As an operator of an offset lithographic press, you have to choose which press to use for each printing job. The number of ink wells on the press must match the number of colors on the printing job. Your supervisor wants each job to be finished in one hour or less, so you must compare the press's number of copies per hour to the number of copies to be printed. Which presses can you use for printing job A745?

A. 101 or 201

B. 201 or 401

C. 301 or 501

D. 401 or 301

E. 501 or 201

16. Your boss needs you to start job A3345. It is needed in three hours. Which press can you use for this job?

F. 101

G. 201

H. 301

J. 401

K. 501

Work Order

Washington and O'Conner Construction, Co.
153 Johnson Ave
Asbury, IA 52002
(555) 820-1837

Work Order Number: 10085
Project ID: EW Glenn Ave.

Customer Name: *Elliot White*
Customer Home Street Address:
15 Maple Glen Ave.
Asbury, IA
Home Zip: 52002
Home Phone: (555) 820-2511
Work Phone: (555) 820-0525

Work for: *Kitchen*

Itemized Description

Location	Description of work
A. Wall with interior door	
B. Wall opposite interior door	
C. Wall with window	
D. Wall opposite windows	

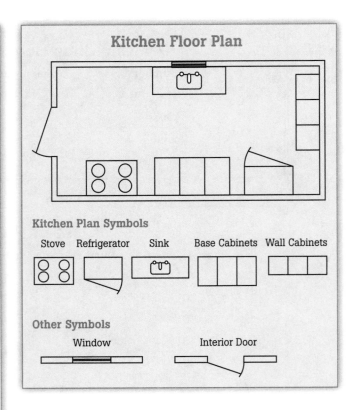

Kitchen Floor Plan

Kitchen Plan Symbols

Stove   Refrigerator   Sink   Base Cabinets   Wall Cabinets

Other Symbols

Window   Interior Door

17. You are an architectural drafter. It is important that you understand the symbols used on floor plans and how to use floor plans to write work orders to the construction crew. To construct Elliot White's kitchen according to the floor plan, what do you write under "Description of work" for location C?

 A. Install stove and connect the gas line

 B. Install and paint base cabinets

 C. Install and paint wall cabinets

 D. Install refrigerator and connect ice maker

 E. Install sink, faucet, and garbage disposal

18. What do you write under "Description of work" for location B?

 F. Install sink, faucet, and garbage disposal

 G. Install and paint wall cabinets

 H. Install refrigerator and connect ice maker

 J. Install and paint base cabinets

 K. Install stove and connect to gas line

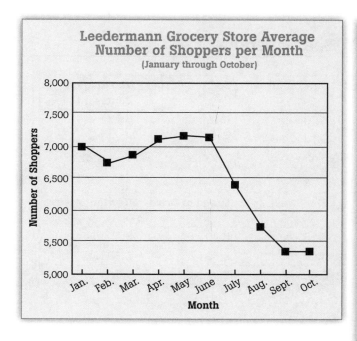

Leedermann Grocery Store Average Number of Shoppers per Month
(January through October)

Year	Fresh Turkeys Sold	Frozen Turkeys Sold	Total Turkeys Sold
Year 1	880	1,320	2,200
Year 2	885	1,328	2,213
Year 3	887	1,330	2,217
Year 4	880	1,980	2,860
Year 5	895	1,350	2,245
Year 6	880	1,345	2,225
Year 7	890	1,346	2,236
Year 8	910	1,365	2,275
Year 9	920	1,380	2,300
Year 10	930	1,400	2,330

Average Turkeys Sold in November

19. As the meat manager at Leedermann Grocery Store, you are in charge of managing inventory. In the past year, a new supermarket opened nearby, impacting your store's sales significantly. Based on the information in the line graph above, in which month did the new supermarket open?

    A. May

    B. July

    C. August

    D. September

    E. October

20. You have kept a careful record of the number of fresh and frozen turkeys sold over the past ten years so that you can order accurately each year for the Thanksgiving holiday. Based on your records and the changes in sales over the past year, about how many total turkeys should you order for November of this year?

    F. 1,750

    G. 1,925

    H. 2,245

    J. 2,300

    K. 2,330

Georgetown Bus Schedule

729 Bus

Fire House	Bay Street	Commuter Rail	Newton Street	Bedford Corner	Washington Boulevard
5:31 P.M.	5:45 P.M.	5:55 P.M.	5:59 P.M.	6:19 P.M.	6:27 P.M.
5:50 P.M.	6:04 P.M.	6:14 P.M.	6:18 P.M.	6:38 P.M.	6:46 P.M.
6:15 P.M.	6:29 P.M.	6:39 P.M.	6:43 P.M.	7:03 P.M.	7:11 P.M.

1280 Bus

Sherman Avenue	9th Street	Market Place	Elm Street	Langden Drive	Newton Street
4:50 P.M.	5:03 P.M.	5:18 P.M.	5:26 P.M.	5:39 P.M.	5:50 P.M.
5:10 P.M.	5:23 P.M.	5:38 P.M.	5:46 P.M.	5:59 P.M.	6:10 P.M.
6:10 P.M.	6:23 P.M.	6:38 P.M.	6:45 P.M.	5:59 P.M.	7:10 P.M.

Georgetown Movie Theater Multiplex Schedule

You Walked In	4:15 P.M.	7:10 P.M.	9:00 P.M.
The Night's Revenge	4:05 P.M.	7:15 P.M.	9:30 P.M.
Maple Falls	4:00 P.M.	7:00 P.M.	9:15 P.M.

21. You write movie reviews for your local newspaper. You need to review new movies that are playing at the Georgetown Multiplex on Newton Street. You decide to first review the latest thriller, *The Night's Revenge*. You need to take the bus to the theater. You live near both the Fire House and Sherman Avenue stops. If you plan to see the 7:15 P.M. showing, which bus will get you there no earlier than 30 minutes before the movie and no later than 5 minutes before the movie?

- **A.** the 729 bus departing at 6:15 P.M.
- **B.** the 729 bus departing at 5:50 P.M.
- **C.** the 1280 bus departing at 5:10 P.M.
- **D.** the 1280 bus departing at 6:10 P.M.
- **E.** the 1280 bus departing at 4:50 P.M.

22. On a different day, you take the 729 bus at 5:31 P.M. and decide to see whatever movie begins closest to the time you get off at the Newton Street stop. What time do you get off at your stop and what movie do you see?

- **F.** 5:50 P.M.; *Maple Falls*
- **G.** 5:59 P.M.; *Maple Falls*
- **H.** 6:27 P.M.; *Maple Falls*
- **J.** 6:10 P.M.; *You Walked In*
- **K.** 7:10 P.M.; *You Walked In*

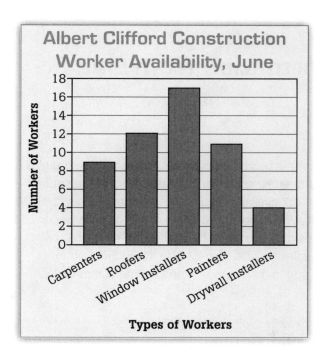

Albert Clifford Construction Worker Availability, June

(Bar graph — Number of Workers vs. Types of Workers)

- Carpenters: 9
- Roofers: 12
- Window Installers: 17
- Painters: 11
- Drywall Installers: 4

Albert Clifford Construction June Schedule

Project Location	Type and Number of Workers
715 Taylor Road	3 painters; 2 roofers; 4 window installers
1101 Lincoln Street, Suite 210	2 drywall installers; 2 painters
821 Polk Avenue	4 carpenters; 2 drywall installers; 4 roofers
Smithfield High School, 1164 Jackson Street	10 window installers; 5 painters

23. You are the manager of Albert Clifford Construction. The bar graph above shows how many workers you have available for the month of June. The schedule shows how many workers are needed for the four projects that are scheduled for June. After you make the schedule, you receive a call from a client who would like to have drywall installed in her house in June. How many workers do you have available to do this work?

    A. 0

    B. 2

    C. 4

    D. 5

    E. 6

24. A colleague of yours has been contracted to build a new home in a nearby town. She asks if you can give her the names of any workers you are not using in June. She needs carpenters, roofers, window installers, painters, and drywall installers. You currently have a bid out for another job and need to keep 3 carpenters and 2 roofers available in case you are awarded the contract. How many carpenters and roofers can you provide your colleague?

    F. 2 carpenters and 4 roofers

    G. 2 carpenters and 8 roofers

    H. 5 carpenters and 4 roofers

    J. 5 carpenters and 8 roofers

    K. 9 carpenters and 12 roofers

Answers are on page 248.

Lesson 5 ■ ■ ■
Summarize Information from One or Two Graphics

Skill: Summarize information from one or two straightforward graphics

When looking at work-related graphics such as diagrams, line graphs, and tables, you need to be able to analyze and make sense of large amounts of information. Many times you will be asked to look over the information and summarize it, or state its main points. For example, when looking at a line graph of sales trends over a period of time, it is more helpful to be able to summarize the overall trend in sales than it is to identify the sales for one specific date. Knowing how to summarize information will help you make sense of graphics that contain a lot of information.

Skill Example

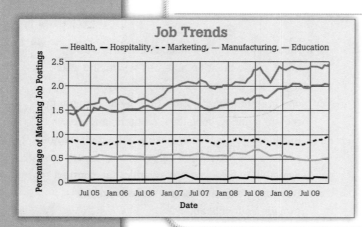

Summarize information from a graphic.

As a job placement associate at a university career center, you must be familiar with trends and opportunities within the industries that you are placing students from your school. You might look at a graph like the one shown on the left to help you identify job trends over a period of time. Being able to summarize this information helps you understand the kinds of placements with which students will have the highest success rates. A summary of this graph would include that the education and health industries experienced the most job growth over the time period shown in the graph.

Skill Practice

Use the graph above to answer the following questions.

1. What kind of jobs will students more likely be able to secure?

   A. hospitality jobs

   B. hospitality and manufacturing jobs

   C. manufacturing jobs

   D. manufacturing and marketing jobs

   E. education and health jobs

2. Why might some jobs be easier to secure than others?

   F. Hospitality jobs might be easier to secure because they are the most plentiful.

   G. Manufacturing jobs might be easier to secure because they are the least plentiful.

   H. All jobs are easier to secure because they are equally as plentiful.

   J. Education jobs might be easier to secure because they are the most plentiful.

   K. Manufacturing jobs might be easier to secure because they are the most plentiful.

Try It Out! ▪ ▪ ▪

You work in the copying and imaging center of an advertising agency and have received the request form on the right. Which statement best summarizes the job that needs to be completed?

A. 42 sets of copies on 3-hole white paper are needed by 5 P.M. on November 24

B. 24 sets of two-sided copies are needed by 11:47 A.M. on November 24

C. 24 sets of two-sided copies are needed on 8.5 x 11 paper by 5:00 P.M. on November 24

D. 24 sets of two-sided color copies on 8.5 x 11, 3-hole white paper are needed by 5:00 P.M. on November 24

E. 42 sets of two-sided copies on color paper are needed by 11:47 A.M. on November 24

Copy Request Form

Today's Date/Time: 11/24 11:47 AM
Requested by: K. Pierce
Department/Cost Center Number: Production

Date/Time Required: 11/24 5:00 PM
Telephone Number: x 5508
Mail Stop: CD-4182

Job Description

| Number of Pages per Original: 42 | Number of Copies/Sets: 24 |

Standard Copies:

B&W ___
Color ☒

☒ 8.5 × 11   ☐ Copy One-Sided
☐ 8.5 × 14   ☐ Copy Two-Sided
☐ 11 × 17   ☒ Copy As Is
☐ Other: ☐ Reduce ____
       ☐ Enlarge ____

Paper:

☐ White   ☒ 3-Hole White

Step 1 — Understand the Problem ▪ ▪ ▪

Complete the *Plan for Successful Solving.*

Plan for Successful Solving

What am I asked to do?	What are the facts?	How do I find the answer?	Is there any unnecessary information?	What prior knowledge will help me?
Summarize the information on the copy request form.	The completed form has specific details about how to complete the job.	Look over the entire form and locate the job details. Summarize the details in a statement.	The areas of the job description where no preference is checked are not needed.	When reading a request form, it is important to scan the form carefully so that the job is completed correctly.

Step 2 — Find and Check Your Answer ▪ ▪ ▪

- Confirm your understanding of the question and revise your plan as needed.

- Based on your plan, determine your solution approach: *The form includes many checked fields that indicate how the employee wants the copy request completed. I will review the preferences that have been checked and will select the answer that best summarizes the employee's copy request.*

- Check your answer. Check each preference on the form with the answer to be sure that it correctly matches the request.

- **Select the correct answer:** D. 24 sets of two-sided color copies on 8.5 x 11, 3-hole white paper are needed by 5:00 P.M. on November 24
  By reviewing each of the preferences checked on the form, it can be determined that this answer best summarizes the employee's copy request.

Problem Solving Tip

When reading forms, it is important to scan carefully in order to locate every piece of information that is needed. In the *Try It Out!* example, answer option C is technically correct. However, the answer does not include two important pieces of information: that the copies be in color and copied onto 3-hole white paper.

Remember!

Forms are used within almost all workplaces to gather and communicate information. They create a standard and easy-to-follow way of indicating preferences. If the requested information was communicated as a paragraph, it would be much more difficult and time-consuming to gather. This is why forms are helpful workplace documents.

On Your Own ▪ ▪ ▪

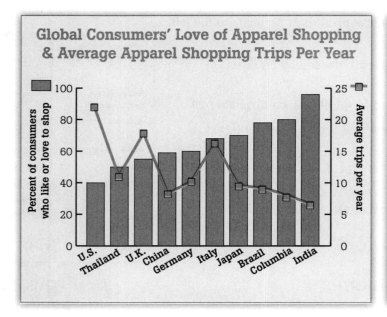

Global Consumers' Love of Apparel Shopping & Average Apparel Shopping Trips Per Year

Per-Capita GDP and Apparel Spending

	Per-Capita GDP ($)	Spent on Apparel ($)	% of GDP Spent on Apparel
Italy	29,200	1,716	5.9
U.K.	30,300	1,605	5.3
Germany	30,400	1,396	4.6
Japan	31,500	1,228	3.9
U.S.	41,800	918	2.2
China	6,800	728	10.7
Columbia	7,900	632	8.0
Brazil	8,400	554	6.6
Thailand	8,300	246	3.0
India	3,300	190	5.8

1. You are a junior clothing buyer for a chain of department stores with international locations. You use consumer reports to gather information about the shoppers who purchase from your stores. According to the graphics,

 A. countries with a low percentage of consumers who say they like or love to shop tend to have a low average number of apparel shopping trips per year.

 B. countries with a high percentage of customers who say they like or love to shop tend to have a high average number of apparel shopping trips per year.

 C. countries with a high percentage of customers who say they like or love to shop tend to spend the most money on shopping.

 D. countries with a high percentage of customers who say they like or love to shop tend to have a low average number of apparel shopping trips per year.

 E. countries with a high average number of apparel shopping trips per year, tend to spend the most money on shopping.

2. Based on the graphics, which of the following accurately summarizes the five countries with the lowest percentage of consumers who say they like or love to shop?

 F. These countries have smaller populations than the countries with a higher percentage of consumers who love to shop.

 G. These countries tend to have a low average number of apparel shopping trips per year.

 H. These countries have smaller salaries than the countries with higher percentage of consumers who love to shop.

 J. These countries spend the least amount of money when shopping for apparel.

 K. These countries tend to have a high average number of apparel shopping trips per year.

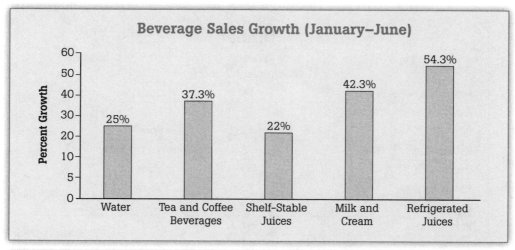

Beverage Sales Growth (January–June)

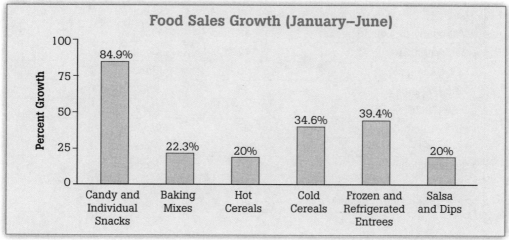

Food Sales Growth (January–June)

3. As a grocery department manager for a supermarket, you are responsible for ordering new and existing products. Based on the graphics, what can you determine about which beverages and foods increased in sales the most?

    A. Fewer beverages had sales growth of more than 35% than foods.

    B. The same amount of beverages had sales growth of more than 35% as foods.

    C. More beverages had sales growth of more than 35% than foods.

    D. Some beverages had sales growth of more than 35%, but no foods.

    E. Some foods had sales growth of more than 35%, but no beverages.

4. Based on the graphics, what can you determine about which beverages and foods had the lowest sales growth?

    F. hot cereals, shelf-stable juices, salsa and dips

    G. hot cereals, shelf-stable juices, candy

    H. individual snacks, shelf-stable juices, salsa and dips

    J. hot cereals, milk, and salsa and dips

    K. hot cereals, refrigerated juices, baking mixes

Timber

Type	Weight (pounds/cubic foot)	Durability
Afromosia	44	Good
Ash	44	Poor
Birch	42	Poor
Cedar (red)	25	Very good
Douglas Fir	33	Moderate
Elm (English)	35	Good
Elm (Wych)	43	Good
Elm (Rock)	51	Good
Iroko	41	Very good
Larch	37	Good
Mahogany (Brazilian)	32	Good
Oak (English)	47	Good
Oak (Japanese)	45	Good
Pine (Parana)	35	Poor
Pine (Pitch)	41	Very good
Pine (British Colombia)	35	Moderate
Redwood	32	Moderate
Sprue (Sitka)	28	Moderate
Teak	42	Excellent
Utile (African)	40	Good

5. As a boat builder, you need to choose carefully which wood to use. You decide that you will only use wood that is rated good, very good, or excellent. You plan to visit a lumber yard this afternoon. How many types of wood in the above graphic would you consider looking at as possible choices for your boat?

A. 13

B. 12

C. 10

D. 9

E. 7

6. Selecting durable wood for a boat depends on the weight per cubic foot. Variations in weights, however, will occur depending on moisture content and other factors. You decide that wood with a weight between 40–44 pounds per cubic foot and a durability rating of very good or excellent will fit the needs of your boat. Which types of woods could you select?

F. Teak, Afromosia, Utile

G. Teak, Ash, Cedar

H. Pine (Pitch), Cedar, Utile

J. Iroko, Cedar, Utile

K. Teak, Pine (Pitch), Iroko

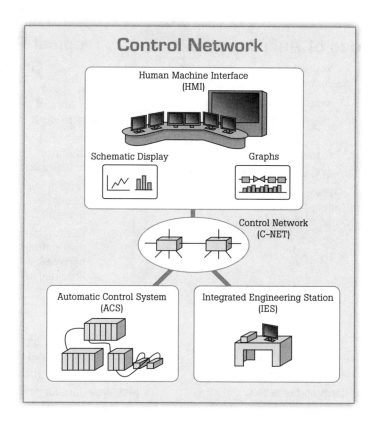

Control Network

Human Machine Interface (HMI)

Schematic Display

Graphs

Control Network (C-NET)

Automatic Control System (ACS)

Integrated Engineering Station (IES)

7. You are an operator at a power plant. You have been asked to install a control network (C–NET). Which of the following statements best describes the role that the C–NET plays?

    A. The C–NET connects the Schematic Display and Graphs to the Human Machine Interface.

    B. The C–NET connects the Integrated Engineering Station to the Human Machine Interface.

    C. The C–NET connects the Automatic Control System and Integrated Engineering Station to the Human Machine Interface.

    D. The C–NET connects the Automatic Control System to the Human Machine Interface.

    E. The C–NET connects the Integrated Engineering Station to the Automatic Display and Graphs.

8. Because you are responsible for keeping the network functioning, what overall factor is important for you to understand about the design of the network?

    F. It has various systems that are independent.

    G. The Automatic Control System is not connected to the Integrated Engineering System.

    H. It has various systems that are interdependent.

    J. The Human Machine Interface is not connected to the Automatic Control System.

    K. It does not have a control network.

Characteristics of Rain Forests

	Tropical Rain Forests	Temperate Rain Forests
Climate	warm	cool
Number of Tree Species	many	few
Types of Leaves	broadleaf	needles
Age of Trees	50–100 years	50–1,000 years
Epiphytes	lots of different kinds, including orchids and bromeliads	mostly mosses and ferns
Decomposition Rate	rapid	slow
Average Rainfall (inches per year)	80–400	100

Tropical Rain Forests Criteria

Criteria
To be a tropical rain forest, forested areas must meet the following criteria:

1	lie between the Tropic of Cancer and the Tropic of Capricorn
2	receive rainfall regularly throughout the year (80–400 inches per year)
3	remain warm and frost-free all year long (mean temperatures are between 70° and 85°F) with very little daily fluctuation

9. You are an assistant research associate working in a conservation office. You are responsible for preparing educational materials for an elementary school science curriculum. Based on the tables, students will learn that

   A. Tropical rain forests are moist and warm and lie between the Tropic of Cancer and the Tropic of Capricorn, while temperate rain forests are cool and have an average of 100 inches of rainfall per year.

   B. Both tropical rain forests and temperate rain forests are moist and warm, lie between the Tropic of Cancer and the Tropic of Capricorn, and have an average of 100 inches of rainfall per year.

   C. Tropical rain forests are dry and warm and lie between the Tropic of Cancer and the Tropic of Capricorn, while temperate rain forests are cool and have an average of 100 inches of rainfall per year.

   D. Tropical rain forests and temperate rain forests are moist and warm, lie between the Tropic of Cancer and the Tropic of Capricorn, and have an average of less than 80 inches of rain per year.

   E. Temperate rain forests are moist and warm and lie between the Tropic of Cancer and the Tropic of Capricorn, and tropical rain forests are cool and have an average of 100 inches of rainfall per year.

10. You must help students understand that not all rain forests are tropical. Based on the tables and criteria, how would you explain the reasons why a temperate rain forest is not categorized as a tropical rain forest?

   F. Although a temperate rain forest receives rainfall within the criteria range; it is cool, not warm; it only has a few tree species.

   G. The temperate rain forest does not receive rainfall within the criteria range, it is cool, not warm.

   H. Although a temperate rain forest receives rainfall within the criteria range, it is warm, not cool; it only has a few tree species.

   J. Although a temperate rain forest receives rainfall within the criteria range, it is cool, not warm.

   K. Although a temperate rain forest receives rainfall within the criteria range, it is warm, not cool.

Employment Trends

Industry Title	2009 Employment	2016 Projected	2009–2016 Change Numeric	2009–2016 Change Percent
Construction	29,312	33,491	4,179	14.3%
Construction of Buildings	7,380	8,403	1,023	13.9%
Heavy and Civil Engineering Construction	3,109	3,618	509	16.4%
Specialty Trade Contractors	18,823	21,470	2,647	14.1%
Wholesale Trade	28,021	31,915	3,894	13.9%
Merchant Wholesalers, Durable Goods	12,059	13,730	1,671	13.9%
Merchant Wholesalers, Nondurable Goods	7,689	8,819	1,130	14.7%
Wholesale Electronic Markets and Agents/Brokers	8,273	9,366	1,093	13.2%
Retail Trade	98,322	105,360	7,038	7.2%
Motor Vehicle and Parts Dealers	12,614	12,488	-126	-1.0%
Furniture and Home Furnishings Stores	3,254	3,498	244	7.5%
Electronics and Appliance Stores	3,731	4,248	517	13.9%
Building Material and Garden Supply Stores	10,236	11,935	1,699	16.6%
Food and Beverage Stores	20,021	20,641	620	3.1%
Health and Personal Care Stores	4,267	4,846	579	13.6%
Gasoline Stations	5,241	5,436	195	3.7%
Clothing and Clothing Accessories Stores	7,734	8,368	634	8.2%
Sporting Goods, Hobby, Book, and Music Stores	5,012	5,221	209	4.2%
General Merchandise Stores	14,769	16,599	1,830	12.4%
Miscellaneous Store Retailers	5,799	6,603	804	13.9%
Non-store Retailers	5,644	5,477	-167	-3.0%
Real Estate and Rental and Leasing	8,083	9,316	1,233	15.3%
Real Estate	5,254	5,982	728	13.9%
Rental and Leasing Services	2,806	3,305	499	17.8%
Lessors of Non-financial Intangible Assets	23	29	6	26.1%
Health Care and Social Assistance	78,250	102,411	24,161	30.9%
Ambulatory Health Care Services	26,582	35,537	8,955	33.7%
Hospitals	26,844	32,185	5,341	19.9%
Nursing and Residential Care Facilities	13,462	17,939	4,477	33.3%
Social Assistance	11,362	16,750	5,388	47.4%

11. You are a manager for a marketing consulting firm. You study projected growth in occupations and industries, as rapid growth can indicate an increase in the demand for marketing services in that industry. How would you describe the employment trends shown in the above table?

A. The highest current employment is in Hospitals; Social Assistance jobs will grow the least.

B. The highest current employment is in Social Assistance; Electronics and Appliance Store jobs will grow the most.

C. The highest current employment is in Food and Beverage Stores; Electronics and Appliance Store jobs will grow the least.

D. The highest current employment is found in Hospitals; Social Assistance jobs are projected to grow the most.

E. The highest current employment is in Non-store Retailers; Social Assistance jobs will grow the most.

12. Based on the information, how should your firm plan to target its services?

F. Increase its focus on Real Estate and Wholesale Trade, while decreasing its focus on Health Care and Social Assistance.

G. Increase its focus on Health Care and Social Assistance and Construction, while decreasing its focus on Wholesale Trade.

H. Increase its focus on Health Care and Social Assistance and Real Estate, while decreasing its focus on Retail Trade.

J. Increase its focus on Health Care and Social Assistance and Retail Trade, while decreasing its focus on Real Estate.

K. Increase its focus on Real Estate and Retail Trade, while decreasing its focus on Wholesale Trade.

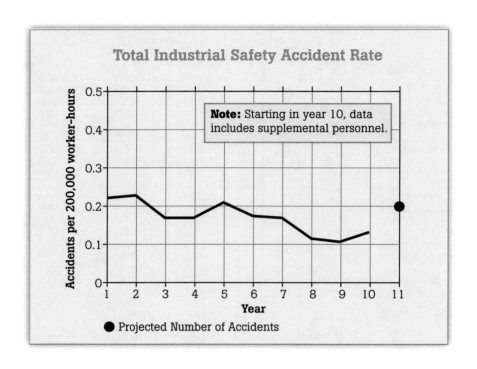

Total Industrial Safety Accident Rate

Accidents per 200,000 worker-hours

Note: Starting in year 10, data includes supplemental personnel.

Year

● Projected Number of Accidents

13. You are an assembly-line monitor. The above graph shows the number of accidents per 200,000 worker-hours. If your supervisor asked you how the year 10 results compare to the year 11 projection, what would you say?

    A. The number of accidents is much higher than the projection.

    B. The number of accidents for year 10 is not shown on the graph.

    C. The number of accidents is equal to the projection.

    D. The number of accidents is slightly higher than the projection.

    E. The number of accidents is less than the projection.

14. Your supervisor also asks you to summarize what the trend in accidents has been over the last five years. What would you say?

    F. The accident rate has been decreasing.

    G. The accident rate has been increasing by a large amount.

    H. The accident rate has been increasing by a small amount.

    J. The accident rate has stayed pretty much the same for the last five years.

    K. The accident rate for the last five years is not shown on the graph.

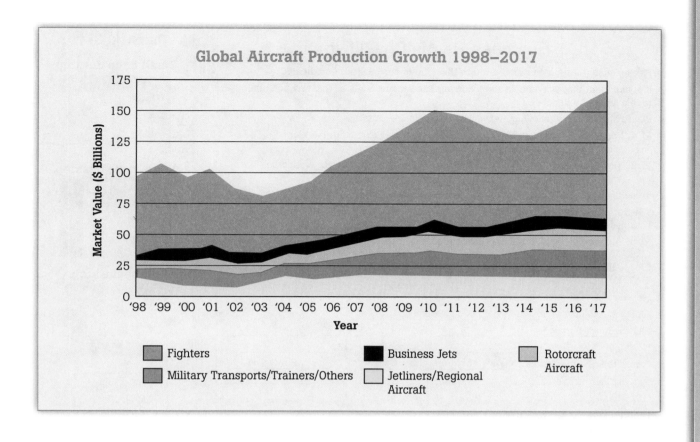

Global Aircraft Production Growth 1998–2017

Legend:
- Fighters
- Military Transports/Trainers/Others
- Business Jets
- Jetliners/Regional Aircraft
- Rotorcraft Aircraft

15. As a manager of aircraft structure assemblers, you are planning next year's production. You would like to work on the best-selling type of aircraft. The above graph shows the market value of sales in the past and estimates of sales for coming years. Which type of aircraft had the biggest market value in '08?

    A. fighters

    B. military transports/trainers/other

    C. business jets

    D. jetliners/regional aircraft

    E. rotorcraft

16. What is the estimate for how many dollars of market value will be earned by business jets in 2017?

    F. 13 billion

    G. 17 billion

    H. 50 billion

    J. 52 billion

    K. 63 billion

Business Ready Checklist

Please follow these instructions & return this form to our Facilities Coordinator.

It is important that you address the following items immediately so that any potential problems can be handled.

Please check-off the following items as you complete each task:

☑ **1.** Test your fax machines, telephone(s) & voicemail.

☑ **3.** Inspect your new furniture for damage or problems.

☑ **2.** Test your computer.

☑ **4.** Unpack & organize your work area & set aside your crates.

If you any assistance, please call the Facilities Helpdesk to assist you (x1132).

When finished with items 1–4, complete the section below and return this form to your Facilities Coordinator.

☑ **5.** All drawers work (don't jam, etc.)
☐ **6.** All keys & locks work
☐ **7.** All task lights (in overhead) work
☑ **8.** No gouges/damage

If you have discovered any problems in regards to the furniture checklist to the left, please circle the number and describe the issue in the space below.

Please stack your unpacked crates by your desk.

All crates should be emptied by 12 P.M. on November 14th.

Name: Janet Sorcar   Extension: 6740

Floor: 7   Location #: 48.222

Furniture and Other Issues: Missing the drawer key, light won't turn on. Printer on wrong side of computer.

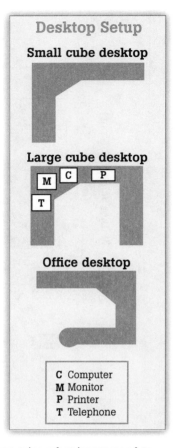

Desktop Setup

Small cube desktop

Large cube desktop

Office desktop

C Computer
M Monitor
P Printer
T Telephone

---

17. As a facilities coordinator, you are responsible for managing the moving of employee work materials and equipment to a new office location. To do this, employees fill out a Desktop Setup form to indicate where equipment should be placed. After being moved, the Business Ready Checklist is completed by the employee indicating whether all items have been moved correctly. Based on the graphics above, summarize what still needs to be done with this employee's computer equipment.

A. The monitor needs to be replaced because it cannot be turned on.

B. The printer needs to be connected to the computer.

C. The printer needs to be moved from the left side of the computer to the right side.

D. The monitor needs to be connected to the computer.

E. Nothing. The equipment was moved correctly.

18. How would you summarize what issues need to be resolved in order for the employee to be business ready?

F. A new file drawer key is needed and a light bulb needs to be replaced.

G. The file drawer needs to be fixed and damage needs to be repaired.

H. The file drawer cannot be unlocked and a jammed drawer needs to be corrected.

J. The computer and printer need to be repaired.

K. Nothing. There are no issues with the new office.

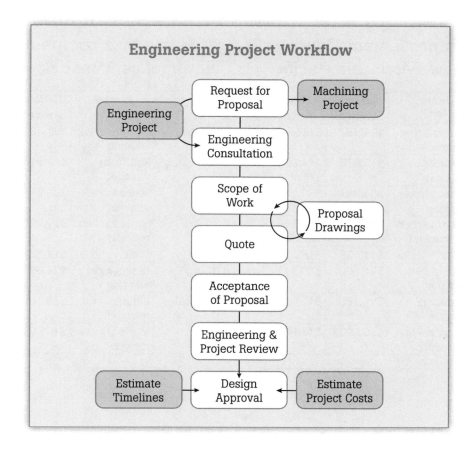

Engineering Project Workflow

- Engineering Project
- Request for Proposal → Machining Project
- Engineering Consultation
- Scope of Work ⇄ Proposal Drawings
- Quote
- Acceptance of Proposal
- Engineering & Project Review
- Estimate Timelines → Design Approval ← Estimate Project Costs

19. You are an engineering project manager. For each of your projects, you follow steps in the Engineering Project Workflow as shown in the graphic. The project manager asks when the estimate of project costs will be ready. You answer that the cost estimate will be done as part of which step?

   A. scope of work

   B. acceptance of proposal

   C. request for proposal

   D. proposal drawings

   E. design approval

20. As shown in the workflow graphic, there are three steps that may take more than one round to complete. What are the three steps?

   F. scope of work, proposal drawings, quote

   G. scope of work, acceptance of proposal, request for proposal

   H. proposal drawings, engineering and project review, engineering consultation

   J. quote, design approval, scope of work

   K. acceptance of proposal, request for proposal, proposal drawings

Home Improvement Costs, National vs. Mountain Pacific

Range	Project	National Average	Mountain Pacific
Midrange	Master suite addition	$94,331	$111,157
	Bathroom remodel	$12,918	$14,889
	Major kitchen remodel	$54,241	$59,716
	Minor kitchen remodel	$17,928	$19,366
	Deck	$14,728	$16,297
	Family room addition	$74,890	$88,371
Upscale	Bathroom remodel	$38,165	$43,050
	Major kitchen remodel	$107,973	$115,549

Home Improvement Costs, National vs. West South Central

Range	Project	National Average	West South Central
Midrange	Master suite addition	$94,331	$84,411
	Bathroom remodel	$12,918	$12,335
	Major kitchen remodel	$54,241	$52,948
	Minor kitchen remodel	$17,928	$17,487
	Deck	$14,728	$14,672
	Family room addition	$74,890	$73,110
Upscale	Bathroom remodel	$38,165	$36,868
	Major kitchen remodel	$107,973	$106,401

21. As a construction worker, you are considering relocating. You are looking at graphics that compare the national average cost of home improvements to the costs in specific locations. Which of the following best summarizes both of these graphics?

    A. Home improvement costs in the West South Central region are higher than the national average.

    B. Home improvement costs are standard no matter what part of the country you are looking at.

    C. Home improvement costs in the Mountain Pacific region are much higher than the national average.

    D. Home improvement costs can vary greatly from the national average depending on the region.

    E. Home improvement costs are much higher in the West South Central region than in the Mountain Pacific region.

22. Which of the following best summarizes the costs of home improvement projects in the upscale range?

    F. A major kitchen remodel costs $115,549 in the Mountain Pacific region.

    G. Regardless of location, a major kitchen remodel is the most expensive home improvement.

    H. Home improvement costs in the Mountain Pacific region are less than the national average.

    J. Regardless of location, a bathroom remodel is the most expensive home improvement.

    K. Regardless of location, a bathroom remodel costs more than a major kitchen remodel.

Invitation To Bid

MHS
Purchasing Department
Building #15/ Stores & Receiving
103 South Farmby Street
Harrisburg, PA 17101

OVERVIEW

Project Description: Construction of the new technology wing

Scope of Work: The successful bidder must present evidence of proper credentials indicating ability to successfully complete the project with workmanship acceptable to MHS as required in the specifications. See additional attached documentation.

BID FORMS

Construction Documents: Bid packages containing Summary of Work, Specifications, and Drawings are attached.

BID SCHEDULE

Mandatory Pre-Bid Meeting: Bidders wishing to submit a bid shall attend a mandatory pre-bid meeting on September 12 at 4 P.M. in the Conference Room, Bldg. #12, MHS. Failure to attend will preclude Bidder from submitting a bid. Subcontractors are welcome to attend, but their attendance is not mandatory.

Bid Opening: October 1 at 4 P.M. in the Conference Room, Building #15/Stores & Receiving.

Place for Receiving Bids: Up until the bid cut-off date, bids will be received in Building #15.

BID SUBMISSION

Sealed Bids: All bids shall be sealed in an envelope and marked as follows in the lower left corner:

Attention: Roger Fahnestock, Purchasing Director
Project: Construction of New Technology Wing

Contact Person: For any questions regarding bid submission, please contact Loraine Night, Construction Manager, at (555) 836-0074.

No Bid: If a bid will not be submitted, return only the Proposal Form with "No Bid" noted in the space for base bid amount. Failure to do so will result in the company's name being removed from future invitations to bid.

---

23. You are a construction contractor hoping to bid on the construction of the new technology wing being built at Midvale High School. Above is the cover page of the bid form. What are the steps in the bidding process?

    A. Attend the pre-bid meeting on September 12 and the bid opening on October 1.

    B. Present credentials and submit your bid.

    C. Return only the proposal form with "No Bid" noted in space for base bid amount.

    D. Present credentials, attend a pre-bid conference, and submit your sealed bid.

    E. Place your bid in a sealed envelope and give it to the purchasing director.

24. Which section of the bid description explains the process of submitting evidence to prove you are the most qualified bidder?

    F. Sealed Bids

    G. Scope of Work

    H. Project Description

    J. No Bid

    K. Construction Documents

Answers are on page 248.

Lesson 6 ■ ■ ■
Identify Trends

Skill: Identify trends shown in straightforward graphics

The ability to identify trends is an important skill needed for many jobs. Recognizing trends can help you make better business decisions by using past information to project future events. For example, when a company recognizes sales trends from previous years, such as increased spending during particular months, it uses this information to make certain marketing and sales decisions during those months that have trended upward in the past.

The graph in *Skill Example 1* was created from the data in the following table.

Year	"Yes" Responses
2001	3,149
2002	3,291
2003	3,504
2004	3,997
2005	3,816

Skill Examples

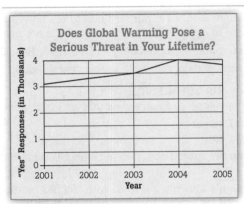

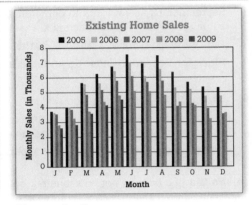

Example 1
Identify trends shown within a line graph.

A line graph is the most common graph used to display information over time. The graph shows that during a five-year period, the number of people polled who believe that global warming will pose a threat during their lifetime increased.

Example 2
Identify trends shown within a bar graph.

To display a trend, one axis must be a time frame. The other axis identifies a value that can change during each time period. The graph shows that housing sales generally increase during spring and summer months, and they peaked in 2005.

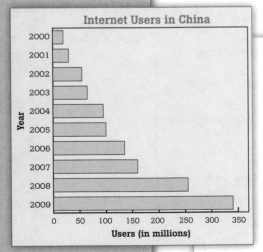

Skill Practice

Use the bar graph to the left to answer the following questions.

1. Which year showed the least growth in Internet users?

   A. 2002–2003

   B. 2004–2005

   C. 2006–2007

   D. 2007–2008

   E. 2008–2009

2. Using the graph, one trend that you can identify is that in China

   F. the number of Internet users has decreased every year.

   G. the number of Internet users has increased every year.

   H. computer equipment sales has doubled every year.

   J. the number of Internet service providers has doubled every year.

   K. the price of Internet access has has increased since 2005.

Try It Out! ■ ■ ■

You are the shipping clerk for a small company that sells specialized pet supplies. In March of this year, your company launched a Web site to sell its products and offered a deal for free shipping for the first four months. The line graph to the right shows the shipping costs paid by your company so far this year, including during the 4-month promotional period. Based on the graph, what trend can you identify in terms of the Web site's impact on sales?

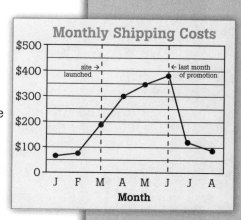

Monthly Shipping Costs

A. Sales in the store are declining while Internet sales are increasing.

B. Internet sales are increasing while shipping expenses are decreasing.

C. Many people have visited the Web site.

D. The Web site has caused a growth in sales.

E. Internet sales are declining.

Step 1 — Understand the Problem ■ ■ ■

Complete the *Plan for Successful Solving.*

Plan for Successful Solving				
What am I asked to do?	**What are the facts?**	**How do I find the answer?**	**Is there any unnecessary information?**	**What prior knowledge will help me?**
Determine the impact of a Web site on sales.	Shipping expenses covered by the company for four months after the launch of the Web site.	Use the graph to compare the amount spent on shipping during the promotion to see if a trend can be identified.	The fact that the company sells pet supplies.	If a line graph goes up as you move left to right, the value it measures has increased over the time period.

Step 2 — Find and Check Your Answer ■ ■ ■

■ Confirm your understanding of the question and revise your plan as needed.

■ Based on your plan, determine your solution approach: *Since the company offered free shipping for the first four months after the Web site's launch, shipping was paid for by the company. The graph shows the company's shipping costs for the first eight months of the year. If I look on the graph for the shipping costs during the promotional period, I can see that the company spent more on shipping every single month. It is likely that this increase was due to a growth in sales caused by the new Web site.*

■ Check your answer. Shipping costs during the two months before and the two months after the promotion were far lower than during the promotion.

■ **Select the correct answer:** D. The Web site has caused a growth in sales. Shipping costs increased dramatically during the free shipping promotion. This indicates a growth in sales due to Internet sales.

Remember!

In a graph containing trend data, the time period must be one of the axes for the graph.

Problem Solving Tip

Though the line graph does not show actual sales, it does show that shipping costs reached about four times as high as normal during the promotional period. Since the trend in shipping costs strongly aligns to the timeframe of the promotion, the cause of this trend is most likely an increase in Internet sales.

On Your Own ▪ ▪ ▪

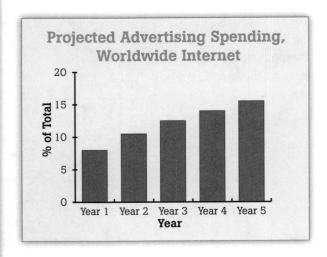

Projected Advertising Spending, Worldwide Internet

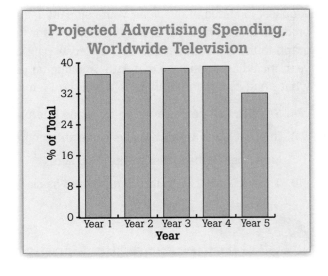

Projected Advertising Spending, Worldwide Television

1. You are an advertising sales agent for a television station. You are preparing a presentation for a potential client. The client wants to know about the relative effectiveness of television advertising and Internet advertising. What do you know about advertising trends based on the information from the bar graphs?

   A. Spending for TV advertising will decline.

   B. Spending for Internet advertising will decline.

   C. Spending for Internet advertising will decline while spending for TV advertising will increase.

   D. Spending for TV and Internet advertising will decline.

   E. Spending for TV and Internet advertising will increase.

2. According to the graphs, the percentage of total advertising for Internet and television is projected to increase between Year 3 and Year 4. Based on this trend, and taking into account that worldwide advertising spending by percentage must always equal 100 percent, what can you assume about the impact on the percent of the total for other types of advertising?

   F. Magazine advertising will drastically decrease.

   G. Cinema advertising will drastically increase.

   H. Radio advertising will drastically decrease.

   J. All of them will increase.

   K. Some of them will decrease.

Average Number of Promotional E-mails Sent by U.S. Online Retailers, by Month

January	9
February	8
March	9
April	9
May	9
June	9
July	9
August	9
September	10
October	10
November	11
December	15

Number of E-mails Received Per Month

January	2,000
February	1,940
March	2,030
April	2,000
May	2,000
June	1,970
July	1,850
August	2,030
September	2,150
October	2,150
November	2,900
December	3,200

3. As an information technology assistant at a large hospital, you are in charge of monitoring the spam filter reports on a monthly basis. Based on the graphs, how would you summarize a yearly trend on your annual report to your supervisor?

   A. While the average number of spam e-mails and total e-mails increased on a monthly basis, it decreased at the end of the year.

   B. While the average number of spam e-mails and total e-mails stayed about the same on a monthly basis, it decreased at the end of the year.

   C. The average number of spam e-mails and total e-mails increased on a monthly basis and also increased at the end of the year.

   D. While the average number of spam e-mails and total e-mails stayed about the same on a monthly basis, it increased at the end of the year.

   E. The average number of spam e-mails and total e-mails decreased on a monthly basis and also decreased at the end of the year.

4. Based on the graphs, why do you think the trend reflected in the graphs occurs?

   F. The trend is due to decreased returns over the holidays.

   G. The trend is due to increased retail activity over the holidays.

   H. The trend is due to increased returns over the holidays.

   J. The trend is due to retail activity staying the same over the holidays.

   K. The trend is due to decreased retail activity over the holidays.

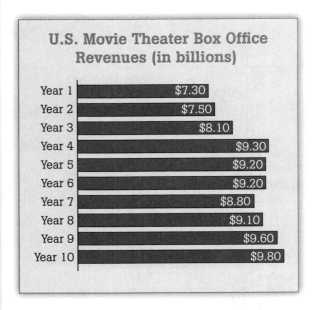

U.S. Movie Theater Box Office Revenues (in billions)

Year 1	$7.30
Year 2	$7.50
Year 3	$8.10
Year 4	$9.30
Year 5	$9.20
Year 6	$9.20
Year 7	$8.80
Year 8	$9.10
Year 9	$9.60
Year 10	$9.80

U.S. Movie Theater Ticket Prices

5. You are a market analyst for a movie theater chain reviewing U.S. box office revenues and average ticket prices over the past ten years. According to the graphs, what is the trend between ticket prices and revenue?

    A. In two years, ticket prices and revenue remained the same.

    B. Both box office revenue and movie theatre ticket prices have generally increased over the past 10 years.

    C. Throughout the ten years, revenue increased as ticket price decreased.

    D. Throughout the ten years, revenue decreased as ticket price increased.

    E. Box office revenue always increases when ticket prices increase.

6. Which of the following is not a possible reason that although ticket prices went up between year 6 and year 7, revenue went down?

    F. Less people went to the movies in year 7.

    G. Some movie theaters closed in year 7.

    H. There were no major blockbusters in year 7.

    J. More people went to the movies in year 7.

    K. People cut back their entertainment expenses in year 7.

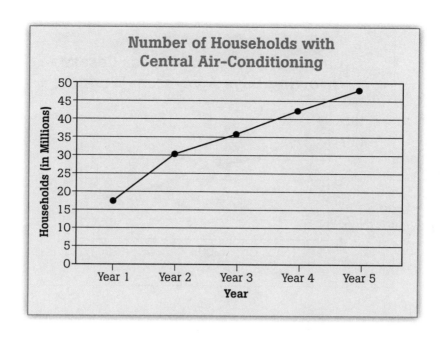

Number of Households with Central Air-Conditioning

Households (in Millions)

Year

---

7. You work as an electrical and electronic equipment assembler for a company that installs air-conditioning systems for commercial and residential customers. Interpreting the data in the above graph will help you understand the trend in the number of households purchasing central air-conditioning. You plan to use this information in a marketing campaign. According to the graph, how many households had central air-conditioning in year 3?

    A. about 30 thousand

    B. about 480 thousand

    C. about 31 million

    D. about 37 million

    E. about 48 million

8. From this graph, what can you tell about the trend in air-conditioning?

    F. The cost of installing central air-conditioning decreased over the five-year period.

    G. The number of homes with central air-conditioning stayed the same over this five-year period.

    H. The number of homes with central air-conditioning steadily decreased over this five-year period.

    J. The number of homes with central air-conditioning steadily increased over this five-year period.

    K. The number of homes with central air-conditioning decreased for the first two years, then steadily increased.

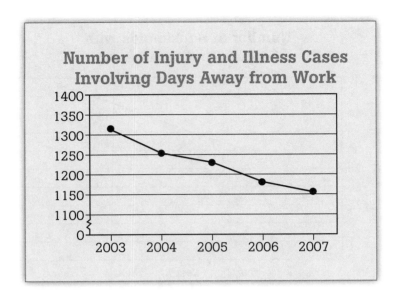

Number of Injury and Illness Cases Involving Days Away from Work

9. As an occupational health and safety specialist, you often use statistics to evaluate the safety record of a particular company or industry. Based on the line graph above, what is the trend in the number of illnesses and injuries that involve days away from work?

   A. The number of cases increased from 2003–2007.

   B. The number of cases doubled from 2003–2007.

   C. The number of cases does not indicate a trend.

   D. The number of cases decreased every year from 2003–2007.

   E. The number of cases increased until 2004 and then decreased every year.

10. Which of the following statements is correct?

   F. All of the injuries and illnesses occurred in a manufacturing facility.

   G. More injuries and illnesses occurred in the final year.

   H. Most of the injuries and illnesses occurred away from the workplace.

   J. Most of the absences were the result of accidents rather than illnesses.

   K. More cases occurred in 2003 than 2007.

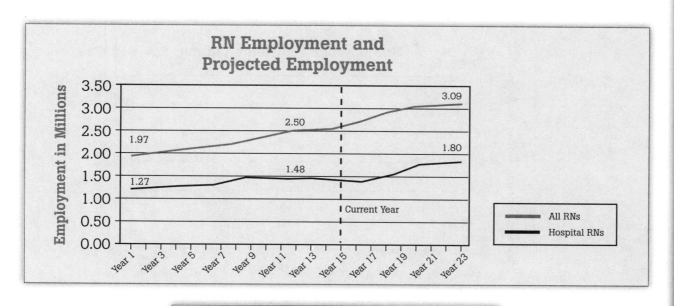

RN Employment and Projected Employment

Employment in Millions

- 1.97
- 2.50
- 3.09
- 1.27
- 1.48
- 1.80

Current Year

All RNs
Hospital RNs

Percentage of Hospital RN Jobs to Total RN Jobs

Year	Percentage
1	64.5%
13	59.2%
21	58.3%

11. You are a registered nurse reporting at a human resources meeting on projected employment opportunities in nursing in the future. What can you learn from the above graph and table?

    A.   Only hospitals hire registered nurses.

    B.   All registered nurses work for hospitals.

    C.   There will be fewer job opportunities for registered nurses in the future.

    D.   Hospitals employ at least half of all registered nurses.

    E.   There will be a shortage of registered nurses in the future.

12. Based on the trends in the line graph and table above, what can you predict about the number of non–hospital nursing jobs over the next 6 years?

    F.   The number of non–hospital nursing jobs will continue to decrease.

    G.   The number of non–hospital nursing jobs will stay the same.

    H.   The number of non–hospital nursing jobs will increase at a faster rate than hospital nursing jobs.

    J.   The number of non–hospital nursing jobs will sharply increase, then decrease.

    K.   You cannot determine anything about the number of non–hospital nursing jobs.

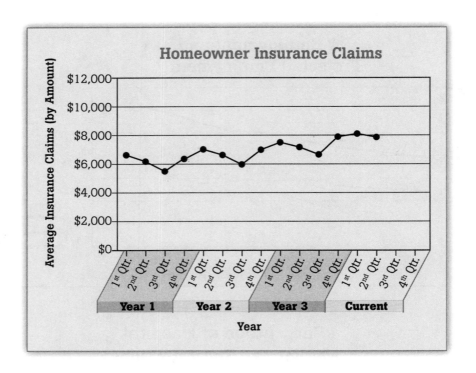

Homeowner Insurance Claims

13. You work as an insurance claims clerk for a company that provides homeowner's insurance. You are just starting the third quarter of the year. Based on the trends illustrated on the graph, what can you expect for the claims filed this quarter?

    A. The graph does not display any information that will help you make predictions about the claims that will be filed this quarter.

    B. The average claim costs for this quarter will be less than the average claim costs last quarter.

    C. The average claim costs for this quarter will be greater than the average claim costs filed last quarter.

    D. More claims will be filed this quarter than last quarter.

    E. Fewer claims will be filed this quarter than last quarter.

14. What is the overall trend for the average cost of homeowner's insurance claims?

    F. The graph does not display enough information to determine an overall trend.

    G. The average cost of the claims filed every year is increasing.

    H. The average cost of the claims filed every year is decreasing.

    J. Fewer claims are filed every year.

    K. More claims are filed every year.

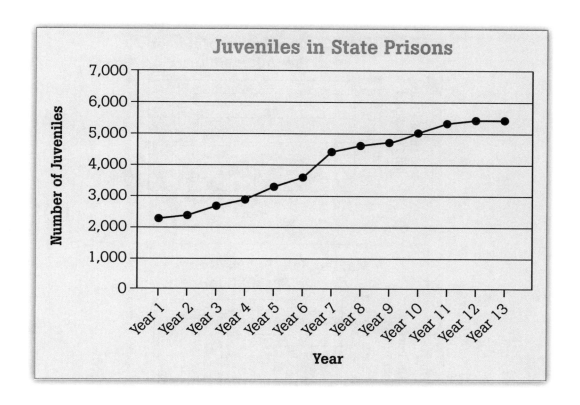

Juveniles in State Prisons

15. You are a social and community service manager who is concerned about methods used to deal with juvenile delinquency. Based on the graph, between which two years did the number of juveniles in state prison increase by the greatest amount?

   A. Year 4 and Year 5

   B. Year 6 and Year 7

   C. Year 9 and Year 10

   D. Year 10 and Year 11

   E. Year 12 and Year 13

16. Based on the graph, what trend can you identify regarding juveniles in state prisons?

   F. The graph does not display enough information to identify any trends.

   G. Juveniles are often released before completing their prison terms.

   H. State prisons can hold only a limited number of juveniles.

   J. Fewer juveniles are sentenced to state prisons every year.

   K. The juvenile population in state prisons has grown nearly every year.

Median Sale Prices of Homes in the United States

Median Sale Price (in Thousands)

$180
$170
$160
$150
$140
$130
$120
$110
$100
0

2001 2002 2003 2004 2005 2006 2007 2008

Year

Median Sale Prices of Homes in Springdale

Median Sale Prices in Springdale (in Thousands)

$220
$210
$200
$190
$180
$170
$160
$150
$140
$130
$120
$110
$100
0

2001 2002 2003 2004 2005 2006 2007 2008

Year

17. As a loan counselor who works for a realtor, you are preparing median sale price information for a client who wishes to purchase a home in Springdale. Reviewing recent reports, you come across two graphs depicting median sale prices for the United States and median sale prices for homes in the town of Springdale. What is the trend in median sales based on these two graphs?

    A. Median sale prices decreased until a sharp increase in 2007.

    B. Median sale prices decreased over time.

    C. Median sale prices increased over time.

    D. Median sale prices varied without establishing a trend.

    E. Median sale prices increased until 2007.

18. Which of the following might be the cause of the change in median sales price between 2007 and 2008?

    F. a housing boom in 2008

    G. a national financial crisis in the late 2000s

    H. steady growth in the economy

    J. a real estate boom throughout the 2000s

    K. extensive inflation every year

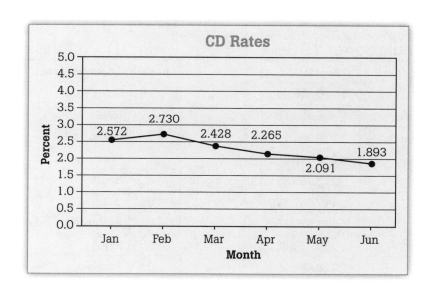

CD Rates

19. You are the teller at a local bank. A customer asks you what the range of certificate of deposit (CD) rates has been so far this year. According to the graph, what is the low–high range for the six months shown?

    A.   2.730–2.572

    B.   2.572–2.730

    C.   2.091–2.265

    D.   1.893–2.572

    E.   1.893–2.730

20. Based on the graph, which statement is true about interest rate trends?

    F.   The interest rate will go up in July.

    G.   The interest rate has decreased nearly every month of the year.

    H.   The interest rate will remain the same in July.

    J.   The interest rate will drop to 0.5 in July.

    K.   There has not been a clear trend.

Top 10 Populations, 1999

Rank	Country/Area	Population
1	China	1,260,106,742
2	India	989,250,189
3	United States	279,294,713
4	Indonesia	210,719,653
5	Brazil	173,763,871
6	Russia	147,352,175
7	Pakistan	143,676,468
8	Bangladesh	134,249,581
9	Japan	126,494,395
10	Nigeria	120,369,199

Top 10 Populations, 2009

Rank	Country/Area	Population
1	China	1,338,612,968
2	India	1,166,079,217
3	United States	307,212,123
4	Indonesia	240,271,522
5	Brazil	198,739,269
6	Pakistan	174,578,558
7	Bangladesh	156,050,883
8	Nigeria	149,229,090
9	Russia	140,041,247
10	Japan	127,078,679

21. You are an editor reviewing an article that contains the two tables above about the top ten most populated countries in 1999 compared to 2009. What is the overall trend in population?

    A. Only the top 5 populations increased between 1999 and 2009.

    B. Almost all of the populations increased between 1999 and 2009.

    C. All of the populations increased between 1999 and 2009.

    D. Almost all of the populations decreased between 1999 and 2009.

    E. All of the populations decreased between 1999 and 2009.

22. What is one possible reason for the population change in Russia between 1999 and 2009?

    F. There were fewer deaths in Russia in 2009 than in 1999.

    G. There was better health care in Russia in 2009 than in 1999.

    H. There were more births in Russia in 2009 than in 1999.

    J. There were more people moving to Russia in 2009 than in 1999.

    K. There were fewer births in Russia in 2009 than in 1999.

College Tuition Inflation

Year	College Inflation	General Inflation	Rate Ratio
2006	5.9%	3.23%	1.83
2005	5.94%	3.39%	1.75
2004	5.97%	2.66%	2.24
2003	5.99%	2.28%	2.63
2002	5.80%	1.58%	3.67
2001	5.48%	2.85%	1.92
2000	5.25%	3.36%	1.56

23. As a financial planner, you help clients save for future college tuition costs based on the trends of tuition inflation. How would you describe the inflation of college tuition represented on the table?

    A. a yearly increase of approximately 10%

    B. a yearly increase of approximately 2.23%

    C. a yearly increase of approximately 6%

    D. a yearly decrease of approximately 6%

    E. a yearly decrease of approximately 10%

24. Based on the table, what trends can you identify regarding the rate of college tuition inflation?

    F. The rate of inflation for college tuition is consistently higher than the general inflation rate.

    G. The general inflation rate is consistently higher than the rate of inflation for college tuition.

    H. The cost of college has gone down nearly every year.

    J. The cost of college has generally stayed the same.

    K. The table does not display enough information to make any conclusions.

Answers are on page 248.

Lesson 7 ■ ■ ■
Compare Information and Trends in Graphics

Skill: Compare information and trends shown in one or two straightforward graphics

When you compare items, you examine the items to find similarities and differences. Many jobs require you to compare several items at the same time. Tasks such as selecting suppliers, placing orders, setting prices, and verifying receipt of the correct items all require the ability to compare information and trends in information that is communicated through graphics.

Skill Example

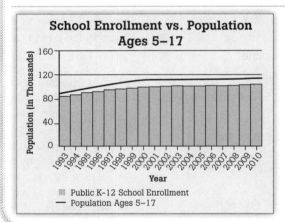

Compare trends within graphs.

Some graphs show different data trends for the purpose of comparison. The graph to the left compares the number of local school-age children to the number of children enrolled in the city's public schools. This data helps city officials understand patterns such as dropout rates and the number of students entering private school. It also helps the city project how many students will be enrolled in future years so they can plan for building new schools as needed.

Desc.	Brass and mahogany	Mahogany desk clock with compass	Brass and hardwood
Size	3.5" × 3.5" × 2	3.5" × 3.5" × 3	3" diameter
Price	$35.00	$100.00	$32.00

Skill Practice

Use the table to the left to answer the following questions.

1. Using the available information, which option can be used to select a compass?

    A. the ship's destination

    B. the size of the compass

    C. the owner's height

    D. how many days it will be used

    E. the ship's traveling speed

2. Based on the available information, compare the compasses to determine why Compass 2 is the most expensive.

    F. It's in a square box.

    G. It's larger.

    H. It's made from brass.

    J. It includes a clock.

    K. It tells the direction better than the other compasses.

Try It Out!

You are an animal caretaker for a veterinary clinic that treats large and small pets. Although you have never had a fish as a patient, you have cared for every other type of animal on the list. Based on the chart, besides fish, what is the most commonly found pet in the American household?

A. dogs   **D.** birds

B. reptiles   **E.** cats

C. horses

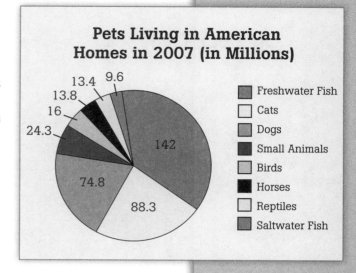

Pets Living in American Homes in 2007 (in Millions)

- 13.4
- 9.6
- 13.8
- 16
- 24.3
- 142
- 74.8
- 88.3

Key:
- Freshwater Fish
- Cats
- Dogs
- Small Animals
- Birds
- Horses
- Reptiles
- Saltwater Fish

Step 1   Understand the Problem

Complete the *Plan for Successful Solving.*

Plan for Successful Solving

What am I asked to do?	What are the facts?	How do I find the answer?	Is there any unnecessary information?	What prior knowledge will help me?
Determine which type of pet, besides freshwater fish, is most common in American households.	Each wedge represents the percentage of each type of pet. There are two categories of fish shown—freshwater and saltwater	Find the largest wedge in the circle graph. If it is fish, find the next largest wedge.	No. The entire graph must be analyzed in order to determine the answer.	The size of a wedge in a circle graph reflects the percentage of the total that the category represents.

Step 2   Find and Check Your Answer

- Confirm your understanding of the question and revise your plan as needed.
- Based on your plan, determine your solution approach: *The circle graph shows a breakdown of the different pets found in American homes. I will first use the key to determine which wedges—fish and saltwater fish—I should ignore. I will then look for the largest wedge of the remaining types of pets. If any wedges are close in size, I will compare the number labels to determine which wedge represents the largest amount. Finally, I will use the key to determine which pet corresponds to the largest wedge.*
- Check your answer. Be sure the key color for the type of animal you have selected matches the largest wedge.
- **Select the correct answer:**   **E.** cats
  Excluding fish, the cat is the most commonly found pet in American households.

Problem Solving Tip

Circle graphs do not always include number labels, particularly when exact quantities are not important. However, when two wedges of a circle graph are similar in size, quantities are helpful for determining which wedge is larger. In the *Try It Out!* example, the number labels help you determine that the number of cats as pets (88.3 million) is greater than the number of dogs as pets (74.8 million).

Remember!

The larger the wedge in a circle graph, the larger the percentage of the total that category represents.

On Your Own ■ ■ ■

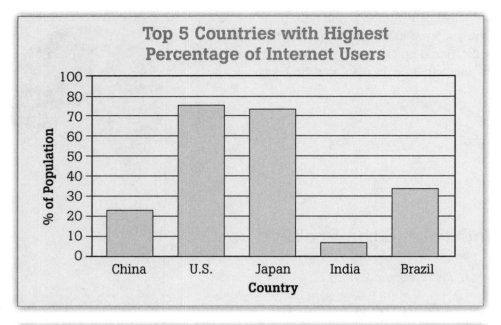

Top 5 Countries with Highest Percentage of Internet Users

Population Statistics

Country	Population (July 2009 est.)
China	1,338,612,968
United States	307,212,123
Japan	127,078,679
India	1,166,079,217
Brazil	198,739,269

1. You are a sales representative for a company that provides Internet access and then sells services through the Internet. Based on the bar graph, which country already has the highest percentage of Internet users?

    A. China

    B. United States

    C. Japan

    D. India

    E. Brazil

2. In order to grow, your company needs to explore markets in countries outside of the U.S. Based on the graph and table, which country has the most potential for growth in Internet use?

    F. China

    G. United States

    H. Japan

    J. India

    K. Brazil

Last Order: June 15
Current Order: June 30

Flavor	Qty. After Last Order	Qty. in Stock
French Vanilla	15	10
Chocolate	9	3
Strawberry	9	4
Fudge Ripple	4	1
Coffee	8	6
Mint Choc. Chip	10	7

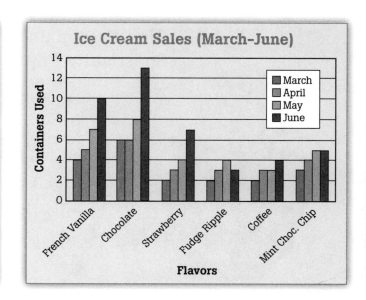

3. As the owner of Marinelli's Ice Cream Parlor, you order ice cream twice a month. You are checking recent sales against current inventory for the upcoming June 30 order. Based on the graphs, for which flavors can you be certain you will not need to order any additional containers?

    A. French Vanilla, Chocolate, Strawberry

    B. Fudge Ripple, Coffee, Mint Chocolate Chip

    C. Strawberry, Fudge Ripple, Mint Chocolate Chip

    D. Chocolate, Strawberry, Coffee

    E. French Vanilla, Coffee, Mint Chocolate Chip

4. Based on the trends so far this year, which flavors need to be most closely watched when ordering, due to changing sales patterns?

    F. French Vanilla, Chocolate, Strawberry

    G. Fudge Ripple, Coffee, Mint Chocolate Chip

    H. Strawberry, Fudge Ripple, Mint Chocolate Chip

    J. Chocolate, Strawberry, Coffee

    K. French Vanilla, Coffee, Mint Chocolate Chip

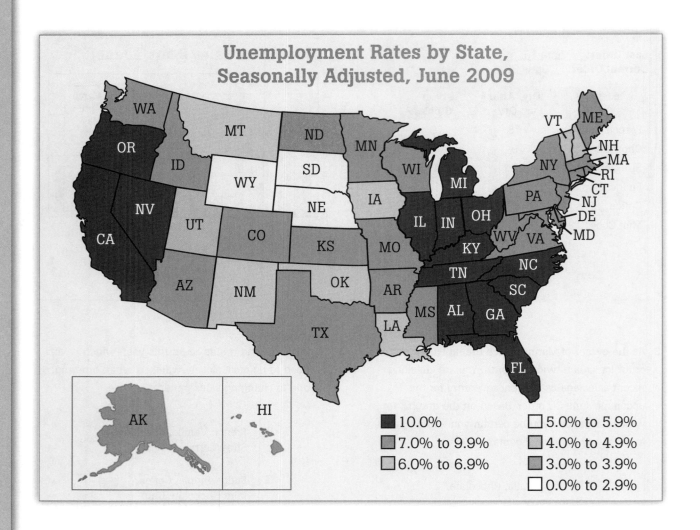

Unemployment Rates by State, Seasonally Adjusted, June 2009

Legend:
- 10.0%
- 7.0% to 9.9%
- 6.0% to 6.9%
- 5.0% to 5.9%
- 4.0% to 4.9%
- 3.0% to 3.9%
- 0.0% to 2.9%

5. You are an employment interviewer for a national personnel firm. Based on the map comparing the unemployment rate in each state, which state has the lowest unemployment rate?

    A. California (CA)

    B. Alabama (AL)

    C. Montana (MT)

    D. Nebraska (NE)

    E. North Dakota (ND)

6. According to the map, which option correctly lists the states from the lowest to the highest unemployment rate?

    F. Wyoming (WY), Florida (FL), Alaska (AK)

    G. Pennsylvania (PA), Montana (MT), Minnesota (MN)

    H. Tennessee (TN), Massachusetts (MA), Illinois (IL)

    J. California (CA), Michigan (MI), Nevada (NV)

    K. Nebraska (NE), Texas (TX), South Carolina (SC)

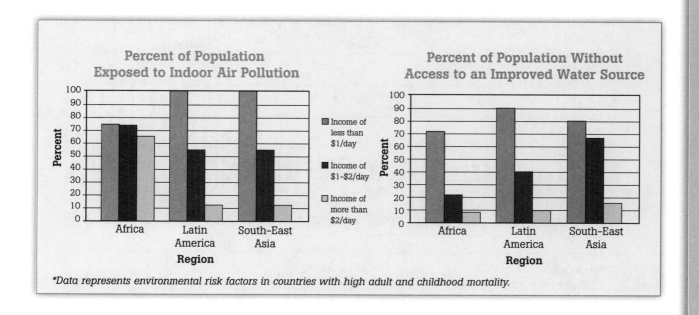

Percent of Population Exposed to Indoor Air Pollution

Percent of Population Without Access to an Improved Water Source

Data represents environmental risk factors in countries with high adult and childhood mortality.

7. You are a manager at a non-profit organization that works to lower vulnerability to health risks caused by exposure to air pollution and limited access to clean water sources. Based on the graphs, what do you know about the relationship between income and vulnerability to health risks?

A. The more income people have, the more likely they are to be exposed to air pollution and lack of an improved water source.

B. The less income people have, the more likely they are to be exposed to air pollution and lack of an improved water source.

C. The less income people have, the less likely they are to be exposed to air pollution and lack of an improved water source.

D. The more income people have, the less likely they are to be exposed to air pollution, and the more likely they are to be exposed to lack of an improved water source.

E. There is no relationship between income and vulnerability to air pollution and lack of an improved water source.

8. What do both graphs tell you about vulnerability to health risks in all three regions?

F. Vulnerability is affected similarly in all three regions based on levels of income.

G. Vulnerability is not affected at all, based on levels of income.

H. Vulnerability is not affected similarly in all three regions, based on levels of income.

J. Vulnerability is affected similarly in Africa and Latin America, based on levels of income.

K. Vulnerability is affected similarly in Africa and South-East Asia, based on levels of income.

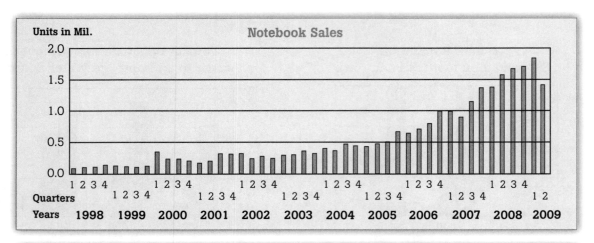

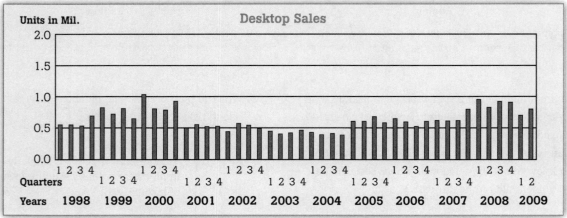

9. You are a computer sales manager. You must monitor customer needs and anticipate inventory needs. Based on the graphs, how would you compare the trends of notebook sales and desktop sales for the time period shown in the graphs?

    A. Notebook sales have fluctuated, while desktop sales have generally increased.

    B. Both notebook sales and desktop sales have steadily increased.

    C. Notebook sales have generally increased, while desktop sales have fluctuated.

    D. Both notebook sales and desktop sales have steadily decreased.

    E. Both notebook sales and desktop sales have had predictable peaks and valleys.

10. Based on the graphs, which type of computer has higher sales?

    F. In 2005, desktop sales surpassed notebook sales and have continued to have higher sales since.

    G. In 2000, notebook sales surpassed desktop sales and have continued to have higher sales since.

    H. Desktop sales have consistently been higher than notebook sales.

    J. Notebook sales have consistently been higher than desktop sales.

    K. In 2005, notebook sales surpassed desktop sales and have continued to have higher sales since.

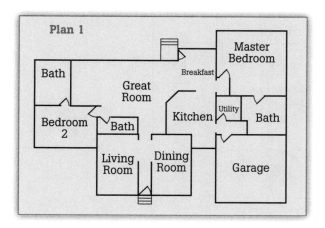

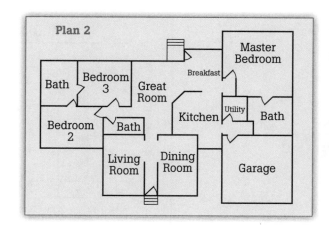

11. You are an architectural drafter who has created two floor plans based on the Smith family's requests. The Smith family approved Plan 2 based on one major change. Compare the floor plans to identify the change.

    A.   garage size and location

    B.   size of living room

    C.   kitchen layout

    D.   number of bathrooms

    E.   number of bedrooms

12. How would you describe the difference between the two plans?

    F.   Both plans have an additional bedroom, which makes the Great Rooms the same in both plans.

    G.   Plan 1 has an additional bedroom, which makes the Great Room smaller in Plan 1 than in Plan 2.

    H.   Plan 2 has an additional bedroom, which makes the Great Room smaller in Plan 2 than in Plan 1.

    J.   Both plans have an additional bedroom, which makes the Great Rooms in each plan a different size.

    K.   Plan 1 has an additional bedroom, which makes the Great Room smaller in both plans.

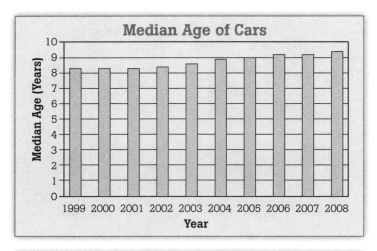

Median Age of Cars

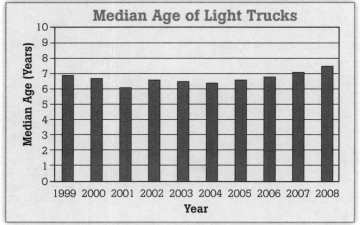

Median Age of Light Trucks

13. As an automotive master mechanic, you are in charge of ordering parts and making recommendations to the store headquarters for supply inventory. Recently you have noticed that many of the parts you order seem to be for older vehicles. Based on the graphs, what conclusions can you draw?

    A. The median age of trucks is higher than the median age of cars.

    B. Trucks and cars are approximately the same age.

    C. Older drivers prefer to drive older cars.

    D. It is expensive to maintain an old car.

    E. Car owners are keeping their vehicles longer.

14. Based on the graphs, what trend can you detect and how should this affect the materials you keep in inventory?

    F. No trend can be detected and no change should be made to your inventory.

    G. People are trading in old cars to buy new trucks. You should keep more parts for new trucks on hand.

    H. People are trading in old cars to buy new cars. You should keep more parts for new cars on hand.

    J. Since 2004, there has been an increase in median vehicle age for both cars and light trucks. You should keep more parts on hand for older vehicles.

    K. Trucks are becoming more popular than cars. You should keep more parts on hand for trucks.

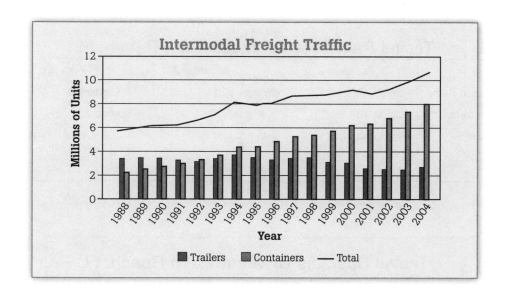

Intermodal Freight Traffic

Millions of Units

■ Trailers ■ Containers —— Total

15. You are a truck driver hauling heavy freight around the country. Intermodal freight consists of freight that travels via truck on the highways and via trains on the railroad. The graph tracks intermodal freight that traveled via trailers on the highway and containers on the railroad. Based on the graph, during what two years was the breakdown about even between trailers and containers?

    A.   1990 and 1991

    B.   1991 and 1992

    C.   1993 and 1994

    D.   1996 and 1997

    E.   2001 and 2002

16. Based on the graph, what can you conclude about intermodal traffic?

    F.   Intermodal traffic is increasing, with the greatest increase being in container freight.

    G.   Intermodal traffic is decreasing, with the greatest decrease being in container freight.

    H.   Initially, there was less trailer traffic than container traffic.

    J.   By 2004, there was more trailer traffic than container traffic.

    K.   Intermodal traffic is increasing, with the greatest increase being in trailer freight.

Travel Packages to West Palm Beach, FL

	Package 1	Package 2	Package 3
Departure date	August 20	August 21	August 22
Return date	August 25	August 25	August 25
Includes	Flight and hotel	Flight and hotel	Flight, hotel transfer, and hotel
Price	$333	$312	$362

Travel Specials to West Palm Beach, FL

	Special 1	Special 2
Valid Dates	August 1st through August 31st (valid for four-night stay only)	August 25th through September 25th (valid for five-night stay only)
Includes	Flight, hotel, hotel transfer, and breakfast	Flight and hotel
Price	$350	$300

17. As a travel agent, you have several corporate customers. For an upcoming conference in West Palm Beach, Florida, a client requests travel options that meet the following criteria: (1) must be in West Palm Beach August 23–24, (2) flight and hotel must be included, (3) the package or special must cost less than $330. Which of the following packages or specials best meets these requirements?

A. Special 1

B. Special 2

C. Package 1

D. Package 2

E. Package 3

18. The client told you that she has a lot of work in the office so she wants to spend as little time in West Palm Beach as possible. Her budget has been increased to up to $400. Which package or special meets this additional request?

F. Special 1

G. Special 2

H. Package 1

J. Package 2

K. Package 3

Turkey Sandwiches

	Brand A	Brand B	Brand C	Brand D	Brand E
Calories	280	480	440	297	950
Total Fat (Grams)	3.5	6	5.5	5	70
Total Carbohydrates (Grams)	47	42	64	43	46

Vegetable Soup

	Brand 1	Brand 2	Brand 3	Brand 4	Brand 5
Calories	120	100	122	110	81
Total Fat (Grams)	1	0.5	1	2.5	1.3
Total Carbohydrates (Grams)	24	21	27	24	13.2

19. You are a dietician dealing with a patient who has specific nutritional needs. Your work involves teaching the patient about selecting meal choices with the lowest fat options possible. Which of the following has the lowest total fat content?

A. Turkey Sandwich Brand A

B. Vegetable Soup Brand 1

C. Turkey Sandwich Brand C

D. Vegetable Soup Brand 2

E. Turkey Sandwich Brand E

20. You meet with another patient the following week, and review how to select the combination of a sandwich and soup with the fewest calories. Based on the tables above, which of the following combinations is the best choice for your patient?

F. Turkey Sandwich Brand A and Vegetable Soup Brand 1

G. Turkey Sandwich Brand A and Vegetable Soup Brand 5

H. Turkey Sandwich Brand B and Vegetable Soup Brand 5

J. Turkey Sandwich Brand C and Vegetable Soup Brand 1

K. Turkey Sandwich Brand D and Vegetable Soup Brand 5

Grass-Type Comparison Based on Environmental Growth Factors

Type	Shade Tolerance	Wear Tolerance	Heat Tolerance	Drought Tolerance
Kentucky Bluegrass	Fair	Good	Fair	Good
Rough Bluegrass	Good	Good	Poor	Poor
Tall Fescue	Good	Good	Good	Excellent
Perennial Ryegrass	Fair	Excellent	Good	Fair
Common Bermuda Grass	Fair	Good	Fair	Excellent

21. As a landscaper, customers frequently ask you which type of grass seed they should plant. The local climate is usually very hot and very dry in the summer. Which type of grass seed should you recommend?

    A. Perennial Ryegrass

    B. Tall Fescue

    C. Rough Bluegrass

    D. Kentucky Bluegrass

    E. Common Bermuda Grass

22. A new client who has several children is worried that the yard will become worn. According to the table, which grass seed should you recommend?

    F. Kentucky Bluegrass

    G. Common Bermuda Grass

    H. Rough Bluegrass

    J. Tall Fescue

    K. Perennial Ryegrass

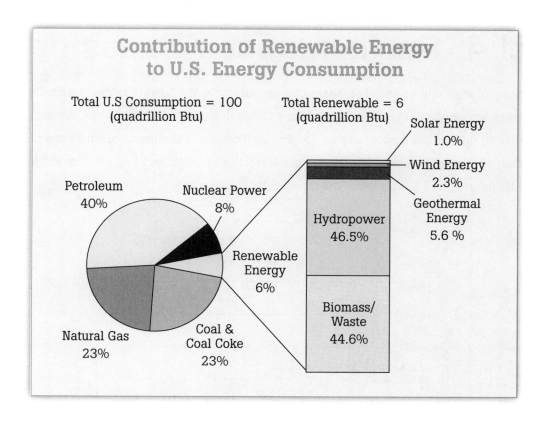

Contribution of Renewable Energy to U.S. Energy Consumption

Total U.S Consumption = 100
(quadrillion Btu)

Total Renewable = 6
(quadrillion Btu)

Petroleum 40%

Nuclear Power 8%

Renewable Energy 6%

Natural Gas 23%

Coal & Coal Coke 23%

Solar Energy 1.0%

Wind Energy 2.3%

Geothermal Energy 5.6 %

Hydropower 46.5%

Biomass/ Waste 44.6%

23. As an environmental compliance inspector, you must have up-to-date knowledge of the current energy sources in the United States. According to the circle graph, which source of energy is the most often used?

   A.   natural gas

   B.   renewable energy

   C.   coal

   D.   nuclear

   E.   petroleum

24. Based on the graph, what is the primary source of renewable energy?

   F.   solar energy

   G.   wind energy

   H.   geothermal energy

   J.   hydropower

   K.   biomass/waste

Answers are on page 249.

−5

Level 4 Performance Assessment

The following problems will test your ability to answer questions at a Level 4 rating of difficulty. These problems are similar to those that appear on a Career Readiness Certificate test. For each question, you can refer to the answer key for answer justifications. The answer justifications provide an explanation of why each answer option is either correct or incorrect and indicate the skill lesson that should be referred to if further review of a particular skill is needed.

1. You are a machinist for a manufacturing company. There have been rumors of a hiring freeze within your company. Based on the graph, what is the trend for employment levels in manufacturing?

    A.   The graph does not display enough information to draw any conclusions.

    B.   Every year, fewer manufacturing workers have full-time jobs.

    C.   Fewer manufacturing workers are hired every year.

    D.   Salaries for manufacturing workers have decreased every year.

    E.   Fewer items are manufactured every year.

2. Based on the graph, what type of manufactured goods is affected by the number of manufacturing workers?

    F.   The graph does not display enough information to draw any conclusions.

    G.   Durable goods are affected.

    H.   Vehicles are affected.

    J.   Machinery is affected.

    K.   All types of manufactured goods are equally affected.

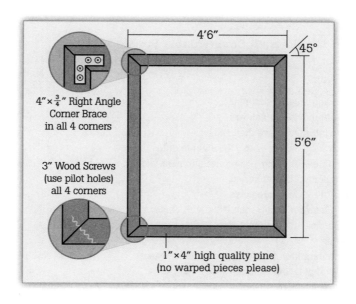

4" × $\frac{3}{4}$" Right Angle
Corner Brace
in all 4 corners

3" Wood Screws
(use pilot holes)
all 4 corners

1" × 4" high quality pine
(no warped pieces please)

4'6"

45°

5'6"

3. As a cabinetmaker, your job is to build the frame
shown in the graphic. Length measures the longer
side of the frame. What is the length of the frame?

    A.   4'6"

    B.   5'6"

    C.   6'4"

    D.   6'5"

    E.   45°

4. Assuming the pieces of pine from which you
are building this frame are all 6 feet long, what
materials will you need in order to build the
frame shown above?

    F.   one 3" wood screw, one 1" × 4" piece
of high quality pine, and one 4" × $\frac{3}{4}$"
right angle corner brace

    G.   one 3" wood screw, four 1" × 4" pieces
of high quality pine, and four $\frac{3}{4}$" right
angle corner braces

    H.   four 3" wood screws, four 1" × 4"
pieces of high quality pine, and four
4'6" right angle corner braces

    J.   four 3" wood screws, four 1" × 4"
pieces of high quality pine, and four
4" × $\frac{3}{4}$" right angle corner braces

    K.   three 3" wood screws, four 1" × 4"
pieces of high quality pine, and four
$\frac{3}{4}$" right angle corner braces

Norwalk County Cable Bundle Packages			
Package Name	Includes	Price Per Month (First 12 Months)	Price Per Month Thereafter
Digital Cable Value Deal	· Over 80 digital cable channels · *Demand It!* movies and shows · *PowerUp* Internet (faster than DSL) · Unlimited local calling with 12 calling features	$99.99	$109.99
High Definition Starter Deal	· Free high definition (no access or equipment fees) · Over 80 digital cable channels · *Demand It!* movies and shows · *PowerUp* Internet (faster than DSL) with *Security Assistance* · Unlimited local and national long distance with 12 calling features · Voice mail	$114.99	$129.99
High Definition Super Deal	· Free high definition (no access or equipment fees) · Over 150 digital cable channels · *Demand It!* movies and shows · *Rocket* Internet (fastest Internet speed) with *Security Assistance* · Unlimited local and national long distance with 12 calling features · Voice mail	$139.99	$159.99

5. As the administrative assistant at a teen recreation center, you are comparing different cable, Internet, and phone packages for use at the center. Which of the following best summarizes the differences between the Digital Cable Value Deal and the High Definition Starter Deal?

   A. The High Definition Starter Deal costs more and has free high definition.

   B. The High Definition Starter Deal has more digital cable channels, free high definition, unlimited local calling, and it costs more.

   C. The High Definition Starter Deal has *Security Assistance*, unlimited national long-distance calling, and it costs more.

   D. The High Definition Starter Deal has free high definition, *Security Assistance*, unlimited national long-distance calling, voice mail, and it costs more.

   E. The High Definition Starter Deal costs more, has *Rocket* Internet, with *Security Assistance*, *Demand It!* movies and shows, and it costs less.

6. Which statement best summarizes the differences in price between the first 12 months and the price thereafter for all of the bundle packages?

   F. As the package gets better, the difference between the price for the first 12 months and the price thereafter decreases.

   G. As the package gets better, the difference between the price for the first 12 months and the price thereafter increases.

   H. As the package gets better, the difference between the price for the first 12 months and the price thereafter is $15.

   J. As the package gets better, the difference between the price for the first 12 months and the price thereafter is $20.

   K. As the package gets better, the difference between the price for the first 12 months and the price thereafter is $40.

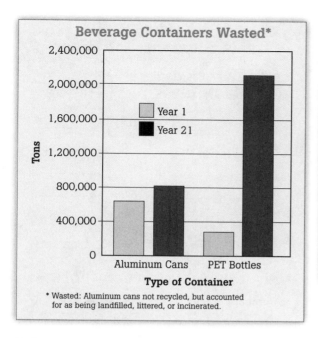

Beverage Containers Wasted*

* Wasted: Aluminum cans not recycled, but accounted for as being landfilled, littered, or incinerated.

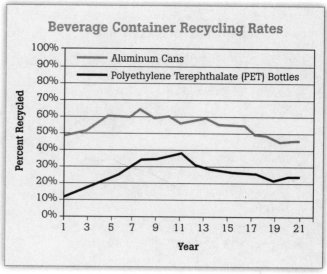

Beverage Container Recycling Rates

7. As a recycling coordinator, you come across a bar graph that shows the amount of beverage containers that are wasted (containers not recycled but accounted for as being landfilled, incinerated, or littered) and a line graph that shows the recycling rate of beverage containers. Which of the following is true based on a comparison of these two graphics?

   A. The amount of aluminum cans wasted has decreased between years 1 and 21, and the recycling rate is lower in year 21 than it was in year 1.

   B. The amount of PET bottles wasted has increased between years 1 and 21, and the recycling rate has decreased between these years.

   C. The amount of aluminum cans and PET bottles wasted has increased between years 1 and 21, and the recycling rate has consistently decreased.

   D. The amount of aluminum cans wasted has increased between years 1 and 21, and the recycling rate is lower in year 21 than it was in year 1.

   E. The amount of aluminum cans and PET bottles wasted has decreased between years 1 and 21, and the recycling rate has consistently increased.

8. Although the recycling rate for PET bottles is higher in year 21 than it was in year 1, the amount wasted is also significantly higher in year 21 than it was in year 1. What is one possible reason for this?

   F. Fewer people are recycling in year 21 than were in year 1.

   G. Fewer people are wasting PET bottles in year 21 than in year 1.

   H. The PET bottles in year 21 weigh more than the ones in year 1.

   J. There are fewer PET bottles being sold in year 21 than there were in year 1.

   K. There are more PET bottles being sold in year 21 than there were in year 1.

Daily Appointments

Time	Appointment	Notes
7:00	Install cable, 12 Emerson Ln.	SB Cable; 2 hours
8:00		
9:00		
10:00	Inspect and test cable lines, 5425 Jefferson St.	∨ ViewCast Cable; 1 hour
10:00		
11:00	Equipment repair, 858 5th Blvd.	∨ ViewCast Cable; 0.5 hour
12:00	Install cable, 580 Elk Rd.	SB Cable; 2.5 hours
1:00		
2:00		
3:00	Lunch	
4:00	Measure signal strength, 815 Marilyn St.	SB Cable; 1.5 hours
5:00		
6:00	Adjust customer equipment, 55 Jackson Ave.	SB Cable; 1 hour

Cable Subcontract Work

Company Name:	SB Cable	
Detailed Description	Invoice: RG-368	
Job: _____	Hrs: _____	
Job: _____	Hrs: _____	
Job: _____	Hrs: _____	
Job: _____	Hrs: _____	
Job: _____	Hrs: _____	
Total Hours Worked	4.5	

Cable Subcontract Work

Company Name:	ViewCast Cable	
Detailed Description	Invoice: RG-724	
Job: _____	Hrs: _____	
Job: _____	Hrs: _____	
Job: _____	Hrs: _____	
Job: _____	Hrs: _____	
Job: _____	Hrs: _____	
Total Hours Worked	1.5	

9. As a cable technician who subcontracts for both SB Cable and ViewCast Cable, you must submit an invoice to each company. It is important to understand how the notes you made in your planner relate to the invoices you complete. Which of the following would you not write under "Detailed Description" for invoice RG-368?

A. Install cable, 580 Elk Rd.

B. Adjust customer equipment, 55 Jackson Ave.

C. Measure signal strength, 815 Marilyn St.

D. Equipment repair, 858 5th Blvd.

E. Install cable, 12 Emerson Ln.

10. What do you write next to "Total Hours Worked" on RG-724?

F. 0.5 hour

G. 1.5 hours

H. 3.5 hours

J. 4 hours

K. 7 hours

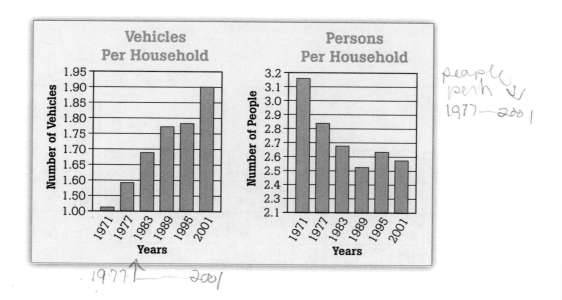

Vehicles Per Household

Persons Per Household

peaple perh ↓ 1977—2001

1977 ↑—————— 2001

11. You are an environmental compliance inspector in a car manufacturing plant. According to the data for the years shown in the graph, which of the following has been the trend in persons per household?

    A. The number of persons per household steadily increased between 1971 and 2001.

    B. The number of persons per household was the same in 1971 as it was in 2001.

    C. The number of persons per household increased between 1971 and 1989 and then decreased between 1989 and 2001.

    D. The number of persons per household was less in 1971 than it was in 2001.

    E. The number of persons per household generally decreased between 1971 and 2001.

12. Based on the two graphs, how has the trend in number of vehicles per household been impacted by the trend in the number of persons per household?

    F. While the number of persons per household remained the same, the number of vehicles per household decreased.

    G. While the number of persons per household decreased, the number of vehicles per household decreased.

    H. While the number of persons per household increased, the number of vehicles per household increased.

    J. While the number of persons per household increased, the number of vehicles per household decreased.

    K. While the number of persons per household decreased, the number of vehicles per household increased.

Periodic Table of Elements

I																	VIII
1 **H**	II											III	IV	V	VI	VII	**2** **He**
3 **Li**	**4** **Be**											**5** **B**	**6** **C**	**7** **N**	**8** **O**	**9** **F**	**10** **Ne**
11 **Na**	**12** **Mg**											**13** **Al**	**14** **Si**	**15** **P**	**16** **S**	**17** **Cl**	**18** **Ar**
19 **K**	**20** **Ca**	**21** **Sc**	**22** **Ti**	**23** **V**	**24** **Cr**	**25** **Mn**	**26** **Fe**	**27** **Co**	**28** **Ni**	**29** **Cu**	**30** **Zn**	**31** **Ga**	**32** **Ge**	**33** **As**	**34** **Se**	**35** **Br**	**36** **Kr**
37 **Rb**	**38** **Sr**	**39** **Y**	**40** **Zr**	**41** **Nb**	**42** **Mo**	**43** **Tc**	**44** **Ru**	**45** **Rh**	**46** **Pd**	**47** **Ag**	**48** **Cd**	**49** **In**	**50** **Sn**	**51** **Sb**	**52** **Te**	**53** **I**	**54** **Xe**
55 **Cs**	**56** **Ba**		**72** **Hf**	**73** **Ta**	**74** **W**	**75** **Re**	**76** **Os**	**77** **Ir**	**78** **Pt**	**79** **Au**	**80** **Hg**	**81** **Tl**	**82** **Pb**	**83** **Bi**	**84** **Po**	**85** **At**	**86** **Rn**
87 **Fr**	**88** **Ra**		**104** **Rf**	**105** **Db**	**106** **Sg**	**107** **Bh**	**108** **Hs**	**109** **Mt**	**110** **Uun**	**111** **Uuu**	**112** **Uub**						

Lanthanides	**57** **La**	**58** **Ce**	**59** **Pr**	**60** **Nd**	**61** **Pm**	**62** **Sm**	**63** **Eu**	**64** **Gd**	**65** **Tb**	**66** **Dy**	**67** **Ho**	**68** **Er**	**69** **Tm**	**70** **Yb**	**71** **Lu**
Actinides	**89** **Ac**	**90** **Th**	**91** **Pa**	**92** **U**	**93** **Np**	**94** **Pu**	**95** **Am**	**96** **Cm**	**97** **Bk**	**98** **Cf**	**99** **Es**	**100** **Fm**	**101** **Md**	**102** **No**	**103** **Lr**

Chemical Element Symbols

Al:	Aluminum	**He:**	Helium
Ar:	Argon	**I:**	Iodine
Br:	Bromine	**Ni:**	Nickel
Cu:	Copper		

13. As the intern in a chemistry laboratory, you need to be able to quickly identify elements. The periodic table of elements is a table that organizes the elements based on their mass and other characteristics. The periodic table above lists the symbol and atomic number for each element. Using the above tables, what is the name of the element that has an atomic number of 35?

A. Bromine

B. Copper

C. Helium

D. Iodine

E. Nickel

14. What is the atomic number for Argon?

F. 2

G. 13

H. 18

J. 28

K. 29

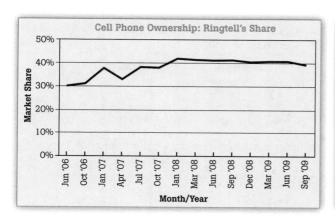

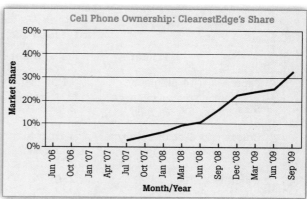

15. You are a market research analyst in charge of conducting consumer surveys to help track marketing and sales trends. Based on the graphs, which show the market share of current, overall cell phone ownership, how would you summarize the ownership trends of the two leading cellular phone brands?

   A. From September 2008 to September 2009, ownership of Ringtell phones increased by 15%, while ownership of ClearestEdge phones slightly decreased.

   B. From September 2008 to September 2009, ownership of ClearestEdge phones decreased by 15%, while ownership of Ringtell phones slightly increased.

   C. From September 2008 to September 2009, ownership of ClearestEdge phones increased by 15%, while ownership of Ringtell phones slightly decreased.

   D. From September 2008 to September 2009, ownership of both ClearestEdge and Ringtell phones increased by 15%.

   E. From September 2008 to September 2009, ownership of both ClearestEdge and Ringtell phones decreased by 15%.

16. How would you describe ClearestEdge market share, compared to Ringtell, since Clearest Edge introduced its new phone in July 2007?

   F. ClearestEdge lost market share while Ringtell slowly gained market share.

   G. ClearestEdge gained significant market share while Ringtell slowly lost market share.

   H. While ClearestEdge's market share remained the same, Ringtell slowly lost market share.

   J. ClearestEdge and Ringtell both slowly lost market share.

   K. ClearestEdge gained market share while Ringtell slowly gained market share as well.

Printer Specifications

	Printer A	Printer B	Printer C	Printer D
Paper	14 pt. glossy	14 pt. matte	14 pt.	14 pt.
Size	2 x 7	2 x 9	2 x 7	2 x 7
Colors	4-color both sides	4-color front, blank back	4-color both sides	4-color front, blank back
Quantity	100	250	200	250
Time	3 days	6 days	1 day	4 days
Price	$64.95	$54.82	$85.72	$74.95

17. As a library manager, you are having bookmarks created for promotional purposes. You are comparing the packages offered by four printers to see which one you should use. The packages offered by the printers are shown in the table above. If your first priority is to receive the bookmarks quickly, which printer(s) should you use?

    A. Printer A

    B. Printer B or Printer C

    C. Printer C

    D. Printer D

    E. Printer B or Printer D

18. You need 100 bookmarks printed so that you can distribute them at a convention in 5 days. Compare the packages to determine the printer(s) that will best fit your needs.

    F. Printer A

    G. Printer A or Printer B

    H. Printer C

    J. Printer D

    K. Printer C or Printer D

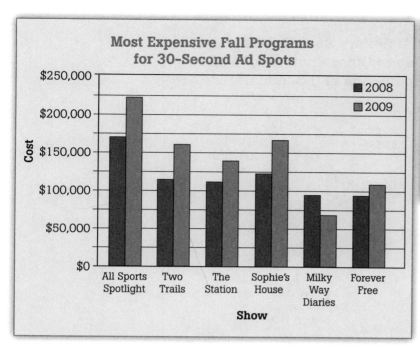

Most Expensive Fall Programs for 30-Second Ad Spots

Legend: ■ 2008 ■ 2009

Y-axis (Cost): $0, $50,000, $100,000, $150,000, $200,000, $250,000

X-axis (Show): All Sports Spotlight, Two Trails, The Station, Sophie's House, Milky Way Diaries, Forever Free

Weekly Viewership (in Millions)		
Show	2007	2008
All Sports Spotlight	18.1	22.4
Two Trails	13.2	14.4
The Station	12.9	13.1
Sophie's House	13.5	15.1
Milky Way Diaries	10.5	9.6
Forever Free	10.4	11.2

19. You are an advertising agent working for a media firm. You are in charge of presenting information to clients in order to create campaigns. Based on the two graphics, how would you describe the overall ad cost trend for fall programming?

A. The programs with the most expensive 30-second ad spots in both 2008 and 2009 were *All Sports Spotlight*, *Sophie's House*, and *The Station*.

B. The programs with the most expensive 30-second ad spots in both 2008 and 2009 were *All Sports Spotlight*, *Sophie's House*, and *Forever Free*.

C. The programs with the most expensive 30-second ad spots in both 2008 and 2009 were *All Sports Spotlight*, *Sophie's House*, and *Milky Way Diaries*.

D. The programs with the most expensive 30-second ad spots in both 2008 and 2009 were *All Sports Spotlight*, *Forever Free*, and *The Station*.

E. The programs with the most expensive 30-second ad spots in both 2008 and 2009 were *All Sports Spotlight*, *Sophie's House*, and *Two Trails*.

20. Based on the two graphics, which show had a change in the price of ad spots that did not match the others, and what is the reason for this change?

F. *Milky Way Diaries*; Weekly viewership increased in 2008.

G. *Milky Way Diaries*; Weekly viewership decreased in 2008.

H. Two Trails; Weekly viewership decreased in 2008.

J. *The Station*; Weekly viewership stayed the same in 2009.

K. *Forever Free*; Weekly viewership increased in 2008.

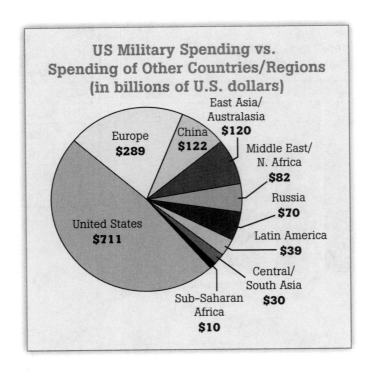

US Military Spending vs. Spending of Other Countries/Regions (in billions of U.S. dollars)

East Asia/Australasia $120
China $122
Europe $289
Middle East/N. Africa $82
Russia $70
United States $711
Latin America $39
Central/South Asia $30
Sub-Saharan Africa $10

21. You are a staff writer working for a major media outlet. Through the research you conducted for an article about trends in military spending, you have learned about how much different nations and regions of the world spend on their militaries. According to the circle graph, which country or region spent the least on its military?

　A. Sub-Saharan Africa

　B. Russia

　C. Latin America

　D. China

　E. Central/South Asia

22. Which of the following assumptions can be eliminated based on the information presented in the graph?

　F. The United States spent more on the military than any other country or region shown.

　G. Russia and China's combined military spending totaled more than half that of the United States.

　H. The budget for nuclear weapons falls under the U.S. Department of Energy.

　J. The European countries reduce military spending every year.

　K. China spent less on its military than Europe spent.

Answers are on page 249.

Level 5 Introduction ...

The lesson and practice pages that follow will give you the opportunity to develop and practice the reading and interpretation skills needed to answer work-related questions at a Level 5 rating of difficulty. The *On Your Own* practice problems provide review and practice of key skills needed for locating information from graphical sources in the workplace. These skills are applied through effective problem solving approaches. The *Performance Assessment* provides problems similar to those you will encounter on a Career Readiness Certificate test. By completing the Level 5 *On Your Own* and *Performance Assessment* questions, you will gain the ability to confidently approach workplace scenarios that require understanding and application of the skills featured in the following lessons:

Lesson 8: Focus on Relevant Information in Graphics

Lesson 9: Find Patterns in Complicated Graphics

Lesson 10: Summarize Information in Complicated Graphics

Lesson 11: Compare Information in Complicated Graphics

These skills are intended to help you successfully use workplace graphics such as instrument gauges, detailed forms, tables, graphs, diagrams, and maps. Locating information in these types of documents and graphics often requires the ability to:

- sort through distracting information,
- understand how to read graphics that have less common formats,
- summarize information in detailed or complicated graphics,
- compare information and trends from multiple graphics.

Through answering document-related questions at this level, you will continue to develop problem-solving approaches and strategies that will help you determine the correct answer in real-world and test-taking situations.

Lesson 8 ▪ ■ ▪
Focus on Relevant Information in Graphics

Skill: Sort through distracting information

Workplace graphics often present far more information than is needed to answer a particular question. When trying to locate information within complex diagrams and tables, you need to sort through information that may be confusing or unnecessary. You can do this by asking yourself questions before searching the graphic. *What do I need to know? What information is not necessary to answer the question?* By identifying what information is needed and what is not, you can focus on the relevant information when interpreting workplace graphics.

Skill Example

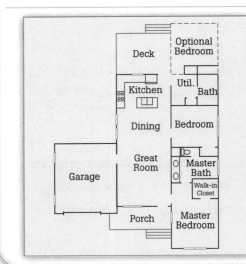

Locate a specific piece of information using symbols.

Graphics such as floor plans include symbols to represent specific pieces of information. Suppose you are a condo sales manager explaining to a potential buyer that an optional bedroom is available. The blueprint shows with dashed lines where the bedroom will go if the buyer chooses it. The rest of the blueprint is not necessary to find the information the buyer needs to make a decision.

US Monthly Average Wheat Prices (per bushel)*						
	Jan.	Feb.	March	April	May	June
2005	3.43 (+.12)	3.36 (+.25)	3.42 (+.29)	3.35 (+.50)	3.31 (−.08)	3.23 (+.74)
2006	3.52 (+.09)	3.66 (+.30)	3.79 (+.37)	3.81 (+.46)	4.09 (+.78)	4.01 (+.78)
2007	4.54 (+1.02)	4.71 (+1.05)	4.75 (+.96)	4.89 (+1.08)	4.88 (+.79)	5.03 (+1.02)
2008	7.93 (+3.39)	9.98 (+5.27)	10.60 (+5.85)	10.00 (+5.11)	8.87 (+3.99)	7.62 (+2.59)
2009	6.21 (−1.72)	5.79 (−4.19)	5.70 (−.4.90)	5.74 (−4.26)	5.84 (−3.03)	5.92 (−1.70)
Numbers in parenthesis indicate change from previous year.						

Skill Practice

Use the table to the left to answer the following questions.

1. You are a crop manager researching past years' wheat sales. What was the price for wheat in June 2008?

   A. $2.59 per bushel

   B. $5.03 per bushel

   C. $7.16 per bushel

   D. $7.62 per bushel

   E. $10.11 per bushel

2. Which month/year had the greatest increase from the previous month/year?

   F. February 2009

   G. April 2008

   H. March 2008

   J. January 2005

   K. February 2008

Try It Out! ▪ ▪ ▪

Part of your job as an administrative assistant is to pay all department bills on time. You are reviewing the corporate credit card statement for one of the employees in your department. A new policy requires all employee corporate credit card accounts to be paid off in full. What payment must be made to this employee's corporate card account in order for the balance to be paid in full?

Prepared For Grant Newsom		Account Number XXXX-XXXXX8421156	Page 1 of 2 Payment Due Date 10/9	
Previous Balance $	Payment Activity $	New Activity $ inc. Adjustments and Finance Charges if any	New Balance $	Minimum Due $
834.93	-325.00	+46.62	556.55	15.00
Credit Line Summary on 09/14	Total Credit Line $20,000.00	Available Credit Line $19,443,45	Cash Advance Limit $ 400.00	Available Cash Limit $ 400.00

Activity	Amount $
08/31/09* COMPUTER PAYMENT RECEIVED - THANK YOU	-25.00
09/09/09* ELECTRONIC PAYMENT RECEIVED - THANK YOU	-300.00
Total of Payment Activity	**-325.00**

A. $15.00   **B.** $46.62   **C.** $325.00   **D.** $556.55   **E.** $834.93

Step 1 Understand the Problem ▪ ▪ ▪

Complete the *Plan for Successful Solving.*

Plan for Successful Solving				
What am I asked to do?	**What are the facts?**	**How do I find the answer?**	**Is there any unnecessary information?**	**What prior knowledge will help me?**
Determine what the total balance is on this employee's corporate credit card account.	The statement includes account balance and payment information.	Identify where the overall account information is located to find the balance.	Most information is not needed to determine the balance.	The balance is typically included with the rest of the payment information.

Step 2 Find and Check Your Answer ▪ ▪ ▪

- Confirm your understanding of the question and revise your plan as needed.
- Based on your plan, determine your solution approach: *I need to determine what balance remains on this employee's corporate credit card account. I know that on most bills or statements there is a section that includes the most current payment information. Usually, the overall balance is also found in this section, which is typically located near the top or the bottom of the statement. I will look for this section to determine the balance.*
- Check your answer. Review all answers to determine if the answer you have selected is the best possible answer.
- **Select the correct answer:** D. $556.55
  By sorting through the information you don't need, you see that the overall balance is listed under New Balance.

On Your Own ▪ ▪ ▪

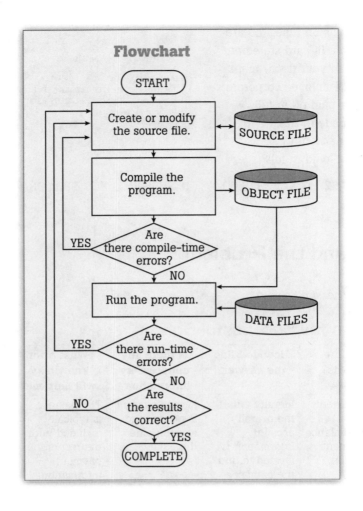

Flowchart

1. As a computer software engineer, you are using this flowchart to create a program. What should you do if there are compile-time errors?

   A. Run the program.

   B. Import information from the data files.

   C. Exchange information with the source file.

   D. Create or modify the source file.

   E. Compile the program.

2. There are no run-time errors. What should you do next?

   F. Check to see if the results are correct.

   G. Check to see if there are any compile-time errors.

   H. Exchange information with the source file.

   J. Create or modify the source file.

   K. Compile the program.

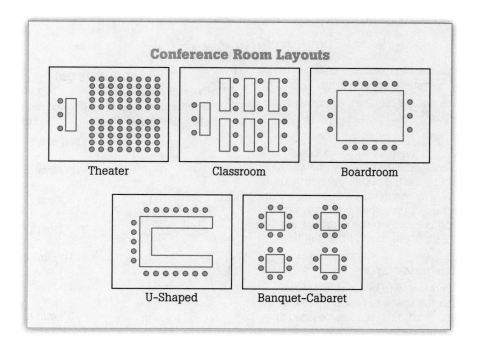

Conference Room Layouts

Theater Classroom Boardroom

U-Shaped Banquet-Cabaret

3. You work as an office manager at a conference center. A client requests a conference room for a one-day panel discussion on accounting. He would like the three-person panel to be seated at the front of the room. He would like the attendees to be able to write notes as they listen to the panel discussion. He also prefers that attendees face the panel during the discussion. Which layout should you choose for the event to best suit the needs of the client?

   A. theater

   B. u-shaped

   C. classroom

   D. boardroom

   E. banquet-cabaret

4. Another client requests the conference room setup that will seat the most people. Which layout do you suggest?

   F. theater

   G. u-shaped

   H. classroom

   J. boardroom

   K. banquet-cabaret

BOILER CLEARANCES

The following minimum clearances must be maintained for operation and servicing.

Additional space will be required for installation, depending upon site conditions.

Side and Rear Flue

a. Provided that the flue hole is cut accurately (e.g., with a core drill), the flue can be easily installed from inside the building where wall thicknesses are no greater than 600 millimeters (mm) (24 inches). If the space into which the boiler is going is less than the length of the flue required, then you must fit the flue from the outside.

Installation from Inside ONLY

b. If a core boring tool is to be used inside the building, then the space in which the boiler is to be installed must be at least wide enough to accommodate the tool.

REAR FLUE ONLY
Minimum top clearance required = 145 mm $(5\frac{3}{4}$ inches)

SIDE FLUE ONLY	
Horizontal length of flue from center line of boiler to outside wall	Top clearance required (minimum) Dim. A
0.5 m	165 mm $(6\frac{1}{2}$ inches)
1.0 m	170 mm $(6\frac{11}{16}$ inches)
1.5 m	185 mm $(7\frac{1}{4}$ inches)
2.0 m	200 mm $(7\frac{7}{8}$ inches)
2.5 m	210 mm $(8\frac{1}{4}$ inches)
3.0 m	225 mm $(8\frac{7}{8}$ inches)
3.5 m	235 mm $(9\frac{1}{4}$ inches)
4.0 m	250 mm $(10\frac{7}{8}$ inches)
4.5 m	260 mm $(10\frac{1}{4}$ inches)
5.0 m	275 mm $(10\frac{13}{16}$ inches)
5.5 m	290 mm $(11\frac{3}{8}$ inches)
6.0 m	300 mm $(11\frac{13}{16}$ inches)

5. As a boiler installer, you have to know the clearance requirements between the boiler and the walls and the top of a ventilating cupboard. If the length of the flue from the center line of the boiler to the outside wall is 3.5 m, what is the minimum top clearance required?

   A. 145 millimeters

   B. 225 millimeters

   C. 235 millimeters

   D. 250 millimeters

   E. 600 millimeters

6. What is the minimum clearance required for the rear flue?

   F. 5 millimeters

   G. 50 millimeters

   H. 100 millimeters

   J. 145 millimeters

   K. 278 millimeters

Utensils in an Informal Place Setting

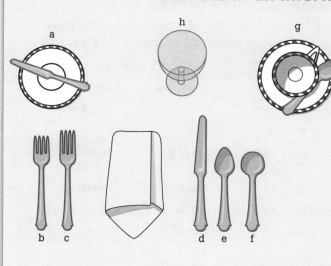

- **Two Forks:** The forks are placed to the left of the plate. The smaller fork is used for a salad or appetizer; the larger of the two forks is used for the main course.
- **Dinner knife:** The dinner knife is set immediately to the right of the plate, cutting edge facing inward. (If the main course is meat, a steak knife should take the place of the dinner knife.)
- **Spoons:** Spoons go to the right of the knife. If soup is being served first, the soupspoon goes to the far (outside) right of the dinner knife.
- **Butter knife:** If used, the bread plate goes above the forks, with the butter knife placed diagonally across the edge of plate, handle on the right side and blade facing down.
- **Coffee cup, saucer, and spoon:** If coffee is served during the meal, the coffee cup, saucer, and spoon are placed above and to the right of the knife and spoons.
- **Water glass:** The water glass is placed directly above the dinner knife and spoons. Water glasses should be filled with ice and water just prior to guest arrival so that cubes are not melted before guests have been seated.

7. As a trainee for a restaurant manager position, you are reading the procedures for how to set places for dinner guests. According to the graphic and description, which utensil is used for a salad or appetizer?

    A. a

    B. b

    C. c

    D. e

    E. f

8. You are not serving soup at tonight's meal. Which utensil is not necessary?

    F. a

    G. b

    H. d

    J. e

    K. f

Westfield High School Class Schedule

Teacher	1st Block 8:15–9:10	2nd Block 9:13–10:56	3rd Block 10:59–11:49	4th Block 12:20–1:10	5th Block 1:13–2:03
Harris	Literature	Prep	Speech	English 9	English 12
Rodriguez	Prep	Algebra 2	Geometry	Study Hall	Geometry 2
Walker	Algebra 1	Consumer Math	Prep	Statistics	Pre-Algebra A
Hall	Band	Music 1	Music 2	Prep	Choir
Lee	Prep	Shop 1	Mechanics	Shop 2	Advanced Mechanics
Nelson	Health 9	Health 10	Prep	Health 11	Health 12
Parkers	Pre-Algebra A	General Math	Pre-Algebra B	Algebra 1	Prep
Walters	Earth Science A	Earth Science B	Prep	Life Science	Biology

9. You are a high-school guidance counselor. A new student needs to take an Algebra 1 course. She would also like to be in the school band. In which block will you enroll her for Algebra 1?

    A. 1st Block

    B. 2nd Block

    C. 3rd Block

    D. 4th Block

    E. 5th Block

10. As the administrative assistant, you are in charge of finding substitute teachers. Ms. Walters will be taking her Earth Science A and B students on a field trip to the museum. She is leaving at noon and will be gone for the remainder of the day. For which courses will you need to schedule a substitute teacher to take over in her absence?

    F. Statistics and Pre-Algebra

    G. Life Science and Biology

    H. General Math and Statistics

    J. Pre-Algebra and General Math

    K. Consumer Math and General Math

Jackson Commons Dining Menu

Week of October 16–22

	Monday	Tuesday	Wednesday	Thursday	Friday	Weekend
Breakfast	*Every Day* Omelets to order, cereal, fruit, bagels, muffins, bacon, sausage, ham, hash browns					
	Daily Feature: Egg and cheese sandwiches to order	**Daily Feature:** Breakfast burritos	**Daily Feature:** Pancakes, hash browns, bacon	**Daily Feature:** Mexican breakfast tacos	**Daily Feature:** Biscuits & gravy, hash browns	**Daily Feature (both days):** Waffles, pancakes, hash browns, corned beef hash
Lunch	*Every Day* Sandwich bar, salad bar, pasta bar, soup bar, stir fry bar, daily grill					
	Daily Feature: Enchiladas bar (meat or vegetarian)	**Daily Feature:** Lemon chicken Alfredo over angel hair pasta, tofu Cobb salad	**Daily Feature:** Southwestern chicken salad, hummus veggie wrap	**Daily Feature:** Grilled chicken sandwich, grilled eggplant sandwich	**Daily Feature:** Meat or vegetable calzones	**Daily Feature (Saturday only):** Philly cheesesteak, Tofu salad
Dinner	*Every Day* Sandwich bar, salad bar, pasta bar, soup bar, stir fry bar, daily grill					
	Daily Feature: Butterfly pork chops, applesauce, vegetarian stir-fry	**Daily Feature:** Popcorn shrimp basket and starch, garden vegetable casserole	**Daily Feature:** Pot pie (chicken or vegetarian), curried vegetables	**Daily Feature:** Chicken or eggplant parmesan	**Daily Feature:** Build-your-own pizza	**Daily Feature: (Saturday only)** Steak tips, grilled polenta with roasted tomatoes, assorted vegetables

11. You are a kitchen manager in a college dining hall. Because you know you will have a smaller staff for two of the lunch shifts this week, you decide to serve a single daily feature on those two days. The single feature must have both meat and vegetarian options. Based on the schedule, which two days will you have a smaller lunch shift staff?

    A.   Monday and Friday

    B.   Wednesday and Friday

    C.   Monday and Wednesday

    D.   Tuesday and Wednesday

    E.   Wednesday and Thursday

12. For which two meals is there no daily feature?

    F.   Sunday dinner, Thursday dinner

    G.   Tuesday lunch, Thursday lunch

    H.   Wednesday dinner, Sunday lunch

    J.   Monday dinner, Wednesday lunch

    K.   Sunday lunch, Sunday dinner

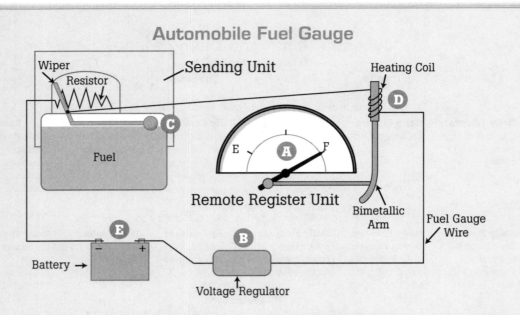

Automobile Fuel Gauge

This fuel gauge consists of a sending unit, located on the fuel tank, and a remote register unit mounted in the instrument cluster. The remote register unit pointer is controlled by a bimetallic arm and heating coil. The sending unit is a rheostat that varies its resistance depending on the amount of fuel in the tank.

Troubleshooting inoperative or erratic gauge.

The gauge has four things that can malfunction to make it inoperative or erratic.

1. Loose or broken fuel gauge wire from the voltage regulator to the remote register unit

2. Defective fuel gauge wire

3. Loose or broken fuel gauge wire from the fuel tank sending unit

4. Defective fuel tank sending unit

---

13. As a calibration technician, you are working on calibrating an erratic fuel gauge. You think there might be a loose or broken wire, as described in number three above. Based on the instructions and diagram, where do you check to determine if this is the problem?

    A A

    B. B

    C. C

    D. D

    E. E

14. The wire is not the problem, so you want to investigate the remote register unit. Based on the instructions and diagram, where do you look to determine if the remote register unit is the problem?

    F. A

    G. B

    H. C

    J. D

    K. E

Pandemic Influenza Preparedness Checklist

Completed	In Progress	Not Started	
❏	❏	❏	Pandemic influenza has been incorporated into emergency management planning and exercises for the organization.
❏	❏	❏	A planning committee[1] has been created to specifically address pandemic influenza preparedness.
❏	❏	❏	A person has been assigned responsibility for coordinating pandemic influenza preparedness planning (hereafter referred to as the pandemic response coordinator) for the organization. (Insert name, title, and contact information.) _____
❏	❏	❏	Members of the planning committee include the following: (Insert below or attach a list with name, title, and contact information for each.)

    ❏ Administration: _____

    ❏ Medical staff: _____

    ❏ EMS providers: _____

    ❏ Phone triage personnel/dispatch center: _____

    ❏ Emergency management officer: _____

    ❏ State/local health official: _____

    ❏ Law enforcement official (for quarantine/security): _____

    ❏ Other member[2]: _____

Completed	In Progress	Not Started	
❏	❏	❏	A point of contact (e.g., internal staff member assigned infection control responsibility for the organization or an outside consultant) for questions/consultation on infection control has been identified. (Insert name, title, and contact information.) _____

[1] *Size of committee can vary, depending on the size and needs of the organization.*

[2] *Some organizations may need or want to include a school official or volunteer coordinator for local civic and preparedness groups.*

---

15. You are an emergency medical technician. Your supervisor asks you who must be on the planning committee to address pandemic influenza preparedness. Based on the checklist, what is your response?

    A. The members must include a school official.

    B. The members must include the people listed under the fourth item.

    C. The members must be doctors and EMS providers.

    D. The organization can choose not to have a planning committee.

    E. The members must include a consultant.

16. Your supervisor asks about the role of the pandemic response coordinator. Based on the checklist, what is this person's role?

    F. Create the planning committee.

    G. Choose the members of the planning committee.

    H. Act as a contact for questions about infection control.

    J. Coordinate the pandemic influenza preparedness planning.

    K. Act as a contact for volunteers from local civic organizations.

US Monthly Average Soybean Prices Received for the 1999–2008 Calendar Years

Year	Jan	Feb	Mar	Apr	May	Jun	Jul	Aug	Sep	Oct	Nov	Dec	Avg*
1999	5.32	4.80	4.61	4.63	4.50	4.44	4.19	4.39	4.57	4.48	4.45	4.43	4.57
2000	4.62	4.79	4.91	5.00	5.19	4.93	4.53	4.45	4.59	4.45	4.55	4.78	4.73
2001	4.68	4.46	4.39	4.22	4.33	4.46	4.79	4.85	4.53	4.09	4.16	4.20	4.43
2002	4.22	4.22	4.38	4.47	4.64	4.88	5.35	5.53	5.39	5.20	5.46	5.46	4.93
2003	5.51	5.55	5.59	5.82	6.07	6.09	5.82	5.68	6.06	6.60	7.05	7.17	6.08
2004	7.35	8.28	9.28	9.62	9.56	9.08	8.46	6.83	5.84	5.56	5.36	5.45	7.56
2005	5.57	5.42	5.95	6.03	6.20	6.58	6.84	6.15	5.77	5.67	5.62	5.77	5.96
2006	5.88	5.67	5.57	5.52	5.68	5.61	5.61	5.23	5.24	5.52	6.07	6.18	5.65
2007	6.38	6.87	6.95	6.88	7.13	7.51	7.56	7.72	8.18	8.36	9.41	10.00	7.75
2008	9.96	11.70	11.50	12.00	12.10	13.20	13.30	12.80	10.70	9.94	9.38	9.24	11.32

*Calendar year average.

17. You are a farm management firm president, and you are looking at a table of soybean prices over the last 10 years. What is the range (high/low) in prices for the summer months (June through August) of 2008?

   A. $4.44/$4.39

   B. $7.72/$7.51

   C. $13.20/$10.70

   D. $13.20/$2.80

   E. $13.30/$12.80

18. In what year was the calendar year average price per bushel lowest?

   F. 1999

   G. 2001

   H. 2003

   J. 2005

   K. 2007

Postage Master 3000

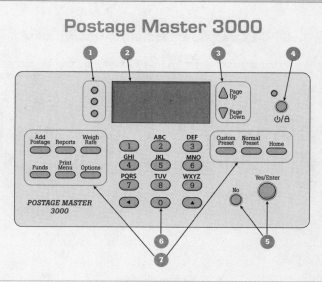

Control Panel

Item	Part/Key	Description
1	Screen Selection Keys	Allows you to select an option on the screen with the corresponding key.
2	LCD Display	Shows the current status of your system and prompts you through all operations.
3	Page Up/Page Down (Scroll Keys)	Allows you to scroll up and down through menu choices.
4	Lock/Power Key	Allows you to power up or power down machine. If the lock code feature has been enabled, you can either power down the machine or put the machine into lock-down mode.
5	Yes/Enter and No Keys	Allows you to confirm an operation or answer "Yes" or "No" to a prompt.
6	Alpha/Numeric Keypad	Allows you to type in numbers and letters for account names, postage values, and other information.
7	Feature Keys	Allows you quick access to key features. See page 8 of this guide for more information.

19. As an administrative support supervisor, you are learning to use a new postage machine that allows you to weigh packages and print out stamp labels with exact cost and shipping specifications. Where is the button located that allows you to power up the machine?

   A. top left

   B. top right

   C. top center

   D. bottom left

   E. bottom right

20. What is the purpose of the buttons in the bottom right-hand corner of the machine?

   F. allows you to select an option

   G. allows you to type in numbers

   H. allows quick access to key features

   J. shows the current status of the system

   K. allows you to answer "Yes" or "No" to a prompt

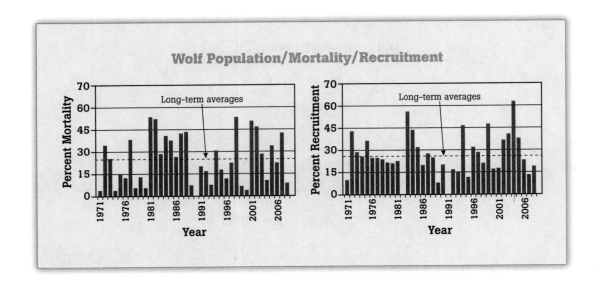

Wolf Population/Mortality/Recruitment

21. You are a natural sciences manager. You are reviewing a study of the wolf population of a wilderness area. Based on the graphs, which year shows no mortality?

    A. 1982

    B. 1989

    C. 1990

    D. 1991

    E. 2000

22. Which year shows the highest percent recruitment, or increase in population?

    F. 1981

    G. 1982

    H. 1994

    J. 1999

    K. 2004

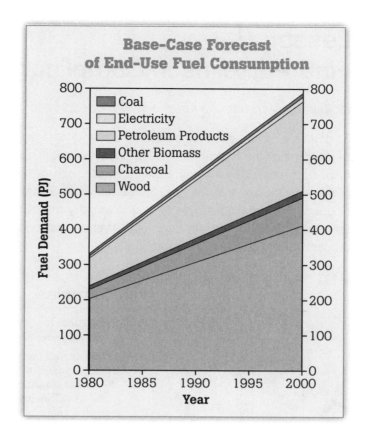

Base-Case Forecast of End-Use Fuel Consumption

23. As an environmental engineering technician, you are reviewing historical data on the use of fuels to analyze the accuracy of the author's fuel consumption predictions. The graph shows projections for the total consumption for each year and is broken down by fuel source. Based on the graph, which fuel source was projected to be used the most from 1980 to 2000?

   A. wood

   B. coal

   C. charcoal

   D. electricity

   E. other biomass

24. A petajoule is a unit of measurement used to measure energy. Which fuel source was projected to grow from about 25 petajoules in 1980 to nearly 100 in 2000?

   F. coal

   G. electricity

   H. petroleum products

   J. charcoal

   K. wood

Answers are on page 254.

Lesson 9 ■ ■ ■
Find Patterns in Complicated Graphics

Skill: Identify trends shown in one or more detailed or complicated graphics

As part of your job, you may be asked to look at data or graphics to identify trends. Trends are typical patterns in behavior that can be identified by looking at data. For instance, by looking at monthly sales of a certain product over a period of a few years, you may see trends in terms of when sales of that product go up or down. Grocery stores must be able to identify trends as to which foods are more popular during certain times of the year. Knowing these trends can help grocers better plan their inventories.

Skill Examples

Weekly Online Holiday Retail Sales

Example 1
Identify trends shown in a graphic.

As you can see from the graph, the general trend from the past five years has been that online retail sales increase gradually each week leading up to Christmas. This information helps retailers project expected sales figures.

Example 2
Identify changes in trends shown in a graphic.

This graph shows that in the current year, sales have been lower in weeks 1 and 2 than they were in year 5. Sales may continue to be lower than year 5 in the upcoming weeks. One possible reason is an economic slump. Retailers carefully plan strategies based on this change in sales trends.

Skill Practice

Use the graph to the left to answer the following questions.

Percent of Asking Price Received for Home Sales
May 2007–November 2008

1. You are a real estate agent looking at sale trends. Based on the graph, what has been the overall trend?

   A. Sellers are receiving a larger percent of their asking price.

   B. Sellers are accepting a smaller percent of their asking price.

   C. The difference between asking prices and selling prices has decreased.

   D. No trend can be identified.

   E. More people are buying than selling.

2. Based on the graph, what are the highest and lowest percentages of typical sale prices?

   F. High = 114%; Low = 69%

   G. High = 114%; Low = 78%

   H. High = 114%; Low = 82%

   J. High = 104%; Low = 77%

   K. High = 100%; Low = 78%

Try It Out! ▪ ▪ ▪

You are an elementary school administrator in a fast-growing county. You have to do some long-range planning about expected changes in student enrollment over the next ten years. To determine population trends, you look at the graph to the right. What likely trend do you predict for the population of Hilliard, Mercer, and Niles between 2010 and 2020?

A. It will stay the same.

B. It will continue to decrease.

C. It will continue to increase.

D. It will decrease dramatically.

E. There is not enough information.

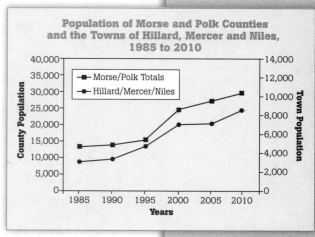

city morse polk
county population

Problem Solving Tip

Some graphs may contain extra information. Start by identifying what you need to know. Then focus only on the information that will help you answer the question. The line graph in the *Try It Out!* example includes two data sets on population—one for counties and one for the three towns that are discussed in the question. By first using the key to identify which set of data you should focus upon, you can eliminate any unnecessary data.

Step 1 Understand the Problem ▪ ▪ ▪

Complete the *Plan for Successful Solving.*

Plan for Successful Solving				
What am I asked to do?	**What are the facts?**	**How do I find the answer?**	**Is there any unnecessary information?**	**What prior knowledge will help me?**
Identify population trends in the towns of Hilliard, Mercer, and Niles.	The data on the graph reflect the population for the last 25 years.	Look at the graph to find patterns in the data and predict the population in 10 years.	The Morse/Polk line is for the counties. This is not needed to answer the question.	Line graphs that go up show increases over time.

Step 2 Find and Check Your Answer ▪ ▪ ▪

▪ Confirm your understanding of the question and revise your plan as needed.

▪ Based on your plan, determine your solution approach: *I need to find trends in the data for the town population only. According to the graph, the population of the three towns has been steadily rising since 1985, with a great increase in growth between 2000 and 2010. Based on the graph, I think the population will continue to increase.*

▪ Check your answer. Review all answers to determine if the answer you have selected is the best possible answer.

▪ **Select the correct answer:**   C. It will continue to increase.
By identifying the line used to plot population data for the towns, you see that the trend for the past 25 years has been for the population to increase. Based on this information, it is likely that the population will continue to increase.

Remember!

Line graphs are often used to show information regarding something that occurs over a period of time. Because of this, they are useful for displaying trend data. In most cases, when the plotted data result in a line that goes up, there is an increasing trend; when the plotted data result in a line that goes down, there is a decreasing trend.

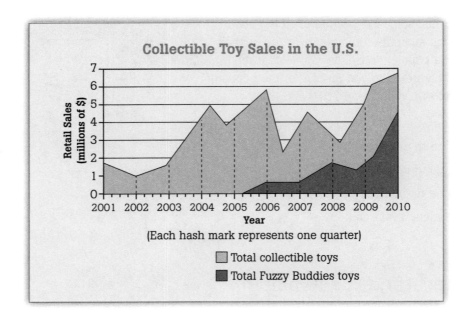

1. As a retail sales manager, you are responsible for understanding trends in sales of particular products. You are tracking sales of Fuzzy Buddies toys over the last few years. What trends do you see in the graphic?

   A. Fuzzy Buddies sales increased significantly in 2009.

   B. Sales of collectible toys have slowed in the last two years.

   C. Fuzzy Buddies sales go up and down consistently.

   D. Fuzzy Buddies sales slowly decreased between 2008–2010.

   E. Sales of collectible toys increased steadily from 2001–2010.

2. In which years did sales of Fuzzy Buddies toys increase in every quarter of the year?

   F. 2006 and 2008

   G. 2006, 2008, and 2009

   H. 2005, 2006, and 2008

   J. 2007 and 2009

   K. 2005, 2007, 2008, and 2009

Corn-Acreage, Production, and Value by leading States: 2005-2007

State	Acreage harvested (1,000 acres)			Yield per acre (bu.)			Production (mil. bu.)			Price ($/bu.)			Farm value (mil. dol.)		
	2005	2006	2007	2005	2006	2007	2005	2006	2007	2005	2006	2007	2005	2006	2007
U.S.	75,117	70,648	86,542	148	149	151	11,114	10,535	13,074	2.00	3.04	4.00	22,198	32,095	52,090
Iowa	12,500	12,350	13,850	173	166	171	2,163	2,050	2,368	1.94	3.03	4.00	4,195	6,212	9,473
Illinois	11,950	11,150	13,050	143	163	175	1,709	1,817	2,284	2.08	3.07	4.05	3,554	5,580	9,249
Nebraska	8,250	7,750	9,200	154	152	160	1,271	1,178	1,472	1.92	3.00	4.00	2,439	3,534	5,888
Minnesota	6,850	6,850	7,800	174	161	146	1,192	1,103	1,139	1.86	2.89	3.85	2,217	3,187	4,384
Indiana	5,770	5,380	6,370	154	157	155	889	845	987	2.00	3.17	4.05	1,777	2,678	3,999

3. You are a farm management advisor looking at trends for growing corn in your area. According to the table, which U.S. values consistently increased from 2005 to 2007?

    A. acreage harvested and production

    B. yield per acre and production

    C. farm value and acreage harvested

    D. acreage harvested and yield per acre

    E. yield per acre, price, and farm value

4. Based on the trends from 2005 to 2007, which state most likely saw a decreased yield in 2008?

    F. Iowa

    G. Illinois

    H. Nebraska

    J. Minnesota

    K. Indiana

Internet Usage and Educational Attainment

	Total households	In the home Percent			No internet use	
		All households	Dial-up	Broadband	Total households	Percent of total
Educational attainment of householder						
Elementary	5,812	18.5	5.4	13.1	4,322	74.4
Some high school	9,264	28.2	7.4	20.5	5,721	61.8
High school diploma/GED	35,295	49.1	12.1	36.8	14,322	40.6
Some college	33,078	68.9	12.1	56.5	6,580	19.9
Bachelors degree or more	34,392	84.1	9.7	74.2	3,187	9.3

Internet Usage and Household Income

Family Income of householder [1] [2]						
Less than $15,000	13,939	82.7	18.5	63.9	8,506	61.0
$15,000 to $24,999	10,848	76.2	20.2	55.7	5,382	49.6
$25,000 to $34,999	11,650	50.9	11.2	39.7	4,085	35.1
$35,000 to $49,999.	13,718	65.7	14.4	51.0	2,995	21.8
$50,000 to $74,999	17,101	80.2	13.8	66.0	1,949	11.4
$75,000 to $99,999	9,872	88.6	11.4	76.8	546	5.5
$100,000 to $149,000	8,481	92.1	8.0	83.7	363	4.3
$150,000 and over	5,570	95.5	5.0	90.3	120	2.2

[1] Includes other groups not shown separately
[2] Does not include households that would not provide income level data.

5. You are a software developer looking to develop a new Web site. You are looking at the data above. What can you determine about the percent of households that have broadband compared to those that have dial-up?

A. For only the first 3 levels of educational attainment and income, a higher percent of households have dial-up.

B. For only the last 2 levels of educational attainment and income, a higher percent of households have broadband.

C. For all ranges of educational attainment and all ranges of income, a higher percent of households have dial-up.

D. For only the first 3 levels of educational attainment and income, a higher percent of households have broadband.

E. For all ranges of educational attainment and all ranges of income, a higher percent of households have broadband.

6. What trend do you notice in the percentage of households with no Internet?

F. As educational attainment and income increase, the percentage of households with no Internet decreases.

G. As educational attainment increases and income level decreases, the percentage of households with no Internet increases.

H. As educational attainment increases and income level decreases, the percentage of households with no Internet decreases.

J. As educational attainment and income increase, the percentage of households with no Internet increases.

K. As educational attainment and income decrease, the percentage of households with no Internet decreases.

INVESTMENTS, LIFE/HEALTH INSURERS, 2005-2007

Investment type	Amount ($ billions)			Percent of Total Investments		
	2005	2006	2007	2005	2006	2007
Bonds	1,889.8	2,134.6	2,164.1	75.09	74.12	73.17
Stocks	95.1	143.5	142.5	3.78	4.98	4.82
Preferred stocks	29.9	64.7	65.7	1.19	2.25	2.22
Common stocks	65.2	78.7	76.8	2.59	2.73	2.60
Mortgage loans on real estate	253.7	294.0	315.1	10.08	10.21	10.65
First liens	252.8	292.9	313.1	10.04	10.17	10.58
Other than first liens	0.9	1.1	2.0	0.04	0.04	0.07

7. As a financial manager, you are interested in where health insurers invested their money between 2005 and 2007. What trend can you identify in the data?

    A.   The percent of total investments in stocks consistently went up.

    B.   The amount invested in bonds went up and then went down.

    C.   The percent of total investments in both stocks and bonds went down in 2007.

    D.   The amount invested in preferred stocks consistently went down.

    E.   The amount invested in common stocks went down and then went up.

8. What trends can you determine about the percentage of total investments during this time period?

    F.   Investment in bonds went down and then went up.

    G.   Investment in mortgage loans went up every year.

    H.   Investment in mortgage loans other than first liens went up sharply.

    J.   Investment in preferred stocks went down sharply.

    K.   Investment in common stocks went down.

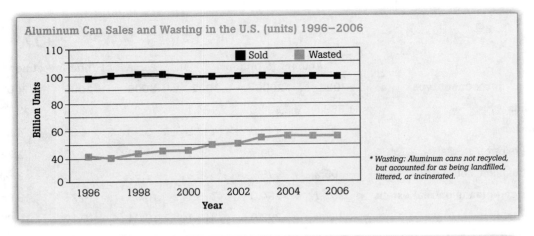

Aluminum Can Sales and Wasting in the U.S. (units) 1996–2006

* Wasting: Aluminum cans not recycled, but accounted for as being landfilled, littered, or incinerated.

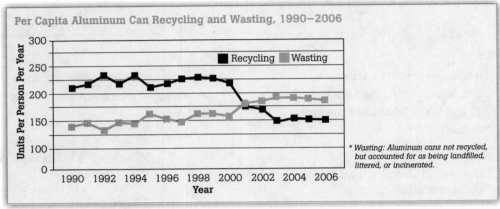

Per Capita Aluminum Can Recycling and Wasting, 1990–2006

* Wasting: Aluminum cans not recycled, but accounted for as being landfilled, littered, or incinerated.

9. As an educational outreach coordinator at a recycling plant, you present information to the community about the benefits of recycling aluminum cans. What is the trend in the first graphic and how does the second graphic help explain this trend?

A. Because more cans are being sold, the amount wasted has increased while recycling has decreased.

B. Despite a relatively stable amount of cans being sold, the amount wasted has increased, and recycling has increased.

C. Despite significantly fewer cans being sold, the amount wasted has increased while recycling has decreased.

D. Despite a relatively stable amount of cans being sold, the amount wasted has increased because recycling has decreased.

E. Despite the fact that more cans are being sold, the amount of waste has decreased because recycling has increased.

10. Based on the graphics, what recommendation would you make for future educational outreach programs about recycling?

F. There is a need for recycling awareness programs. Aluminum recycling has dropped significantly since the late 1990s.

G. There are no additional recycling programs needed. People are recycling more aluminum now than ever before.

H. There is a need for recycling awareness programs. Aluminum recycling began declining steadily in 1990.

J. There are no additional recycling programs needed. The amount of aluminum recycled has stayed consistent since 1990.

K. There is a need for recycling awareness programs. The amount of aluminum wasted has consistently been higher than the amount recycled.

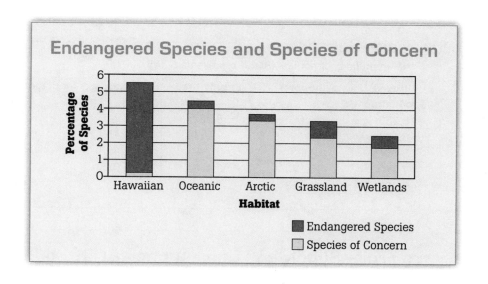

Endangered Species and Species of Concern

11. As a biological research assistant, you are helping to prepare a report on endangered species for a grant application. Which habitat has more endangered species than species of concern?

    A.   arctic

    B.   oceanic

    C.   wetland

    D.   Hawaiian

    E.   grassland

12. What trend do you see by looking at the graph?

    F.   Hawaiian areas have few endangered species.

    G.   There are more endangered species than species of concern.

    H.   Most habitats have about equal numbers of species of concern.

    J.   Almost all the habitats have more species of concern than endangered species.

    K.   Habitats on dry land have more endangered species than areas surrounded by water.

Citrus Fruit—Supply and Consumption 2002 to 2006

In millions of pounds (8,355 represents 8,355,000,000)

Year	Utilized Production	Imports	Supply total	Exports	Consumption total
2002	8,256	707	8,963	2,245	6,718
2003	8,442	969	9,411	2,456	6,955
2004	8,156	993	9,149	2,495	6,654
2005	7,320	1,123	8,443	2,035	6,408
2006	7,306	1,163	8,469	2,021	6,448

Noncitrus Fruit—Supply and Consumption 2002 to 2006

In millions of pounds (8,355 represents 8,355,000,000)

Year	Utilized Production	Imports	Supply total	Exports	Consumption total
2002	12,833	11,552	24,385	2,902	21,483
2003	13,386	12,164	25,550	2,835	22,715
2004	14,335	12,325	26,660	3,079	23,581
2005	14,389	12,460	26,849	3,479	23,370
2006	13,955	13,109	27,064	3,055	24,009

13. As a farm manager, you need to track demand for different types of fruit. You are looking at trends in both citrus and noncitrus fruits. Based on the tables, which of the following trends is true for the years shown?

A. Consumption was consistently lower for noncitrus fruits than for citrus fruits.

B. More citrus fruits were exported than noncitrus fruits.

C. Exports for both citrus and noncitrus fruits consistently went up.

D. Consumption was consistently higher for noncitrus fruits than for citrus fruits.

E. More citrus fruits were produced each year than noncitrus fruits.

14. Which of the following trends is true about the demand for citrus and noncitrus fruit?

F. There was a constant decrease in demand for citrus fruit and a constant increase in demand for noncitrus fruit.

G. There was an overall decrease in demand for citrus fruit and a consistent increase in demand for noncitrus fruit.

H. In general, there was an increase in demand for citrus fruit and a decrease in demand for noncitrus fruit.

J. The demand for both citrus and noncitrus fruit fluctuated up and down throughout the years.

K. There was a constant increase in demand for both citrus and noncitrus fruit.

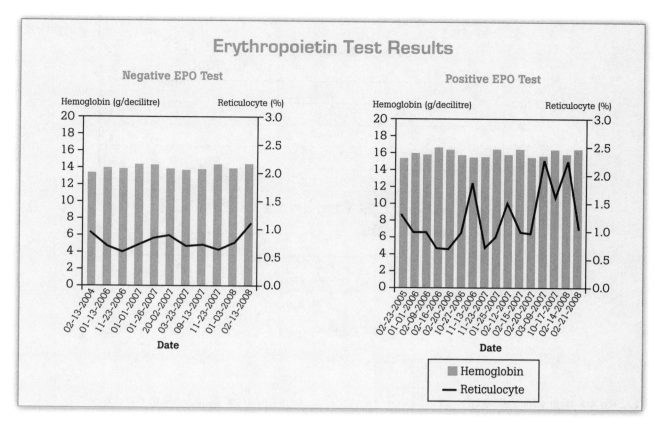

Erythropoietin Test Results

Negative EPO Test

Hemoglobin (g/decilitre)   Reticulocyte (%)

Date

Positive EPO Test

Hemoglobin (g/decilitre)   Reticulocyte (%)

Date

■ Hemoglobin
— Reticulocyte

15. You are a medical laboratory technician learning how to read EPO tests. This test determines if a patient has bone marrow disorders or kidney disease. What trend do you see in reticulocyte levels?

A. The negative test shows levels with sharp peaks and valleys, while the positive test shows relatively consistent levels.

B. The negative and positive tests both show relatively consistent levels.

C. The positive test shows widely varying levels, while the negative test shows levels with sharp peaks and valleys.

D. The positive test shows levels with sharp peaks and valleys, while the negative test shows relatively consistent levels.

E. The positive test shows levels with sharp peaks and valleys, while the negative test shows a sharp increase in the level.

16. What trend do you notice in the amount of hemoglobin in the positive and negative EPO test results?

F. Hemoglobin is consistently higher in the negative EPO test.

G. Hemoglobin is consistently higher in the positive EPO test.

H. Hemoglobin is identical in the positive and negative EPO tests.

J. Hemoglobin consistently increases in both the positive and negative EPO test.

K. Hemoglobin consistently decreases in both the positive and negative EPO test.

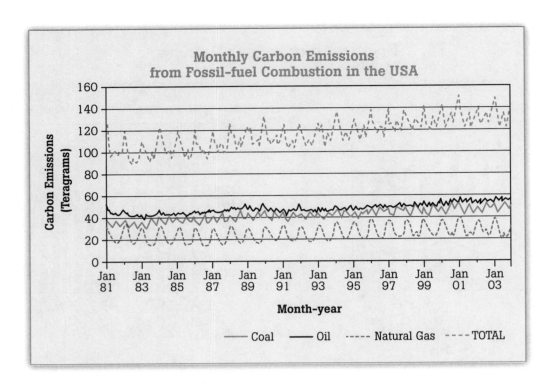

Monthly Carbon Emissions from Fossil-fuel Combustion in the USA

17. You are an environmental specialist, and you are looking at historical carbon emissions trend data in the United States. What was the general trend in total carbon emissions for the time period shown in the graph?

    A. They decreased over time.

    B. They increased gradually over time.

    C. They remained consistent over time.

    D. They had a pattern similar to oil use.

    E. They decreased consistently over time.

18. What trend do you see in natural gas emissions?

    F. They peak in both the summer and the winter.

    G. They peak only in the summer.

    H. They are consistent year round.

    J. They gradually decrease over time.

    K. They increase sharply, and then decrease again.

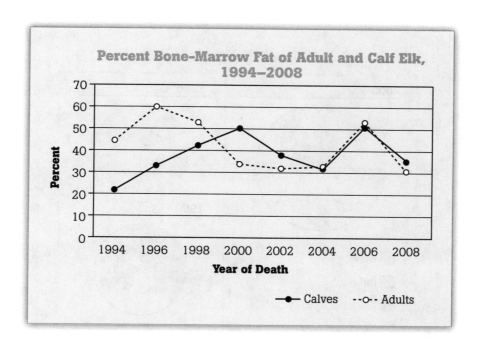

Percent Bone-Marrow Fat of Adult and Calf Elk, 1994–2008

19. You are working at Yellowstone National Park as an environmental science and protection technician. You track the health of the park's elk herds. You can look at the amount of fat in the bone marrow to tell the health of an animal at its time of death. What can you conclude about the bone marrow fat in calves?

   A. It steadily goes up over time.

   B. It went up between 1994 and 2000.

   C. It went down between 1994 and 2002.

   D. It went up sharply between 2000 and 2006.

   E. It went down then up between 1994 and 2006.

20. During which time period was the trend for calves most similar to the trend for adults?

   F. 1994–2000

   G. 1996–2002

   H. 2000–2004

   J. 2002–2008

   K. 2004–2008

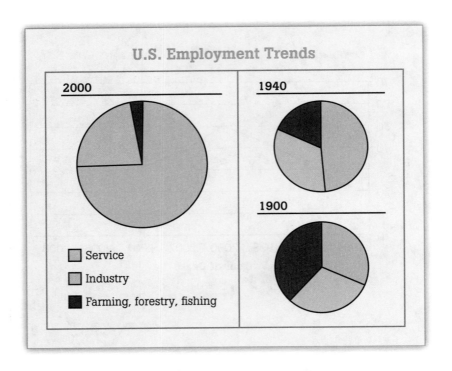

U.S. Employment Trends

2000

1940

1900

- Service
- Industry
- Farming, forestry, fishing

21. In your work as a labor relations specialist, you are looking at how employment has changed during U.S. history. What trend do you see between 1900 and 1940?

    A. reduction in the percentage of service jobs

    B. growth in the percentage of service jobs

    C. no change in the percentage of service jobs

    D. growth in the percentage of farming, forestry, and fishing jobs

    E. no change in the percentage of farming, forestry, and fishing jobs

22. Based on these graphics, what trend in employment percentages would you expect to see in the year 2040?

    F. no industry; growth of farming, fishing, and forestry; reduction in service

    G. mostly industry; growth of farming, fishing, and forestry; reduction in service

    H. growth of farming, fishing, and forestry; reduction in service; almost no industry

    J. mostly service; reduction in industry; almost no farming, fishing, and forestry

    K. mostly industry; reduction in service; almost no farming, fishing, and forestry

Florida Seaside Flycatcher and Brown-bellied Kestrel Nests

Seaside Flycatcher Nests		Population of Brown-bellied Kestrels	
Year	Nests	Year	Number of Kestrels
1	683	1	153
2	756	2	346
3	235	3	278
4	782	4	125
5	1,154	5	261
6	835	6	375
7	323	7	272
8	812	8	175
9	863	9	264
10	878	10	305
11	425	11	312
12	856	12	148
13	1,325	13	202
14	921	14	372
15	612	15	301

■ Low   □ High

23. You are an environmental manager studying the seaside flycatcher. What trend do you see in the data about the seaside flycatcher nests?

   A. It levels off from year 9 to year 12.

   B. It hits a low almost every four years.

   C. It hits a high about every five years.

   D. It grew most quickly from year 5 to year 8.

   E. It remained steady from year 1 to year 4 and then rose.

24. The seaside flycatcher's primary predator is the brown-bellied kestrel. What general trend can you see in the relationship between the two?

   F. The kestrel population matches the number of flycatcher nests.

   G. The number of flycatcher nests drops the year after a peak in the number of kestrels.

   H. The kestrel population grows the year after there is a drop in the number of flycatcher nests.

   J. The number of flycatcher nests drops the year after a drop in the number of kestrels.

   K. The number of flycatcher nests goes up the year after an increase in the number of kestrels.

Answers are on page 254.

Lesson 10 ■ ■ ■
Summarize Information in Complicated Graphics

Skill: Summarize information from one or more detailed graphics

Sometimes, rather than simply locating a piece of information, you may be asked to look at the information in one or more graphics or texts and make a decision. In order to do this, you need to be able to read the graphic, understand what information is displayed, and provide a summary of that information. A summary is typically presented in short written form or through a presentation. A summary is the retelling of the main ideas of the information. Summarizing information presented in graphics or text is an important workplace skill that aids in the decision-making process.

Skill Example

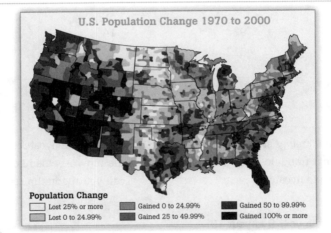

U.S. Population Change 1970 to 2000

Population Change
- Lost 25% or more
- Lost 0 to 24.99%
- Gained 0 to 24.99%
- Gained 25 to 49.99%
- Gained 50 to 99.99%
- Gained 100% or more

Summarize information from complicated graphics.

It is important for service industry businesses to understand population trends. Suppose a restaurant chain is expanding. Based on a summary of the map, the restaurant chain would benefit most by expanding in the west, southwest, or east coast.

Skill Practice

Use the ad rates tables to the left to answer the following questions.

Package 1
Classified Open Rates
City News, Tribune, & Weekend Planner

Lines	1 Day	3 Days	5 Days	7 Days
3	20.01	24.51	26.88	30.42
4	26.68	32.68	35.84	40.56
5	33.35	40.85	44.80	50.70

Total Daily Circulation: 103,418

Package 2
Classified Open Rates
Gazette Ad Sheet, Marketplace, & Extra!

Lines	1 Day	3 Days	5 Days	7 Days
3	23.13	27.63	30.00	33.54
4	30.84	36.84	40.00	44.72
5	38.550	46.05	50.00	55.90

Total Daily Circulation: 133,371

1. You are an ad salesperson for a local newspaper. A customer calls in with a 4-line ad and a $42 budget. She wants to run her ad for as long as possible and in as many places as possible. What package do you suggest?

   A. package 1, 5 days

   B. package 2, 5 days

   C. package 1, 7 days

   D. package 2, 7 days

   E. package 1, 3 days

2. Another customer asks if she can pay $40 for a 1-day ad of 5 lines. Which package should she pick and why?

   F. package 1, because it costs less

   G. package 2, because it costs less

   H. package 1, because it will have greater circulation

   J. package 2, because it will have greater circulation

   K. package 1, because it costs more

Try It Out! ▪ ▪ ▪

As a systems administrator, you are reviewing trends in computer shipments. Which statement best summarizes the information in the graphic?

A. Brand B is more popular than brand A.

B. Brand B shipments have grown at a much faster pace than brand A shipments.

C. Brand B shipments have consistently slowed over the last nine fiscal quarters.

D. Brand A shipments have consistently slowed over the last nine fiscal quarters.

E. More people buy brand A, but they pick them up at the store rather than shipping them.

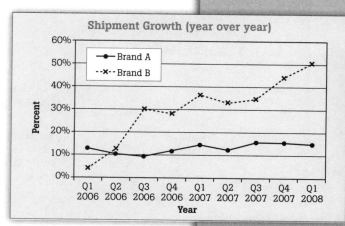

Step 1 Understand the Problem ▪ ▪ ▪

Complete the *Plan for Successful Solving.*

Plan for Successful Solving				
What am I asked to do?	**What are the facts?**	**How do I find the answers?**	**Is there any unnecessary information?**	**What prior knowledge will help me?**
Summarize the information in the graphic.	The line graph shows shipment growth for brands A and B.	Identify, interpret, and summarize the data trends.	No. All of the information is relevant for finding the answer.	The slope of a line on a line graph shows the trend.

Step 2 Find and Check Your Answer ▪ ▪ ▪

▪ Confirm your understanding of the question and revise your plan as needed.

▪ Based on your plan, determine your solution approach: *I first need to determine what the data on the line graph shows. The title indicates that the data shows how much computer shipments have grown. Since all of the percentages are positive, both brands have had shipment growth. The line for brand B shows that the percentage of increase in shipping is much faster than for brand A. I will review each answer to see which one best matches this summary.*

▪ Check your answer. Review all answers to determine if the answer you have selected is the best possible answer.

▪ **Select the correct answer:** B. Brand B shipments have grown at a much faster pace than brand A shipments
The brand B line has risen steadily and is higher than the brand A line.

Problem Solving Tip

Sometimes it may seem that more than one answer might be correct. In order to choose the correct answer in such situations, it is important to review all of the answer options to determine which answer is the best option.

Remember!

When summarizing information from a graphic, remember that a summary should provide a factual overview of what the data shows. In the *Try It Out!* example, answers A, B, and E may all be correct. However, only answer option B is correct based solely on what is shown in the graph. Although option A could be correct, we do not know the actual sales numbers, just the growth rates. Brand B has been shipping at faster rates of growth than brand A, but brand A could still have greater overall sales. While answer option E could possibly be correct, this cannot be determined based solely on the data shown in the graph.

On Your Own ▪ ▪ ▪

Vacation Time Accruals

Union	Vacation Accrual at Completion of 6 Months	7th thru 60th Vacation Service Month	Maximum Accrual for 7th thru 60th Month	61st thru 120th Vacation Service Month	Maximum Accrual for 61st thru 120th Month	121st + Vacation Service Month	Maximum Accrual for 121st Month
APA	48 hours	8 hours per month	120 hours	12 hours per month	180 hours	16 hours per month	240 hours
APSA	48 hours	8 hours per month	120 hours	12 hours per month	180 hours	16 hours per month	240 hours
AP Conf	48 hours	8 hours per month	120 hours	12 hours per month	180 hours	16 hours per month	240 hours
CTU	48 hours	8 hours per month	120 hours	12 hours per month	180 hours	16 hours per month	225 hours
CTU Conf	48 hours	8 hours per month	120 hours	12 hours per month	180 hours	16 hours per month	225 hours
1585	48 hours	8 hours per month	128 hours	12 hours per month	192 hours	16 hours per month	240 hours
999	48 hours	8 hours per month	120 hours	12 hours per month	180 hours	16 hours per month	240 hours
547	48 hours	8 hours per month	120 hours	12 hours per month	180 hours	16 hours per month	240 hours
274	48 hours	8 hours per month	120 hours	12 hours per month	180 hours	16 hours per month	225 hours
Nurses	48 hours	8 hours per month	128 hours	12 hours per month	192 hours	16 hours per month	240 hours
FOP	48 hours	8 hours per month	120 hours	12 hours per month	180 hours	16 hours per month	240 hours
Ext Prog	48 hours	8 hours per month	120 hours	12 hours per month	180 hours	16 hours per month	225 hours
Res Adv	48 hours	8 hours per month	120 hours	12 hours per month	180 hours	16 hours per month	240 hours

1. You are a human resources specialist. You are reading a vacation accrual schedule for unions. Which unions have the best vacation plans in terms of maximum accrual of hours through both months 60 and 120?

    A. Union 1585 and the APA

    B. Union 547 and Union 999

    C. Union 547 and the CTU

    D. Nurses' Union and the FOP

    E. Union 1585 and the Nurses' Union

2. For most unions, what is the maximum accrual for the seventh through sixtieth months of service?

    F. 8 hours

    G. 48 hours

    H. 120 hours

    J. 128 hours

    K. 180 hours

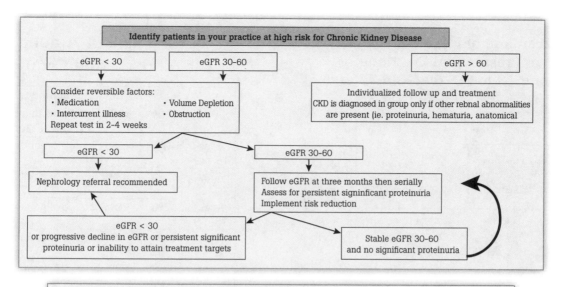

Stages of Kidney Disease

Stage	Description	Glomerular Filtration Rate (GFR)
1	Kidney damage (e.g., protein in the urine) with normal GFR	90 or above
2	Kidney damage with mild decrease in GFR	60 to 89
3	Moderate decrease in GFR	30 to 59
4	Severe reduction in GFR	15 to 29
5	Kidney failure	Less than 15

3. You are a clinical nurse specialist monitoring patients at risk for chronic kidney disease. How would you summarize the overall diagnosis and treatment of a woman with a GFR between 30 and 59?

A. She possibly has Stage 3; tests should be repeated in 3 months once reversible factors are considered.

B. She possibly has Stage 1; tests should be repeated in 2–4 weeks once reversible factors are considered.

C. She possibly has Stage 5; tests should be repeated in 3 months once reversible factors are considered.

D. She possibly has Stage 3; tests should be repeated in 2–4 weeks once reversible factors are considered.

E. She possibly has Stage 2; tests should be repeated in 2–4 weeks once reversible factors are considered.

4. Based on the charts, how would you summarize the relationship between chronic kidney disease and a patient's GFR number?

F. As chronic kidney disease progresses, the GFR number changes from less than 60, to greater than 30, to 30–60.

G. As chronic kidney disease progresses, a patient's GFR number decreases.

H. As chronic kidney disease progresses, the GFR number changes from less than 15, to 30–60, to greater than 60.

J. As chronic kidney disease progresses, a patient's GFR number increases.

K. As chronic kidney disease progresses, a patient's GFR number does not change.

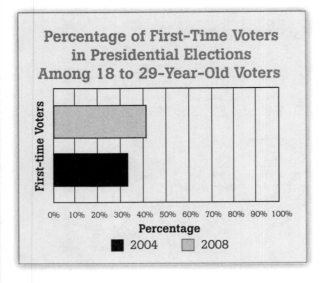

Percentage of First-Time Voters in Presidential Elections Among 18 to 29-Year-Old Voters

First-time Voters

Percentage

0% 10% 20% 30% 40% 50% 60% 70% 80% 90% 100%

■ 2004　■ 2008

Voter Turnout Among Citizens, by Age Group

	Presidential Elections		
	2004	**2008**	**% Point Increase (2004 to 2008)**
Ages 18–29	40%	49%	9% points
Ages 30–44	59%	62%	4% points
Ages 45–59	67%	70%	3% points
Ages 60–74	72%	73%	1% points
Ages 75+	67%	69%	2% points

5. You are a research assistant working for a voter registration campaign in your home state. How would you summarize the information presented in the above graphics on your state's statistics?

    A. Neither young voter turnout nor the percentage of first-time voters among 18- to 29-year-old voters rose from 2004 to 2008.

    B. Both young voter turnout and the percentage of first-time voters among 18- to 29-year-old voters rose from 2004 to 2008.

    C. Both young voter turnout and the percentage of first-time voters among 18- to 29-year-old voters decreased from 2004 to 2008.

    D. Both young voter turnout and the percentage of first-time voters among 18- to 29-year-old voters remained the same from 2004 to 2008.

    E. Young voter turnout rose and the percentage of first-time voters among 18- to 29-year-old voters decreased from 2004 to 2008.

6. As part of your work, you are required to formulate recommendations for the campaign. Based on both graphs, you recommend that resources should be dedicated to

    F. reaching out to voters ages 18–29.

    G. reaching out to voters ages 30–44.

    H. reaching out to voters ages 45–59.

    J. reaching out to voters ages 60–74.

    K. reaching out to voters ages 75+.

Unemployment Claims

	Initial Claims January	Initial Claims February	Initial Claims March	Initial Claims April	Initial Claims May	Initial Claims June
Total	11,703	12,586	15,491	10,381	6,927	9,144
Total Claims by Gender						
Male	7,099	6,607	9,163	4,974	3,926	4,292
Female	4,604	5,979	6,328	5,407	3,001	4,852
Age						
Under 22	304	346	565	286	245	281
22–24	561	655	920	556	472	480
25–34	2,278	2,276	3,290	1,811	1,431	1,897
35–44	2,691	2,664	3,507	2,184	1,545	2,088
45–54	3,147	3,493	3,973	2,910	1,713	2,346
55–59	1,243	1,404	1,477	1,086	695	943
60–64	852	961	1,085	810	466	600
65 or over	626	787	676	739	360	509
Education						
Less than 9th Grade	514	417	512	339	282	256
9th to 12th, no diploma	1,013	1,199	1,419	995	676	746
High School Graduate	4,403	5,273	5,964	4,265	2,703	3,490
Some College	1,686	2,150	2,890	1,832	1,297	1,605
Bachelor's Degree	797	848	1,330	805	621	994
Beyond Bachelor's	824	911	1,439	766	644	1,081
Information Not Available	2,466	1,788	1,937	1,380	704	972

7. As an employment adjudicator in the state employment department, part of your job is to determine who is eligible for unemployment insurance benefits. You are examining recent unemployment claims data. How can you summarize the data on education?

   A. The largest group of people who were laid off have no more than a high school education.

   B. Most people who were laid off do not have a high school diploma.

   C. The smallest number of people who were laid off have more than a bachelor's degree.

   D. People with bachelor's degrees were laid off more often than those with just high school diplomas.

   E. Fewer people who have some college education were laid off than those who have a degree higher than a bachelor's degree.

8. What can you conclude based on the age data?

   F. Most people who were laid off were between 45 and 54 years of age.

   G. Most people who were laid off were between 25 to 34 years of age.

   H. Fewer people between 22 and 24 years of age were laid of than those under 22.

   J. Most people who were laid off were 65 or older.

   K. More people between ages 55 to 59 were laid off than those aged 35 to 44.

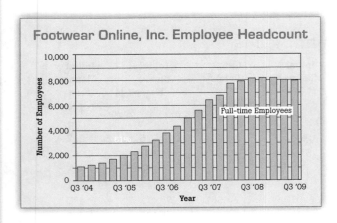

Footwear Online, Inc. Employee Headcount

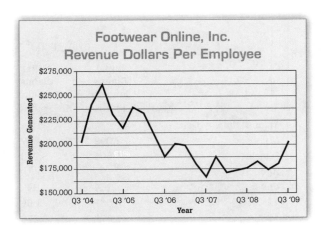

Footwear Online, Inc. Revenue Dollars Per Employee

9. You are an accounting manager working for Footwear Online, Inc. When you are asked to prepare information on employee productivity, you use the graphs above to report that

A. as hiring declined and revenue continued to grow, the amount of revenue Footwear Online, Inc. made per employee decreased.

B. as hiring leveled off and revenue continued to grow, the amount of revenue Footwear Online, Inc. made per employee decreased.

C. as hiring leveled off and revenue continued to grow, the amount of revenue Footwear Online, Inc. made per employee increased.

D. as hiring leveled off and revenue continued to decrease, the amount of revenue Footwear Online, Inc. made per employee increased.

E. as hiring decreased and revenue continued to decline, the amount of revenue Footwear Online, Inc. made per employee decreased.

10. Based on the graphs, how would you describe the productivity of the employees of Footwear Online, Inc.?

F. The employees are the least productive they have been in three years, and as of the most recent quarter they have generated just over $200,000 per employee.

G. The employees are the least productive they have been in three years, and as of the most recent quarter they have generated just over $250,000 per employee.

H. The employees are the most productive they have been in three years, and as of the most recent quarter they have generated just over $150,000 per employee.

J. The employees are the most productive they have been in three years, and as of the most recent quarter they have generated just over $200,000 per employee.

K. The employees are the least productive they have been in three years, and as of the most recent quarter they have generated just over $100,000 per employee.

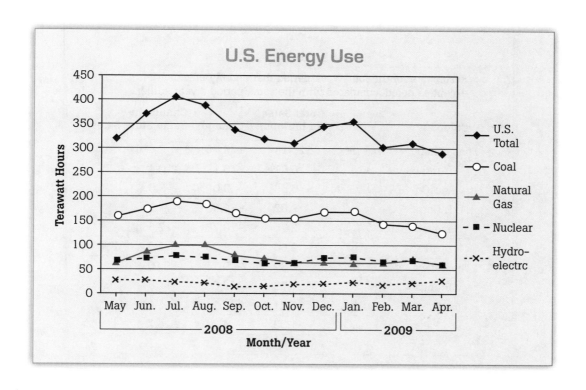

U.S. Energy Use

11. As an environmental engineering technician, you monitor energy use. You are looking at energy use patterns. What can you determine based on the graph?

    A.   U.S. total energy usage is going up.

    B.   U.S. total energy usage fluctuates dramatically.

    C.   Hydroelectric is the most important energy resource.

    D.   Nuclear energy is an important resource for the future.

    E.   Use of natural gas and coal had the greatest variation during the year.

12. How does U.S. dependency on coal as a source of energy compare to other sources?

    F.   There is more dependency on coal than on any other source of energy.

    G.   There is less dependency on coal than on hydroelectric power.

    H.   There is no more dependency on coal than on nuclear power.

    J.   There is less dependency on coal than on natural gas.

    K.   The amount of dependency on coal is about the same as it is for natural gas.

Retail Sales in December

Results are for the four-week period that ended December 24, except as noted, compared with the same period a year earlier.

Company		Total Sales (in billions)	Change	Change in Same Store Sales	
Shop-Smart	4 weeks to Jan. 2	$26.15	+ 5.7%	+ 3.4%	
Arrow		6.61	– 6.1	–10.4	
PriceCo	4 weeks to Jan. 2	6.55	– 3.0	– 5.0	
H.P. Garp		2.82	–11.5	–11.9	
Smoltz's		2.75	–13.7	–17.5	
RFX		2.60	– 9.0	–12.0	
The Valley		2.39	– 9.7	–10.0	
Legacy Brands		1.76	–12.0	–12.0	
Eastwater		1.71	–12.1	–15.9	
Paks		1.33	– 4.2	– 5.2	

13. You are a sales supervisor for a major retailer. You are looking at retail trends for the four-week period before December 24, as compared with the same period during the previous year. How would you summarize the data?

    A. Paks's sales changed the least.

    B. All stores experienced lower sales.

    C. Only Shop-Smart's sales increased from last year.

    D. Smoltz's and Legacy Brands saw the greatest difference in sales.

    E. Eastwater's and H.P. Garp's sales went down the most.

14. You decide to investigate the holiday sales practices of the stores whose sales were least negatively impacted during the holiday season. Which stores do you research?

    F. PriceCo, Arrow, and Paks

    G. Shop-Smart, PriceCo, and Paks

    H. Shop-Smart, Paks, and The Valley

    J. The Valley, RFX, and Arrow

    K. Shop-Smart, PriceCo, and Smoltz's

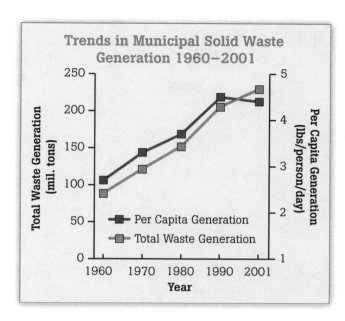

Trends in Municipal Solid Waste Generation 1960–2001

Waste Recycling Rates 1960–2001

15. As an environmental engineering assistant, you are helping to prepare information for a group of recycling advocates working on an effort to address trends in municipal solid waste. Based on the graphs above you report that

- **A.** since 1960, total waste generation has nearly tripled in the United States and recycling rates have dramatically increased as well.

- **B.** since 1960, total waste generation has dramatically declined in the United States and recycling rates have decreased as well.

- **C.** since 1960, total waste generation has nearly tripled in the United States but recycling rates have steadily decreased.

- **D.** since 1960, total waste generation has remained the same in the United States and recycling rates have dramatically increased.

- **E.** since 1960, total waste generation has nearly tripled in the United States but recycling rates have remained the same.

16. In your work gathering information for the group of recycling advocates, you report that overall total waste generation

- **F.** decreased at the same time per capita waste generation increased; a higher percentage of waste is recycled and more waste is sent to landfills each year.

- **G.** decreased at the same time per capita waste generation decreased; a higher percentage of waste is recycled and more waste is sent to landfills each year.

- **H.** increased at the same time per capita waste generation increased; a lower percentage of waste is recycled and more waste is sent to landfills each year.

- **J.** increased at the same time per capita waste generation increased; a higher percentage of waste is recycled and more waste is sent to landfills each year.

- **K.** decreased at the same time per capita waste generation increased; a higher percentage of waste is recycled but less waste is sent to landfills each year.

Lipid Panel Results

Tests	Result	Reference interval
Lipid Panel		
Cholesterol, Total	126 mg/dL	100–199
Triglycerides	155 mg/dL	0–149
HDL cholesterol	28 mg/dL	40–159
VLDL Cholesterol Cal	31 mg/dL	5–40
LDL Cholesterol Calc	67 mg/dL	0–99

National Cholesterol Education Program (NCEP)

Total cholesterol	
Desirable	· Less than 200 milligrams per deciliter (mg/dL)
Borderline high	· 200–239 mg/dL
High	· 240 mg/dL or higher
HDL cholesterol	
High (desirable)	· More than 60 mg/dL
Acceptable	· 40–60 mg/dL
Low (undesirable)	· Less than 40 mg/dL
LDL cholesterol	
Optimal:	· Less than 100 mg/dL
Near optimal:	· 100–129 mg/dL
Borderline high:	· 130–159 mg/dL
High:	· 160–189 mg/dL
Very high:	· 190 mg/dL or higher
VLDL cholesterol	
Optimal:	· 30 mg/dL or less
Triglycerides	
Normal:	· Less than 150 mg/dL
Borderline high:	· 150–199 mg/dL
High:	· 200–499 mg/dL
Very high:	· 500 mg/dL or higher

17. You are a medical laboratory technician. You are reading a patient's lipid test results. Which two lipid levels should the patient concentrate on changing?

A. HDL and LDL

B. LDL and triglycerides

C. triglycerides and HDL

D. LDL and total cholesterol

E. Triglycerides and total cholesterol

18. Which levels in this patient's test results are within desirable parameters as defined by National Cholesterol Education Program (NCEP)?

F. HDL and LDL

G. LDL and triglycerides

H. triglycerides and HDL

J. LDL and total cholesterol

K. HDL and total cholesterol

Ronaghan's Gym

* Extra cost

Membership	Details	Price	Amenities
1 Year Term Commitment	enrollment fee $69 for all new members	$44 per month	· Full use of all 29 affiliated gyms throughout the state · Strength training equipment and cardiovascular machines
No Commitment	enrollment fee $99 for all new members	$49 per month	· Fitness Classes · Free Weights · Steam & Sauna · Child Care* · Tanning* · Pro Shop*
Paid in Full Membership	No enrollment fee	$499 per year	· Juice Bar*

Northton Sports Center

* Extra cost

Membership	Details	Price	Amenities
1 Year Term Commitment	No enrollment fee	$59 per month	· Includes use of primary gym center. · Limited use of other affiliated gyms during off-peak hours. Use of other gyms during peak hours requires additional fee.
No Commitment	$20 enrollment fee	$69 per month	· Strength training equipment and cardiovascular machines · Pool · Group exercise classes · Free Weights · Racquet Sports · Child Care* · Tanning* · Pro Shop* · Cafe*

* Extra cost

19. You are a marketing analyst hired by Ronaghan's Gym to see how their membership packages compare to their competitor's membership packages. How would you summarize the amenities of the two gyms based on the tables above?

    A. Ronaghan's Gym has better amenities, such as free weights and fitness classes, than Northton Sports Center.

    B. Ronaghan's Gym has free amenities, including tanning and child care, that Northton Sports Center charges for.

    C. Northton Sports Center has better options for use of other gyms, while Ronaghan's Gym has more amenities such as a pool and racquet sports.

    D. Ronaghan's Gym has more amenities that are available at an extra cost than Northton Sports Center.

    E. Ronaghan's Gym has better options for use of other gyms, while Northton Sports Center has more amenities such as a pool and racquet sports.

20. Which of the following best summarizes the difference in price for a 1-year membership between the two gyms?

    F. Even though the enrollment fee is less at Northton Sports Center, the membership packages cost more than Ronaghan's Gym.

    G. The enrollment fees are less at Northton Sports Center, and the membership packages cost less than Ronaghan's Gym.

    H. Because the enrollment fees vary for both gyms, certain memberships are less at each gym.

    J. Even though the enrollment fee is less at Ronaghan's Gym, the membership packages cost more than Northton Sports Center.

    K. The enrollment fees are more at Ronaghan's Gym, and the membership packages cost more than Northton Sports Center.

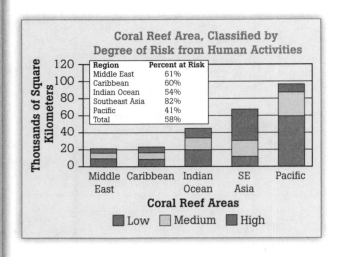

Coral Reef Area, Classified by Degree of Risk from Human Activities

Region	Percent at Risk
Middle East	61%
Caribbean	60%
Indian Ocean	54%
Southeast Asia	82%
Pacific	41%
Total	58%

Coral Reef Areas: Middle East, Caribbean, Indian Ocean, SE Asia, Pacific

■ Low ▢ Medium ■ High

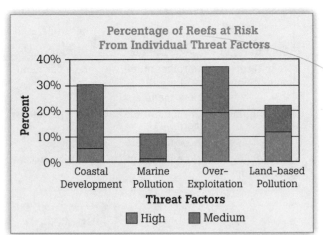

Percentage of Reefs at Risk From Individual Threat Factors

Threat Factors: Coastal Development, Marine Pollution, Over-Exploitation, Land-based Pollution

■ High ■ Medium

21. As an educational outreach coordinator at an aquarium, you are in charge of presenting information about the environment to the community. Based on the graphs, how would you describe the threat to coral reefs?

A. More than half of world reefs are at risk from human activity, and marine pollution and coastal development pose the greatest potential threat to reefs.

B. Less than half of world reefs are at risk from human activity, and marine pollution and land-based pollution pose the greatest potential threat to reefs.

C. More than half of world reefs are at risk from human activity, and overexploitation and coastal development pose the greatest potential threat to reefs.

D. Less than half of world reefs are at risk from human activity, and overexploitation and land-based pollution pose the greatest potential threat to reefs.

E. Less than half of world reefs are at risk from human activity, and overexploitation and coastal development pose the greatest potential threat to reefs.

22. Based on the information in both graphs, how would you summarize what is most urgent in terms of protecting the coral reefs?

F. The reefs of Southeast Asia have the least percent at risk; efforts to enforce expansion of coastal development and increase awareness about pollution and overexploitation are needed.

G. The reefs of Southeast Asia have the greatest percent at risk; efforts to encourage coastal development and increase awareness about pollution and overexploitation are needed.

H. The reefs of Southeast Asia have the least percent at risk; efforts to encourage coastal development and decrease awareness about pollution and overexploitation are needed.

J. The reefs of Southeast Asia have the greatest percent at risk; efforts to enforce restriction of coastal development and increase awareness about pollution and overexploitation are needed.

K. The reefs of Southeast Asia have the greatest percent at risk; efforts to encourage coastal development and decrease awareness about pollution and overexploitation are needed.

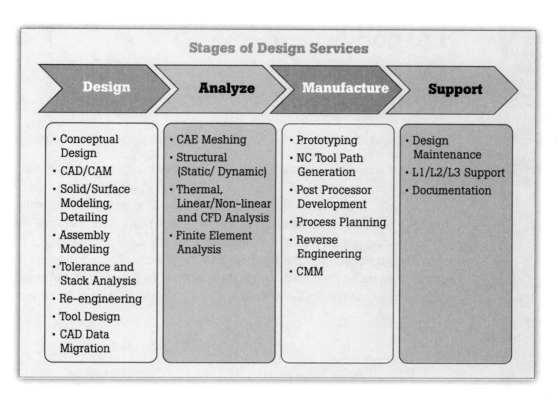

Stages of Design Services

Design	Analyze	Manufacture	Support
• Conceptual Design • CAD/CAM • Solid/Surface Modeling, Detailing • Assembly Modeling • Tolerance and Stack Analysis • Re-engineering • Tool Design • CAD Data Migration	• CAE Meshing • Structural (Static/ Dynamic) • Thermal, Linear/Non-linear and CFD Analysis • Finite Element Analysis	• Prototyping • NC Tool Path Generation • Post Processor Development • Process Planning • Reverse Engineering • CMM	• Design Maintenance • L1/L2/L3 Support • Documentation

23. You are a project coordinator at a mechanical engineering firm. Your company gives you this flowchart and requests that you summarize the stages of design services. What are these stages?

    A. design, support, document, prototype

    B. design, analyze, manufacture, support

    C. design, prototype, documentation, reverse engineering

    D. conceptual design, CAD/CAM, CAE meshing, prototyping

    E. conceptual design, CAE meshing, prototyping, design maintenance

24. Which statement best summarizes the final phase of the process?

    F. The last phase deals with testing and verifying.

    G. The last phase deals with idea creation and prototypes.

    H. The last phase deals with research and testing.

    J. The last phase deals with support and reporting problems.

    K. The last phase deals with building and physical creation.

Answers are on page 254.

compare look for similarities
contrast look for differences

Lesson 11 ■ ■ ■
Compare Information in Complicated Graphics

Skill: Compare information and trends from one or more complicated graphics

As part of your job, you may be asked to compare information in graphics. You may have to compare individual data, or you may have to identify and compare trends. For example, when determining whether to provide a small business with a line of credit, a banker compares trends in similar businesses within the same industry. By comparing industry data, the banker can determine if the industry is doing well and, therefore, whether the business has the potential to be strong enough to honor the terms of the loan. The ability to compare information and trends among graphics is helpful for making more informed decisions in the workplace.

Remember!

When you compare two or more things, you look for the similarities among them. When you contrast two or more things, you look for differences among them. In the workplace, when you are asked to analyze trends or information within complicated graphics, you are typically expected both to compare and contrast the data. Although the terms *compare* and *contrast* technically mean opposite things, people often use the term *compare* to refer to looking both for similarities and differences.

Skill Example

Ticket Sales (in mil.)

	2003	2004	2005	2006
Broadway shows:				
New productions	36	39	39	39
Attendance (mil.)	11.4	11.6	11.5	12.0
Playing weeks	1,544	1,451	1,494	1,501
Gross ticket sales ($)	721	771	769	862
Broadway road tours:				
Attendance (mil.)	12.4	12.9	18.2	17.1
Playing weeks	877	1,060	1,389	1,377
Gross ticket sales ($)	642	714	934	915

Compare trends and information shown in complicated graphics.

You are a public relations specialist in the arts. You are looking at trends in Broadway theater data. Look at the attendance for Broadway shows. Then look at attendance for Broadway road tours. You can see that the attendance for Broadway road tours is higher across all years.

Skill Practice

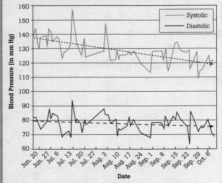

Use the graph to the left to answer the following questions.

1. As a medical laboratory technician, you are comparing changes in a patient's morning systolic and diastolic blood pressure readings to see how his new medication is working. Which comparison is true?

   A. The overall values have remained the same.

   B. Systolic values decreased more than diastolic values.

   C. Systolic values increased more than diastolic values.

   D. Diastolic values decreased more than systolic values.

   E. Diastolic values increased more than systolic values.

2. What statement can be made about both the systolic and diastolic blood pressure readings in early October compared with late June?

   F. Both values were lower in October than in June.

   G. Both values were higher in October than in June.

   H. Only the diastolic values were higher in October than in June.

   J. Only the systolic values were higher in October than in June.

   K. Only the systolic values were lower in October than in June.

71 - 59

Try It Out! ■ ■ ■

As an insurance sales agent, you are reviewing the table to the right to decide how much insurance senior citizens need. Compare the information for ages 65 to 69. What comparisons can you make based on the data listed in the table?

	Male			Female		
Exact age	Death probability*	Number of lives studied	Life expectancy (add'l years expected to live)	Death probability*	Number of lives studied	Life expectancy (add'l years expected to live)
65	0.017609	79,061	16.73	0.011366	87,051	19.49
66	0.019066	77,669	16.02	0.012397	86,062	18.70
67	0.020735	76,188	15.32	0.013571	84,995	17.93
68	0.022655	74,608	14.63	0.014910	83,842	17.17
69	0.024826	72,918	13.96	0.016419	82,592	16.42
70	0.027295	71,108	13.30	0.018160	81,235	15.69
71	0.030012	69,167	12.66	0.020086	79,760	14.97
72	0.032897	67,091	12.04	0.022104	78,158	14.27

Probability of dying within one year

A. Men have a longer life expectancy than women. No

B. Women have a longer life expectancy than men. yes

C. The number of lives studied goes up every year for both sexes. no

D. Between ages 65 and 67, women have a much higher death probability than men. no

E. The probability of dying within one year is lower for men than for women. No

Step 1 Understand the Problem ■ ■ ■

Complete the *Plan for Successful Solving*.

Plan for Successful Solving

What am I asked to do?	What are the facts?	How do I find the answer?	Is there any unnecessary information?	What prior knowledge will help me?
Compare the values in the table for people aged 65 to 69.	The table gives the death probability, number of lives, and life expectancy for people aged 65 to 72.	Look for data within the table that is related and determine what comparisons can be made.	I do not need the data for ages 70 to 72.	I know that reading the footnotes provides clarification or additional information about the data.

Step 2 Find and Check Your Answer ■ ■ ■

- Confirm your understanding of the question and revise your plan as needed.

- Based on your plan, determine your solution approach: *Because each answer choice refers to different data, I have to evaluate each answer by itself. The "Life expectancy" column shows that life expectancy for men is lower than it is for women. So A is false and B is true. The number of lives studied drops every year, so C is not correct. Option D is false because the death probability is higher for men than women between ages 65 and 67. Finally, the probability of dying is higher for men than for women. Therefore, E is not correct.*

- Check your answer. Review all answers to determine if the answer you have selected is the best possible answer.

- **Select the correct answer:** B. Women have a longer life expectancy than men. The table shows women's life expectancy is consistently higher for ages 65 to 69.

On Your Own ■ ■ ■

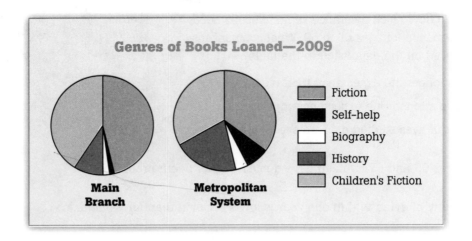

Genres of Books Loaned—2009

Main Branch Metropolitan System

- ☐ Fiction
- ■ Self-help
- ☐ Biography
- ☐ History
- ☐ Children's Fiction

1. As a librarian, you sometimes are asked to compare circulation trends among library branches. You are analyzing the kinds of books that the main branch loans out as compared to the metropolitan system as a whole. Which comparison statement is true of history books?

 A. History is less popular system wide than at the branch.

 B. History is more popular at the branch than system wide.

 C. History is nearly equal in popularity to fiction at the branch and system wide.

 D. History is the most popular kind of book at both the branch and system wide.

 E. History is more popular than self-help and biography at both the branch and system wide.

2. Which comparison is true of both the main branch and the metropolitan system?

 F. Children's books are more popular than fiction at both.

 G. Children's books and fiction are nearly equal in popularity.

 H. Self-help and biography are the least popular genres at both.

 J. Fiction books are as popular at the branch as they are in the larger system.

 K. History books are as popular at the branch as in the larger system.

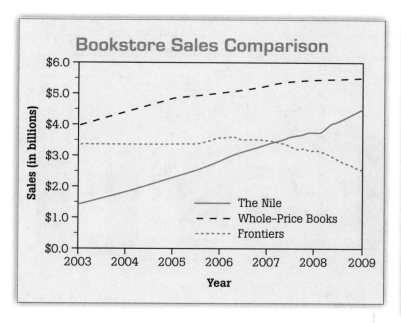

Bookstore Sales Comparison

Sales (in billions)

$6.0, $5.0, $4.0, $3.0, $2.0, $1.0, $0.0

2003 2004 2005 2006 2007 2008 2009

Year

— The Nile
– – Whole–Price Books
····· Frontiers

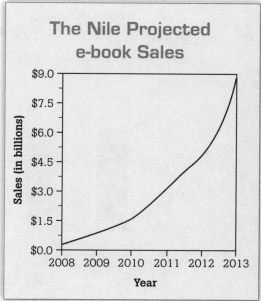

The Nile Projected e-book Sales

Sales (in billions)

$9.0, $7.5, $6.0, $4.5, $3.0, $1.5, $0.0

2008 2009 2010 2011 2012 2013

Year

3. You are a sales manager for Whole-Price Books. You compare your chain's sale to two other chains, Frontiers (a traditional bookstore similar to your own) and The Nile (an online bookstore that began selling e-books in 2006). Based on the two graphs, what comparison can you predict between Whole-Price Books and The Nile?

    A. If e-books continue with their projected sales, Whole-Price Books will continue to sell more than the Nile.

    B. If e-books continue with their projected sales, Whole-Price Books and The Nile will have equal sales.

    C. If e-books continue with their projected sales, The Nile's sales will decline and Whole-Price Books' sales will increase.

    D. If e-books continue with their projected sales, The Nile will sell more than Whole-Price Books by 2010.

    E. If e-books continue with their projected sales, The Nile's and Whole-Price Books' sales will both decrease.

4. Which do you think will be true for 2010 and what kind of recommendation would you make to your company about development of titles available in e-book format?

    F. The Nile will continue to increase its sales; you recommend your company continue to not sell e-books on the store Web site.

    G. Although the Nile's sales will likely decrease, you recommend that your company begin to sell e-books on the store Web site.

    H. Frontiers will rise to take the lead in sales; you recommend that your company continue to not sell e-books on the store Web site.

    J. The Nile will continue to increase its sales; you recommend your company begin to sell e-books on the store Web site.

    K. Whole-Price Books will remain the leader in sales; you recommend your company continue to not sell e-books on the store Web site.

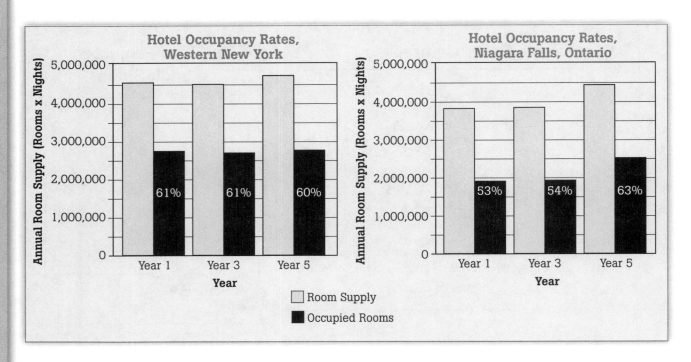

5. You are a hotel sales manager comparing room availability in Western New York to Niagara Falls, Ontario. Which of the following correctly compares the room supply between the two?

A. Western New York's room supply consistently rises; Niagara Falls, Ontario's room supply consistently lowers.

B. Western New York consistently has a lower room supply than Niagara Falls, Ontario.

C. Western New York's and Niagara Falls, Ontario's room supply both consistently lower.

D. Western New York consistently has a higher room supply than Niagara Falls, Ontario.

E. Western New York's and Niagara Falls, Ontario's room supply both consistently rise.

6. Which of the following is true about the percentage of occupied rooms?

F. The percentage of occupied rooms has increased every year in Niagara Falls, Ontario and stayed the same or decreased in western New York, and Niagara Falls, Ontario consistently has a higher percentage of occupied rooms.

G. The percentage of occupied rooms has increased ever year in Niagara Falls, Ontario and in western New York.

H. The percentage of occupied rooms has increased every year in Niagara Falls, Ontario and stayed the same or decreased in western New York, but western New York consistently has a higher percentage of occupied rooms.

J. The percentage of occupied rooms has decreased every year in Niagara Falls, Ontario and stayed the same or decreased in western New York, and western New York consistently has a lower percentage of occupied rooms.

K. The percentage of occupied rooms has decreased every year in Niagara Falls, Ontario and increased in western New York, and western New York consistently has a higher percentage of occupied rooms.

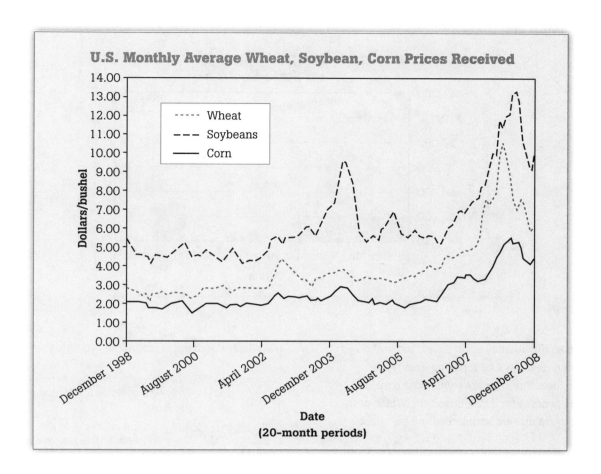

U.S. Monthly Average Wheat, Soybean, Corn Prices Received

Dollars/bushel

- - - - - Wheat
- - - Soybeans
—— Corn

Date
(20-month periods)

7. As a field operations farm manager, you are tracking trends in agricultural product prices over the time period shown on the graph. Compare the prices. Which trend was true for all three?

    A.   Prices went up in 2004.

    B.   Prices went up in 2003.

    C.   Prices went down in 2005.

    D.   Prices were at their highest in 2008.

    E.   Prices remained steady between 2003 and 2006.

8. During which period were the data trends most different for the three crops?

    F.   1999 to 2002

    G.   2002 to 2005

    H.   2005 to 2008

    J.   2005 to 2007

    K.   2007 to 2008

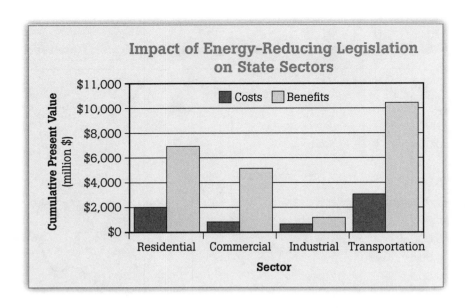

Impact of Energy-Reducing Legislation on State Sectors

9. You are an environmental engineer. You are reviewing new laws for reducing energy consumption. The new laws will incur costs and produce benefits for different sectors. Which of the following statements summarizes the bar graph?

  A. The new laws will be expensive.

  B. The costs far outweigh the benefits for some sectors.

  C. The benefits far outweigh the costs for nearly all sectors.

  D. The laws will have a total benefit of $10,000.

  E. The costs and benefits are almost the same for certain sectors.

10. Which statement is true about the new laws?

  F. They will cost the residential sector the most.

  G. They will benefit the residential sector the most.

  H. They will benefit the commercial sector the most.

  J. They will benefit the transportation sector the most.

  K. They will cost the industrial sector more than the transportation sector.

Diversity in the Workplace, by Gender

Job Category	Total Employees	Men	Women
Officials/Mgrs	16,822	71%	29%
Professionals	49,185	66%	34%
Technicians	8,483	88%	12%
Marketing	39,402	73%	27%
Office/Clerical	4,084	25%	75%
Craft Workers	1,022	64%	36%
Operatives	1,229	65%	35%
Totals*	**120,227**	**69%**	**31%**

* Totals for each gender indicate the percentage of the total number of employees for that group.

Diversity in the Workplace, by Race
(percentages by race based on total white and minority)

Job Category	Total	Minorities (percentage of total)	Percentage of Total (by minority group)			
			Black	Asian	Hispanic	Native American
Officials/Mgrs	16,822	18%	5%	9%	3%	1%
Professionals	49,185	26%	7%	14%	4%	1%
Technicians	8,483	22%	9%	6%	6%	1%
Marketing	39,402	27%	7%	15%	4%	1%
Office/Clerical	4,084	34%	22%	4%	7%	1%
Craft Workers	1,022	16%	8%	5%	2%	1%
Operatives	1,229	16%	6%	6%	3%	1%
Totals*	**120,227**	**25%**	**7%**	**13%**	**4%**	**1%**

*Totals for each individual group indicate the percentage of the total number of employees who have identified themselves as part of that group.

11. Part of your responsibility as a human resources specialist is to analyze diversity in the workplace. Which of the following pairs of job categories are the least diverse based on the above gender and race statistics?

   A.   Marketing and Office/Clerical

   B.   Professionals and Marketing

   C.   Officials/Managers and Technicians

   D.   Professionals and Office/Clerical

   E.   Technicians and Marketing

12. You have been asked to prepare a 5-year plan for bringing diversity percentages of minorities and women for all job categories to 20% or higher. For which job categories do you recommend the company focus on promoting diversity?

   F.   Officials/Managers, Technicians, Craft Workers, Operatives

   G.   Officials/Managers, Professionals, Technicians, Office/Clerical

   H.   Officials/Managers, Office/Clerical, Craft Workers, Operatives

   J.   Professionals, Technicians, Marketing, Craft Workers

   K.   Professionals, Technicians, Craft Workers, Operatives

Natural Gas Consumption by End Use (Million Cubic Feet)						
	2003	2004	2005	2006	2007	2008
Total Consumption	403,991	372,533	378,067	370,665	408,759	375,123
Pipeline & Distribution Use	1,988	1,755	1,810	1,499	1,737	1,862
Volumes Delivered to Consumers	402,003	370,778	376,257	369,116	407,022	373,261
Residential	125,879	112,780	118,617	103,882	115,199	113,198
Commercial	62,590	56,879	56,665	52,283	61,504	56,963
Industrial	44,128	43,546	47,774	43,316	46,334	46,811
Vehicle Fuel	154	173	772	715	754	762
Electric Power	169,252	157,400	152,429	168,970	183,231	155,527

13. You are a customer services representative for a natural gas company. The table shows natural gas use for 2003 through 2008. Based on the information shown in the table, what comparison can be made between residential and industrial gas use?

   A. Both fell consistently from 2003 to 2006.

   B. Both rose consistently from 2003 to 2006.

   C. Industrial varied less than residential from 2003 to 2006.

   D. Residential was lower in 2005 than industrial.

   E. Residential rose and fell more often than industrial from 2003 to 2006.

14. Which of the following timespans included the most drastic change in end use consumption?

   F. Industrial, 2003 to 2004

   G. Residential, 2004 to 2005

   H. Vehicle fuel, 2004 to 2005

   J. Commercial, 2006 to 2007

   K. Pipeline & Distribution Use, 2006 to 2007

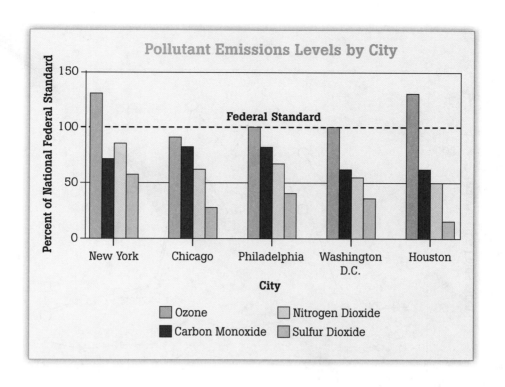

Pollutant Emissions Levels by City

15. You work for the Environmental Protection Agency as an environmental engineering technician. You are comparing pollutants. What can you determine by looking at the graph?

   A. All cities are above the federal standard for ozone.

   B. Philadelphia has the highest levels of nitrogen dioxide.

   C. New York City has the highest level of carbon monoxide.

   D. Houston needs to reduce its levels of sulfur dioxide.

   E. Between Chicago and New York, Chicago has fewer pollutants.

16. Which pollutant is highest in all cities?

   F. ozone

   G. nitrogen dioxide and sulfur dioxide

   H. sulfur dioxide

   J. nitrogen dioxide

   K. carbon monoxide

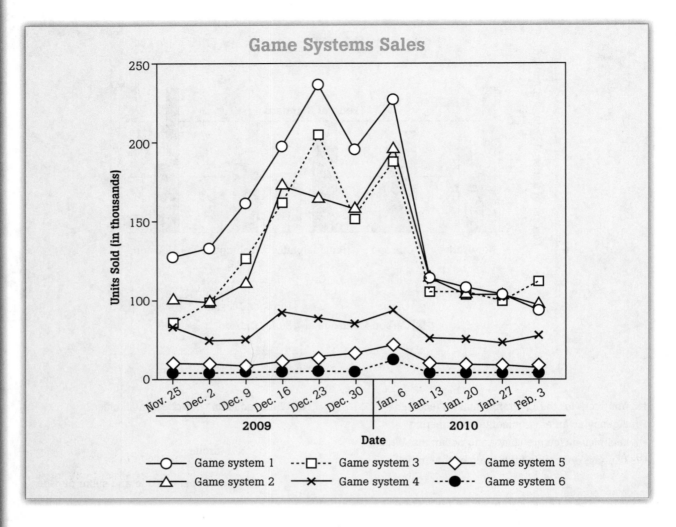

Game Systems Sales

Units Sold (in thousands)

Game system 1 ──○──
Game system 2 ──△──
Game system 3 ---□---
Game system 4 ──✕──
Game system 5 ──◇──
Game system 6 ---●---

17. You are a retail products research assistant for an electronics company. You are analyzing winter sales for six similar game systems. Based on the above graph, what comparisons can be made between sales of game system 2 and game system 3?

    A. Sales for game system 2 were higher overall.

    B. Game system 2 had greater sales throughout January.

    C. Game system 3 had greater sales from December 9 to 23.

    D. Game system 3 consistently had fewer sales.

    E. Sales for the two systems were drastically different throughout January.

18. Which statement is true for all products?

    F. January 6 was a peak sales date.

    G. Sales fell on December 23.

    H. Sales ended higher than they started.

    J. Sales declined sharply in late December.

    K. Sales leveled off in the middle of the period.

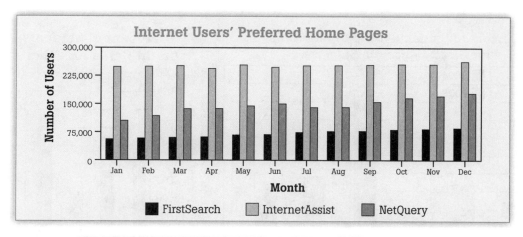

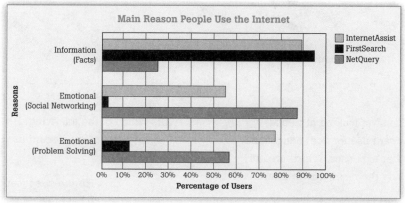

19. As a computer software marketing consultant, you are studying Internet behaviors and the three most popular Web sites people use as their home page. Based on the above graphs, which of the following comparisons is true?

A. While the number of users who prefer InternetAssist has increased, the number of users who prefer the other two Web sites has decreased.

B. FirstSearch is preferred for the widest range of uses; NetQuery is preferred for finding information.

C. InternetAssist is preferred for the widest range of uses; FirstSearch is preferred for finding information.

D. Although NetQuery is the most preferred home page for Internet users, the number of users who prefer FirstSearch has increased.

E. There are no comparisons that can be made based on the graphs.

20. Based on the data presented in the two graphs, what is one trend you predict will occur in the upcoming year?

F. There will be a decrease in the number of people who use NetQuery as their home page.

G. The number of users who use the Internet for social networking will continue to grow.

H. There will be a decrease in the number of people who use InternetAssist as their home page.

J. There will be a dramatic increase in the number of people who use InternetAssist as their home page.

K. People will stop using the Internet to find solutions to problems.

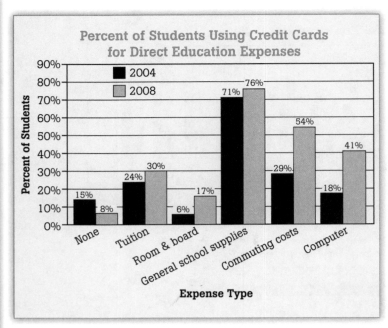

Percent of Students Using Credit Cards for Direct Education Expenses

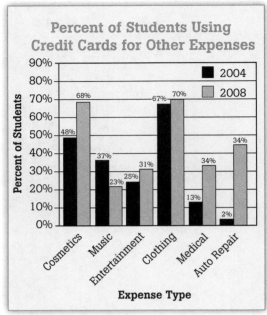

Percent of Students Using Credit Cards for Other Expenses

21. You are a credit analyst looking at trends in student credit card use for both educational expenses and other expenses. Which area of credit card use saw the most growth from 2004 to 2008?

    A.   medical

    B.   room and board

    C.   cosmetics

    D.   commuting costs

    E.   auto repair

22. Which of the following describes the overall trend in students' credit card use?

    F.   For direct education expenses, the percentage of students using credit cards increased; for other expenses, the percentage of students using credit cards decreased.

    G.   For both direct education expenses and other expenses, the percentage of students using credit cards has decreased in almost all categories.

    H.   For both direct education expenses and other expenses, the percentage of students using credit cards has decreased in half of the categories.

    J.   For direct education expenses, the percentage of students using credit cards decreased; for other expenses, the percentage of students using credit cards increased.

    K.   For both direct education expenses and other expenses, the percentage of students using credit cards has increased in most categories.

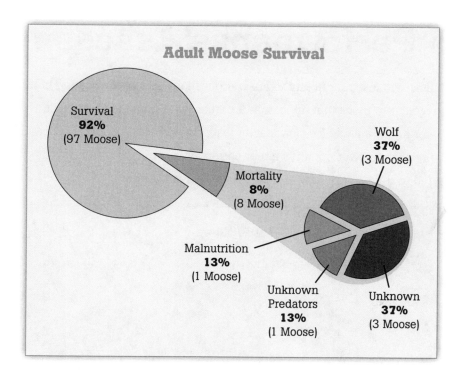

Adult Moose Survival

Survival
92%
(97 Moose)

Mortality
8%
(8 Moose)

Wolf
37%
(3 Moose)

Malnutrition
13%
(1 Moose)

Unknown
Predators
13%
(1 Moose)

Unknown
37%
(3 Moose)

23. As a environmental education specialist, you are studying the reasons for death of adult moose in Rocky Mountain National Park. Over the course of three years, you have tagged and tracked the survival of 105 moose in the park. What information does the circle graph show you?

    A. Most moose died of malnutrition.

    B. Most moose were killed by unknown causes.

    C. Malnutrition killed more moose than unknown predators.

    D. More moose were killed by wolves than by unknown predators.

    E. Equal numbers of moose died due to unknown causes and malnutrition.

24. What can you tell by looking at the two circle graphs?

    F. The moose population grew in 2009.

    G. The total number of moose studied is 92.

    H. The total number of moose studied is 97.

    J. In 2009, more moose died than survived.

    K. The total number of moose studied is 105.

Answers are on page 254.

−4

Level 5 Performance Assessment

The following problems will test your ability to answer questions at a Level 5 rating of difficulty. These problems are similar to those that appear on a Career Readiness Certificate test. For each question, you can refer to the answer key for answer justifications. The answer justifications provide an explanation of why each answer option is either correct or incorrect and indicate the skill lesson that should be referred to if further review of a particular skill is needed.

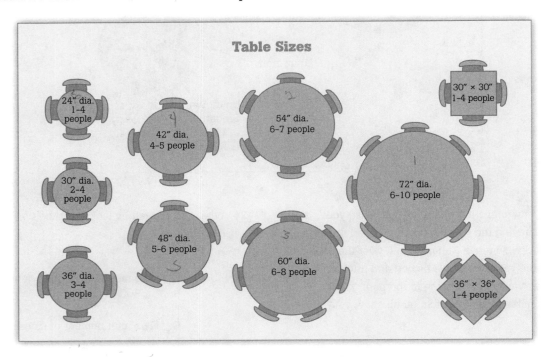

Table Sizes

24" dia. 1–4 people

42" dia. 4–5 people

54" dia. 6–7 people

30" × 30" 1–4 people

30" dia. 2–4 people

72" dia. 6–10 people

48" dia. 5–6 people

36" dia. 3–4 people

60" dia. 6–8 people

36" × 36" 1–4 people

1. As a banquet manager, you need to decide which tables to use for an upcoming event. You need tables that can seat at least six people. Using the sketch, how many different-sized tables can you use?

   A. 2

   B. 3

   C. 4

   D. 5

   E. 6

2. For another event, you need square tables that seat four people. How many tables fit this description?

   F. 1

   G. 2

   H. 3

   J. 4

   K. 6

Formal Place Setting

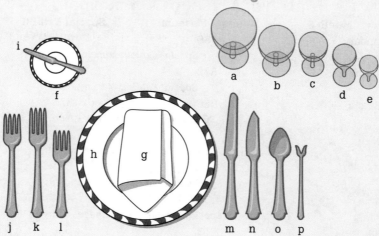

- **Service Plate:** This large plate, also called a charger, serves as an under plate for the plate holding the first course, which a server will bring to the table.
- **Butter Plate:** The small butter plate is placed above the forks at the left of the place setting. On top of it is the butter knife.
- **Glasses:** There can be up to five glasses, and they are placed so that the smaller ones are in front. The water goblet is placed directly above the knives and to its right is the champagne flute. Beside these are placed a red and/or white wine glass and a sherry glass.

- **Napkin:** The napkin is placed on top of the charger (if one is used) or in the space for the service plate.
- **Utensils:** The forks are arranged to the left of the service plate according to when you need to use them, following an "outside-in" order. First is a fish fork, followed by the dinner fork, and then the salad fork for meals where salad is served last. The other utensils are placed to the right of the service plate, following the "outside-in" order. These are an oyster fork for shellfish, a soup spoon, a fish knife, and a dinner knife.

---

3. You work as a server for a catering company. You are learning how to set the table for a formal banquet. Which item on the table will be used for champagne?

    A. a

    B. b

    C. c

    D. d

    E. e

4. Which item is placed on top of the charger?

    F. white wine glass

    G. sherry glass

    H. butter plate

    J. napkin

    K. service plate

Marshall Museum Admissions

Month	General Museum	Special Exhibit
January	786	454
	Special Exhibit: Mummies	
February	832	505
	Special Exhibit: Mummies	
March	885	326
	Special Exhibit: Inspiring Fashion	
April	923	463
	Special Exhibit: Inspiring Fashion	
May	1,023	551
	Special Exhibit: American Presidents	
June	1,089	404
	Special Exhibit: American Presidents	
July	1,132	621
	Special Exhibit: Pirates!	
August	1,148	530
	Special Exhibit: Pirates!	
September	923	475
	Special Exhibit: The Ancient Americas	
October	867	464
	Special Exhibit: The Ancient Americas	
November	886	415
	Special Exhibit: Surrealist Sculptures	
December	724	385
	Special Exhibit: Surrealist Sculptures	

5. As a museum curator, you are looking at attendance data from last year to look for trends in attendance. Based on the data, what trend do you see in last year's general museum attendance?

A. Attendance was highest in the fall.

B. Attendance was highest in the spring.

C. Attendance was highest in the winter.

D. Attendance was highest in the summer.

E. There were no patterns in attendance.

6. Which special exhibit had the largest overall attendance?

F. Mummies

G. Inspiring Fashion

H. American Presidents

J. Pirates!

K. The Ancient Americas

Subcutaneous Fluid Volume to Administer to Kittens and Cats (mL)

Body weight in lbs.	% Dehydration 5-6	% Dehydration 7-8	% Dehydration 9-10
0.5	15	20	25
1	30	40	50
1.5	45	60	75
2	60	80	100
2.5	75	100	125
3	90	120	150
3.5	105	140	175
4	120	160	200
4.5	135	180	225
5	150	200	250
6	180	240	300
7	210	280	350
8	240	320	400
9	270	360	450
10	300	400	500

7. You are a veterinary laboratory technician looking up information about administering fluid for dehydrated cats. How does dehydration affect the amount of fluid that you give?

   A. The level of dehydration is not important.

   B. The amount of fluid needed increases as dehydration levels increase.

   C. The amount of fluid needed increases as dehydration levels decrease.

   D. The amount of fluid needed decreases as dehydration levels increase.

   E. The amount of fluid needed increases and then decreases as dehydration levels decrease.

8. How does body weight affect the volume of fluid that you give?

   F. Body weight is not important.

   G. The amount of fluid needed decreases as body weight increases.

   H. The amount of fluid needed increases as body weight decreases.

   J. The amount of fluid needed decreases as body weight decreases.

   K. The amount of fluid needed increases and then decreases as body weight increases.

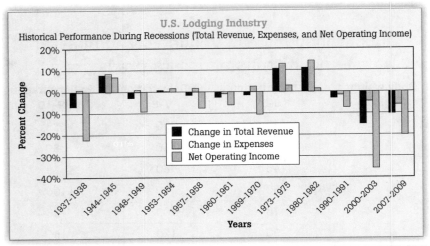

U.S. Lodging Industry
Historical Performance During Recessions (Total Revenue, Expenses, and Net Operating Income)

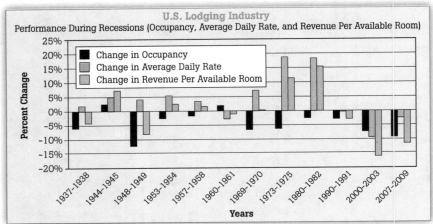

U.S. Lodging Industry
Performance During Recessions (Occupancy, Average Daily Rate, and Revenue Per Available Room)

9. You are a research analyst for a hospitality research center. Currently you are reviewing historic trends in the hotel industry to see what patterns you notice during a recession. What is one trend you notice in the graphics?

A. Most of the time, when there is a drop in occupancy, there is a drop in total revenue.

B. Every time there is a rise in occupancy, there is a rise in total revenue.

C. A drop or rise in occupancy has no related effect to a drop or rise in total revenue.

D. Every time there is a rise in occupancy, there is a drop in total revenue.

E. When there is a drop in occupancy, there is never a drop in revenue.

10. In which range of years did hotels see the most significant decline in total revenue, expenses, net operating income, occupancy, average daily rate, and revenue per available room?

F. 1944–1945

G. 1969–1970

H. 1990–1991

J. 2000–2003

K. 2007–2009

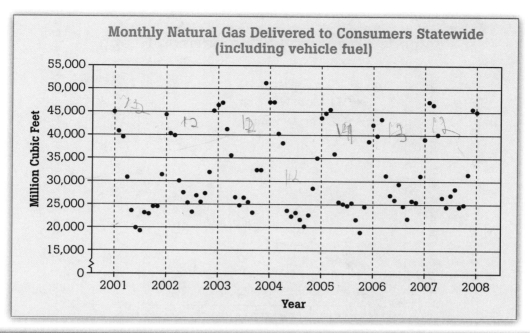

Monthly Natural Gas Delivered to Consumers Statewide (including vehicle fuel)

Natural Gas Delivered to Consumers Statewide, Including Vehicle Fuel (Million Cubic Feet)												
Year	Jan	Feb	Mar	Apr	May	June	Jul	Aug	Sep	Oct	Nov	Dec
2001	45,181	40,868	39,690	30,815	23,495	19,798	19,305	23,154	22,753	24,627	24,646	31,456
2002	44,559	40,420	40,295	29,989	27,757	25,316	23,254	26,957	25,422	27,484	31,958	45,435
2003	46,732	47,096	41,405	35,646	26,400	24,827	26,581	25,461	23,294	32,416	32,407	51,504
2004	47,337	47,355	40,517	38,312	23,705	22,360	23,202	21,585	20,120	22,710	28,310	35,091
2005	43,684	45,004	45,737	36,162	25,515	25,040	24,822	25,383	21,751	18,920	24,651	38,819
2006	42,251	39,967	43,664	31,251	26,934	25,998	29,288	24,626	21,947	25,785	25,506	31,234
2007	39,141	47,516	46,572	40,133	26,516	24,423	26,937	28,310	24,665	24,748	31,610	45,696
2008	45,147	43,916	41,148	35,077	22,777	23,431	27,030	21,291	19,990	22,120	30,040	40,534

11. You are a customer service representative for a natural gas company. You are looking at data for gas delivery in your state. What trend do you see?

- **A.** Delivery goes up in the winter and down in the summer.

- **B.** Delivery goes up in the summer and down in the winter.

- **C.** Delivery is about the same throughout the year.

- **D.** Delivery was most consistent from 2001 to 2003.

- **E.** Delivery varies a lot from year to year.

12. The highest monthly total for gas delivery within each of the years shown has always occurred during which four months?

- **F.** December, January, February, March

- **G.** January, February, March, April

- **H.** September, October, November, December

- **J.** June, July, August, September

- **K.** March, April, May, June

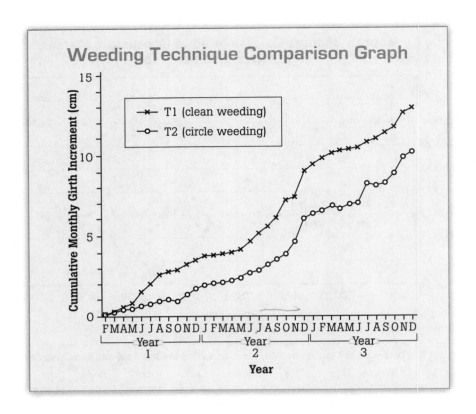

Weeding Technique Comparison Graph

13. You are a tropical crop farm manager. You are studying two weeding techniques: clean weeding involves removing all weeds from around a plant, and circle weeding involves allowing some weeds to grow in a certain area around a plant. You have graphed the data you collected. An increase in girth indicates an increase in growth. What trend do you see in the data?

A. Clean weeding allows for plants to grow more.

B. Circle weeding allows for plants to grow more.

C. Both weeding patterns allow for identical rates of plant growth.

D. Plants that are clean weeded grow more quickly in the winter months.

E. Plants that are circle weeded grow more quickly in the winter months.

14. What trend do you see from November to December of Year 2?

F. The growth of both kinds of plants slowed.

G. The growth of both kinds of plants increased.

H. Clean-weeded plants grew at a much slower rate than circle-weeded plants.

J. The growth for both kinds of plants was almost the same as the earlier months.

K. Clean-weeded plants grew at a much greater rate than circle-weeded plants.

Fresh Fruits and Vegetables Supply and Use: 2002–2007

(In millions of pounds)

Year	Imports [1]	Exports [1]	Total consumption
VEGETABLES AND MELONS			
2002	7,697	4,265	49,388
2003	8,076	4,251	49,944
2004	8,193	4,363	50,700
2005	8,932	4,264	51,658
2006	9,522	3,953	53,590
2007	10,208	3,815	55,220
POTATOES			
2002	883	693	12,757
2003	872	590	13,631
2004	755	479	13,457
2005	788	639	12,577
2006	817	626	12,601
2007	940	565	13,200

[1] Fiscal year for fruits

Beef—Supply and Use: 2002–2007

(In millions of pounds)

	Imports	Exports	Consumption
2002	2,356	1,006	24,031
2003	3,032	2,468	27,338
2004	3,679	460	27,750
2005	3,599	697	27,754
2006	3,085	1,145	28,139
2007	3,048	1,431	28,137

15. As a farm manager, you are looking at trends in crops and beef over the past few years to help you decide which new crops to plant and how much beef you will need to supply this year. What trend do you see in both the vegetable and melon data and the beef data?

A. increased imports and consumption

B. decreased imports and consumption

C. increased imports and decreased consumption

D. no change in consumption; decreased imports

E. decreased consumption; no change in imports

16. What trend in data do you see for exports of vegetables, melons, potatoes, and beef?

F. Exports have increased consistently every year.

G. Exports have decreased consistently every year.

H. Exports have increased every other year.

J. Exports have decreased every other year.

K. There is no consistent trend in export data.

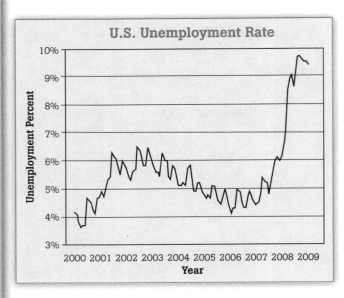

U.S. Unemployment Rate

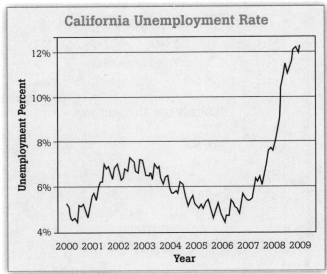

California Unemployment Rate

17. You are a journalist writing an article on unemployment trends since 2000. Which of the following correctly summarizes the overall unemployment trend in both graphics?

    A. Unemployment was low in 2000, and it has been steadily increasing since 2001.

    B. Unemployment was low in 2000, it rose from 2001 to 2003, and it began to decline in 2007.

    C. Unemployment was high in 2000, it rose from 2001 to 2003, it began to decline in 2004, and it began to rise sharply in 2005.

    D. Unemployment was low in 2000, it rose from 2001 to 2003, it began to decline in 2004, and it began to rise sharply in 2007.

    E. Unemployment was high in 2000, and it has declined and risen in predictable sharp peaks and valleys since then.

18. Which of the following statements best summarizes how the trend in the unemployment rate in California compared to that of the rest of the United States for the years shown?

    F. The unemployment rate in both California and the rest of the United States reached its lowest point at the end of the decade.

    G. While the unemployment rate in California rose dramatically toward the end of the decade, it decreased significantly for the rest of the Untied States.

    H. Whenever the unemployment rate in the United States increased, it generally decreased in California.

    J. Whenever the unemployment rate in the California increased, it generally decreased in the rest of the United States.

    K. While the unemployment rates in California and the United States have followed similar patterns, the rate has been consistently higher in California.

Life Insurance Features Comparison

PLAN PROVISIONS	PLAN NAME				
	Life Insurance	Individual & Family	Term Life Option 1	Term Life Option 2	Accidental Death & Dismemberment
Employee Coverage	Minimum: 1 times Retirement System (RS) reported earnings. Maximum: 5 times RS reported earnings.*	Initially, you may purchase $5,000 increments to a maximum of $20,000. At annual open enrollment or through evidence of insurability, additional amounts may be purchased to a maximum of $200,000.	Decreasing term based on age.	Decreasing term based on age.	Maximum coverage: $250,000. May not exceed 10 times your annual salary.
Dependent Coverage	Minimum: $5,000 per dependent Maximum: $10,000 per dependent Spouse and Dependent Coverage are combined. You cannot purchase separately. To end of year attaining age 25	Initially, you may purchase $2,500 increments to a maximum of $5,000. At annual open enrollment or at any time through evidence of insurability, additional amounts may be purchased. To end of month attaining age 25	No	No	Coverage amount based on percentage of employee's coverage. To age 25
Domestic Partner Coverage	No	Yes. See spouse coverage information.	No	No	Yes. See spouse coverage information.
Accidental Death Benefit	Employee Coverage Doubles	No	No	No	Yes
Premium Waiver	Yes, if disabled.	Yes, if disabled.	No	No	No

Based on previous year's RS covered earnings unless years prior to the previous were higher (highest coverage is retained).

19. As an insurance sales agent, you are explaining different term life plans to a customer. She would like a plan that offers a premium waiver and an accidental death benefit. Which plan do you recommend to her?

    A. Accidental Death & Dismemberment

    B. Term Life Option 2

    C. Individual & Family

    D. Term Life Option 1

    E. Life Insurance

20. A man with two children wants a plan that has dependent coverage until the children reach age 25. Which plans do you offer him?

    F. Life Insurance; Term Life Option 2; Individual & Family

    G. Term Life Option 2; Term Life Option 1; Individual & Family

    H. Life Insurance; Individual & Family; Accidental Death & Dismemberment

    J. Term Life Option 2; Term Life Option 1; Accidental Death & Dismemberment

    K. Life Insurance; Term Life Option 1; Accidental Death & Dismemberment

Summary of Domestic Travel by U.S. Resident Households: 1999–2005

[In millions of trips]

Type of trip	1999	2000	2001	2002	2003	2004	2005
All travel: [1]							
Household trips	995.5	1,008.9	993.8	994.9	978.2	1,002.6	1,019.1
Individual trips	1,856.7	1,892.1	1,869.9	1,919.1	1,890.3	1,953.3	1,992.4
All overnight travel:							
Household trips	488.5	493.0	480.7	475.2	470.5	482.2	499.0
Individual trips	873.4	895.6	878.3	884.1	903.2	941.8	968.3
Business travel (multi-night):							
Household trips	400.5	401.0	393.0	364.8	346.8	349.5	345.7
Individual trips	559.9	566.6	545.3	512.0	502.1	513.0	510.0
Leisure travel (multi-night): [2]							
Household trips	595.1	607.9	600.8	630.1	631.4	653.1	673.5
Individual trips	1,296.8	1,325.4	1.324.6	1,407.1	1,388.2	1,440.4	1,482.5

[1] Includes personal and other trips (e.g. medical, funerals, weddings) not shown separately. All domestic travel included. Ninety-five percent of U.S. resident person-trips are domestic.

[2] Includes visiting friends/relatives, outdoor recreation, entertainment, and travel for other pleasure/personal reasons, etc.

21. You work in advertising for a hotel chain. You are researching travel trends to see about a special to offer to your clients. Based on the table, which would be a best-selling deal?

    A. a deal for a multi-night, household, leisure trip

    B. a deal for an overnight, individual trip

    C. a deal for a multi-night, individual, business trip

    D. a deal for an overnight, household trip

    E. a deal for a multi-night, individual, leisure trip

22. How would you summarize the data overall?

    F. U.S. domestic travel went down from 1999 to 2005.

    G. U.S. domestic travel was higher in 2001 than it was in 2005.

    H. U.S. domestic travel was higher in 1999 than it was in 2005.

    J. U.S. domestic travel consistently increased every year.

    K. U.S. domestic travel has gone up and down, but was higher in 2005 than it was in 1999.

Answers are on page 254.

Level 6 Introduction ...

The lesson and practice pages that follow will give you the opportunity to develop and practice the reading and interpretation skills needed to answer work-related questions at a Level 6 rating of difficulty. The *On Your Own* practice problems provide review and practice of key skills needed for locating information from graphical sources in the workplace. These skills are applied through effective problem-solving approaches. The *Performance Assessment* provides problems similar to those you will encounter on a Career Readiness Certificate test. By completing the Level 6 *On Your Own* and *Performance Assessment* questions, you will gain the ability to confidently approach workplace scenarios that require understanding and application of the skills featured in the following lessons:

Lesson 12: Draw Conclusions Based on Graphics

Lesson 13: Apply Information from Graphics to Situations

Lesson 14: Use Information from Graphics to Make Decisions

These skills are intended to help you successfully use workplace graphics such as charts, tables, graphs, floor plans, flowcharts, instrument gauges, and forms. Locating and interpreting information from these types of graphics often require the ability to:

- draw conclusions from the information presented in graphics,
- apply information from graphics to specific situations,
- make decisions requiring judgment based on the information presented in graphics.

Through answering document-related questions at this level, you will continue to develop problem-solving approaches that will help you determine the correct answer in real-world and test-taking situations.

Lesson 12 ▪ ▪ ▪
Draw Conclusions Based on Graphics

Skill: Draw conclusions based on one complicated graphic or several related graphics

In the workplace, you often need to do more than simply find information in graphics. Based on the information that is presented, it is sometimes necessary to draw conclusions about the information that a graphic shows. For example, when creating a budget for a new project, you might look at data tables for past projects to see what the costs were. You might also look at graphs that show profit projections. By drawing conclusions from these and other related graphics, you can create an accurate budget for the new project.

Remember!

When using graphics, always begin by reading the title and any labels. Then, you can skim over the information in the graphics. These steps will help you identify the type of information the graphic contains and help you correctly locate and analyze the information you need.

Skill Examples

Nutritional Values of Juices (per 12-ounce serving)

	Orange Juice	Apple Juice	Cranberry Juice	Grape Juice
Total Carbohydrates	39 g	42 g	36 g	60 g
Sugar	8 tsp.	10 tsp.	9 tsp.	15 tsp.
Calories	165	165	180	240

Example 1
Determine what conclusions can be drawn from a graphic.

The title of the table tells you that the table contains nutritional information about various juices. The table provides information that can be used to draw conclusions about the nutritional values of these juices.

Example 2
Use several pieces of information from graphics to draw conclusions.

Tables are helpful graphics for drawing conclusions based on comparisons. The information in the table above can be used to draw conclusions about the comparative nutritional values of any of the juices listed.

Skill Practice

Use the table above to answer the following questions.

1. As a clinical dietician, which juice would you select for a patient who should intake less than 9 teaspoons of sugar and no more than 180 calories?

   A. orange juice

   B. apple juice

   C. cranberry juice

   D. grape juice

   E. all juices are acceptable

2. What conclusion might you draw about why a doctor recommends grape juice for a patient?

   F. to lower sugar intake

   G. to lower carbohydrates

   H. to increase calorie intake

   J. to limit intake to 180 calories

   K. to limit intake to 10 tsp. sugar

Try It Out!

You are a loan officer comparing CD interest rates among different countries. Based on the graph, what conclusions can you draw about CD interest rates in Australia, New Zealand, and the United States?

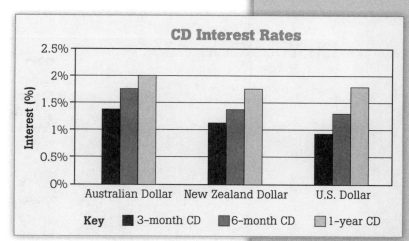

CD Interest Rates

Key ■ 3-month CD ■ 6-month CD ■ 1-year CD

A. Australia has the highest overall CD interest rates.

B. One-year CDs have a 2% or greater interest rate in all three countries.

C. CD interest rates are going up in all three countries.

D. CD interest rates are going up in Australia only.

E. CD interest rates have the fastest growth in the United States.

Step 1 Understand the Problem ■ ■ ■

Complete the *Plan for Successful Solving.*

Plan for Successful Solving

What am I asked to do?	What are the facts?	How do I find the answer?	Is there any unnecessary information?	What prior knowledge will help me?
Draw conclusions based on CD rates in three different countries.	Interest rates for 3-month, 6-month, and 1-year CDs are shown in the graph.	Identify and compare CD interest rates.	No. All of the information is necessary.	Bar graphs are often used to compare information.

Step 2 Find and Check Your Answer ■ ■ ■

- Confirm your understanding of the question and revise your plan as needed.

- Based on your plan, determine your solution approach: *This graph compares interest rates for 3-month, 6-month, and 1-year CDs in Australia, New Zealand, and the United States. The bars for Australia seem to be highest for all three types of CDs. I will select the answer that draws the conclusion that Australia's CD interest rates are the highest of the three countries shown.*

- Check your answer. Review all the answers to determine if the answer you have selected is the best possible answer.

- **Select the correct answer:** A. Australia has the highest overall CD interest rates.
  The CD interest rates for 3-month, 6-month, and 1-year CDs are all highest in Australia among the three countries shown.

Remember!

The key, or legend, within a bar graph identifies what each of the symbols or colors in the graph represents.

Problem Solving Tip

Be sure that you understand the information being shown in the graph before drawing conclusions. In the *Try It Out!* example, the bars on the graph all go up for each of the countries shown. Answer options C, D, and E all draw conclusions based on the idea that this pattern indicates an increase in rates over a period of time. However, the graph does not display information about trends or growth over time; instead, it displays the interest rates for three different CD products for the purpose of comparison. By first identifying the purpose of the graph and what information is being shown, you can better understand what types of conclusions can be drawn.

On Your Own ▪ ▪ ▪

Soil Classification

Seive	Size (millimeters)	Size Classification
	500	Cobbles
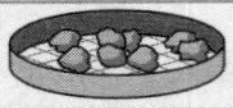	76.20	Course Gravel
	19.05	Fine Gravel
	4.75	Course Sand
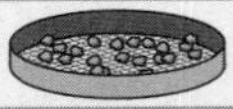	2.00	Medium Sand
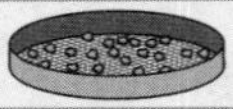	0.425	Fine Sand
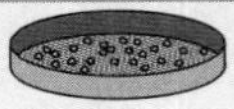	0.075	Silt or Clay

Soil Type	Desired Uses (+ best use, − worst use, = reasonable use)				
	Rolled Earth Fill Dams		Canals	Roadways	
	Embankments	Shells	Earth Lining	Fill Pot Holes	Surfacing
Gravels	−	+	−	+	=
Sands	−	=	=	=	+
Clays	=	−	−	−	−
Silts	−	−	−	−	−

1. You are a city engineer and have analyzed soil the city has stored for construction purposes. Your analysis shows that the stored soil is a mixture that contains 25% particles that are 4.75 mm in diameter, 40% particles that are 2.0 mm in diameter, and 35% particles that are 0.425 mm in diameter. You need to identify the project that is best for this soil mixture. Based on the information shown, what is the best project for this soil mixture?

   A. Embankments

   B. Shells

   C. Earth lining

   D. Fill pot holes

   E. Surfacing

2. The city needs to purchase additional material to fill potholes. What are the best material sizes to purchase?

   F. 76.20 and 4.75

   G. 4.75 and 2.00

   H. 19.05 and 0.075

   J. 76.20 and 19.05

   K. 4.75 and 0.075

Complaints					
Remedy Ticket Number: HD0001748050					
User ID: Selena_Q			**Complaint ID:** #3604C_VID		
Problem Description: The video will not upload properly. The video begins to upload, but then my screen freezes.					
Office	**Software Format**	**Processor**	**Video Length**	**Video Size**	
Nashville	.mov file	1.75 GHz Core Duo	39.16 minutes	133 MB	

Remedy Ticket Number: HD0001749263					
User ID: Bobby_V			**Complaint ID:** #3604D_SPE		
Problem Description: The video begins to upload, but then slows down. It takes nearly an hour to upload a single video.					
Office	**Video Software**	**Processor**	**Video Length**	**Video Size**	
St. Louis	.eqq file	2.5 GHz Core Duo	90 minutes	698 MB	

Instruction Manual—Troubleshooting Difficulties with Video Uploads		
What the User Is Experiencing	*Probable Cause*	*What the User Should Try*
The video begins to upload but takes a very long time.	The user may be uploading a video in the wrong format.	Inform the user that only the following video formats can be uploaded: mov, mp4, m4v
The uploading gets started, but then gets "stuck," or the screen freezes.	The user's processor speed may be too slow.	Instruct the user to make sure that the computer has at least a 2GHz processor.
	The user's browser may be too slow.	Inform the user that if his or her processor is at least 2GHz, then he or she should clear the cache, empty the cookies, and try again.
The video uploads, but then the user cannot view it.	The user may have tried to upload a video that was too large.	Inform the user that the video should be less than 5,000 MB. Users should go back to their video software and export the video again in a smaller form.

3. You work for a Web site as a data development engineer. A user named Selena_Q has difficulty uploading a video to the Web site. Based on the user's description of the problem and the troubleshooting instruction manual, which of the following could be causing the user's problem?

    A. The user's video is in the .mp4 format, which is the wrong format.

    B. The video is too large to upload to the Web site.

    C. The user's processor speed is 1.75 GHz, which is not fast enough.

    D. The user's video is in the .mov format, which is the wrong format.

    E. The user's problem is not addressed in the troubleshooting instruction manual.

4. In order to resolve ticket number HD0001749263, you must instruct the user on how to fix the problem. Based on the user's description of the problem and the troubleshooting instruction manual, what is the source of his problem?

    F. His processor is not fast enough to load videos.

    G. The video is too long to be uploaded to the Web site.

    H. His video is in .eqq format, which is not a supported video format.

    J. His video is in .mov format, which is not a supported video format.

    K. The video is too large to be uploaded to the Web site.

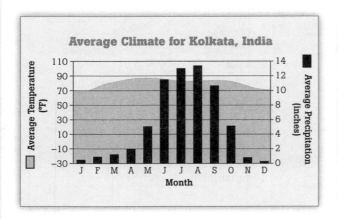

Average Climate for Kolkata, India

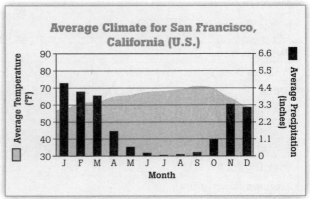

Average Climate for San Francisco, California (U.S.)

5. You work as a travel agent. A customer would like to travel to a warm, dry location in September. Based on the time of year that the customer is traveling, which of the two locations would be best and why?

    A. Kolkata, India, because the average temperature is about 72°F in September.

    B. San Francisco, California, because the average temperature is about 70°F in September and there is very little precipitation.

    C. Kolkata, India, because the average temperature is about 85°F in September and it is the driest time of the year.

    D. San Francisco, California, because the average temperature is about 38°F and the average precipitation is about 6.5 inches in September.

    E. Kolkata, India, because the average temperature is about 100°F and the average precipitation is about 8.8 inches in September.

6. A newly married husband and wife are researching places for a vacation. They have learned that California has a "Mediterranean" type of climate. They do not know what this means. Based on the climate graph of San Francisco, California, how do you describe a Mediterranean type of climate?

    F. It has a fairly warm temperature all year round.

    G. It is hot and wet for most of the year.

    H. It is rainiest during the hottest part of the year.

    J. It is driest during the coldest part of the year.

    K. It has about the same average rainfall throughout the year.

Camera Specifications

CAMERA	Camera A	Camera B	Camera C	Camera D
List Price	$129.99	$139.99	$279.99	$399.99
Megapixels	12.2	10.2	10.1	12.1
Image Resolution	Up to 4,000 x 3,000 pixels	Up to 3,688 x 2,770 pixels	Up to 3,648 x 2,736 pixels	3,264 x 2,446 pixels
Optical Zoom	3x	3x	10x	20x
Digital Zoom	5.7x	5x	2x	4x
Lens Focal Length(s)	35mm equivalent 32-96mm	35mm equivalent 38-190mm	35mm equivalent 38-380mm	35mm equivalent 28-560mm
Viewfinders	LCD only	LCD only	LCD only	Color TFT
Image Stabilization	Yes	Yes, digital	Yes, optical	Yes, optical
Face Detection	Yes	Yes	Yes	Yes
Panorama Mode	No	No	No	Yes
Internal Memory	10MB	32MB	11MB	No
Compatible Memory Formats	Secure Digital (SD) Secure Digital High Capacity (SDHC)	Secure Digital (SD) Secure Digital High Capacity (SDHC)	Memory Stick Duo Memory Stick PRO Duo	MultiMedia Card Secure Digital (SD) Secure Digital High Capacity (SDHC)
Shutter Speeds	8 sec – 1/1,400 sec	1.4 sec – 1.5 sec	Auto: 2 – 1/2,000 sec	15 – 1/3,200 sec
Flash Range	2' – 11.5' (wide) 2' – 6.6' (telephoto) 1' – 2.6' (macro)	ISO 400:2' –13.1' (wide) 2' – 8.2' (telephoto)	0.7' – 23' (wide) 3' – 18' (telephoto)	1.6' – 22'
Flash Modes	Auto, red-eye reduction, forced flash, suppressed flash, slow synchro	Auto, fill-flash, red-eye reduction, flash off	Auto, flash on, flash off, red-eye reduction on/off, slow sync	Auto, slow synchro, red-eye reduction, flash off
Batteries	Rechargeable lithium-ion battery NP-45 (included)	Rechargeable lithium-ion battery	Rechargeable lithium-ion NP-BG1	4 AA alkaline

7. You work as a salesperson in the camera department. A customer comes in with a budget of $300 looking for a camera with at least 10 megapixels, a high optical zoom, red-eye reduction flash mode, and face detection software. Based on the camera specifications chart, which camera do you recommend?

    A. Camera A

    B. Camera B

    C. Camera C

    D. Camera D

    E. None of the cameras in the chart fit these specifications.

8. Looking at the table above, what is one conclusion you can draw about why Camera D is the most expensive camera?

    F. It is the most expensive because it has the most megapixels and can take the highest quality pictures.

    G. It is the most expensive because it has the most internal memory.

    H. It is the most expensive because it has auto flash and red-eye reduction modes.

    J. It is the most expensive because of special features such as a very high optical zoom and a panorama mode.

    K. It is the most expensive because it has the highest image resolution.

Costal Warning Display Signals

Type of Warning	Flag (Red and Black)	Information
No Warning	None	No maritime warning issued.
Small Craft Advisory	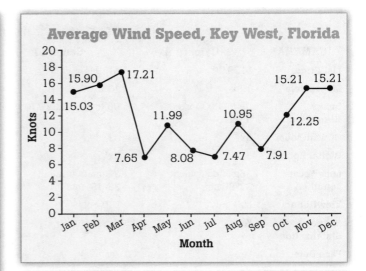	Sustained winds or frequent gusts of 20–33 knots and waves of 4–10 feet are forecast for the area. Required winds and wave heights differ based on the geographic area.
Gale Warning		Winds of 37–47 knots are forecast for the area.
Storm Warning		Winds of 48 knots or more are forecast for the area.
Hurricane Warning		Winds of 64 knots or more are forecast for the area; issued only in connection with a tropical storm (hurricane).

Average Wind Speed, Key West, Florida

High Wind Speed, Key West, Florida

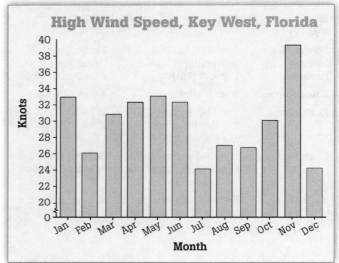

9. As a member of the Maritime Weather Service in Key West, you are responsible for analyzing weather data. Your conclusions can be used directly or combined with other data. Based on the data for wind speed in Key West, when are gale warnings more likely to be issued?

   A. March

   B. May

   C. November

   D. August

   E. February

10. Based on the average wind speed, which coastal warning display flag is usually flying?

    F. No flag is flying.

    G. The Small Craft Advisory flag is flying.

    H. The Gale Warning flag is flying.

    J. The Storm Warning flag is flying.

    K. The Hurricane Warning flag is flying.

Wire Information			
Standard Wire Gauge	Diameter (in inches)	Mass per length (in pounds per foot)	Current Capacity/A (750 kcmil/A)
00000 (5/0)	0.43	0.57	249
0000 (4/0)	0.40	0.49	213
000 (3/0)	0.37	0.42	185
00 (2/0)	0.34	0.37	161
0 (1/0)	0.32	0.32	140
1	0.30	0.27	120
2	0.28	0.23	102
3	0.25	0.19	84.7
4	0.23	0.16	71.8
5	0.21	0.13	59.9

CURRENT TESTS   Initials: L.K.

SITE A
ADDRESS: 2134 South Render Street
CAPACITY REQUIRED: ≥ 240

Test	Current Detected
1	213
2	211
3	212

SITE B
ADDRESS: 3264 Maharesset Avenue
CAPACITY REQUIRED: ≥ 70

Test	Current Detected
1	71
2	71.8
3	70.9

11. You work as an electrical engineer, and your supervisor has given you the results of a current test run on various wires. Using the table and the test results, what is most likely the gauge of the wire at Site A?

A. 5/0

B. 4/0

C. 3/0

D. 2/0

E. 1/0

12. Your supervisor informs you that the wire gauge needed for Site A differs from the wire gauge needed for Site B. Using the table and the test results, why are different wire gauges needed?

F. The wires at Site B should be longer.

G. The wires at Site B should weigh less.

H. The budget for Site A is higher.

J. Site B requires more capacity.

K. Site A requires more capacity.

Electricity Consumption and Plug Types

Rank Per Electricity Consumption	Country	Annual Electricity Consumption (in kilowatt-hours)	Population	Plug Type
1	United States	3,873,000,000,000	307,212,123	A, B
2	China	2,835,000,000,000	1,338,612,968	A, C, I
3	Japan	1,007,000,000,000	127,078,679	A, B
4	Russia	840,400,000,000	140,041,247	C, F
5	India	568,000,000,000	1,166,079,217	C, D, M
6	Germany	547,300,000,000	82,329,758	C, F
7	Canada	536,100,000,000	33,487,208	A, B
8	France	447,200,000,000	64,057,792	E
9	Brazil	404,300,000,000	198,739,269	A, B, C, I
10	South Korea	385,100,000,000	48,508,972	A, B, C, F
11	United Kingdom	345,800,000,000	61,113,205	G
12	Italy	315,000,000,000	58,126,212	C, F, L
13	Spain	276,100,000,000	40,525,002	C, F
14	Taiwan	233,000,000,000	22,974,347	A, B
15	Australia	222,000,000,000	21,262,641	I
16	South Africa	215,100,000,000	49,052,489	D, M
17	Mexico	200,900,000,000	111,211,789	A
18	Saudi Arabia	165,100,000,000	28,686,633	A, B, C, G
19	Iran	153,800,000,000	66,429,284	C, F
20	Turkey	153,700,000,000	76,805,524	C, F

13. As an electrical engineering intern, you are reviewing information about electricity around the world. Based on the information, which plugs appear to be the most widely used?

    A.   Plugs A, C, and I

    B.   Plugs A, B, and C

    C.   Plugs C, F, and I

    D.   Plugs C, D, and M

    E.   Plugs D, M, and I

14. According to the table above, what conclusions can you draw about Mexico?

    F.   Despite having a relatively large population, it has relatively low annual electricity consumption.

    G.   It has a small population and low annual electricity consumption.

    H.   It has a large population and high annual electricity consumption.

    J.   Despite having a relatively small population, it has relatively high annual electricity consumption.

    K.   It has the largest population and the least amount of annual electricity consumption.

Beef Grading Information

Grade of Beef	Info
Prime Grade	• Only 2% of all the beef produced in the United States is certified as USDA prime. • USDA prime beef is served by the finest upscale restaurants. • Prime roasts and steaks are excellent for dry-heat cooking.
Choice Grade	• High quality meat • Choice roasts and steaks from loin and rib will be tender, juicy, and flavorful. • Suited to dry-heat cooking • Less tender cuts (from rump, round, and blade chuck) can also be cooked with dry heat, but will be most tender if braised
Select Grade	• Uniform in quality and leaner than the higher grades • Tender, but may lack juiciness and flavor • Best when marinated before cooking or braising to obtain maximum tenderness and flavor
Standard and Commercial Grades	• Sold as ungraded or store brand meat

Beef Cuts Sold

Beef Cut	Info	Cooking Method	Price per Pound
Filet Mignon	• Most tender beef cut • Lean • Buttery texture • Also known as tenderloin steak	• Broiling • Grilling • Sautéing	$19.56
Cowboy Steak	• Fine-grained, juicy rib steak with rich flavor • Very tender • Known as rib steak bone-in and rib-eye bone-in	• Broiling • Grilling • Sautéing	$16.49
Center Cut Sirlon Steak	• Moderately tender • Lean and well-flavored • Versatile	• Broiling • Grilling • Sautéing	$16.29
Chuck Eye Steak	• Less flavor and tenderness than rib-eye • Marinate before grilling. • Also known as boneless chuck filet steak	• Braising • Grilling • Sautéing	$7.85

15. You work as a meat clerk at a local grocery store. Based on the information above, which item would be hardest to find at the grocery store?

   A. choice filet mignon

   B. select center cut sirloin steak

   C. standard filet mignon

   D. prime rib-eye bone-in

   E. choice cowboy steak

16. What conclusion can you draw about the grade and cut of beef as it relates to price?

   F. The grade of beef does not affect price.

   G. A better grade of beef is more expensive.

   H. The grade determines how the beef is cooked.

   J. The grade determines freshness.

   K. The grade affects the cut of beef.

Sewage by Region

Regional Code	Zoning	Sewage
Area 1	Residential	Toilets, baths, showers, sinks, lawn clippings, garbage
Area 2	Commercial—Grade 1	Food scraps, food packages, cleansers
Area 3	Commercial—Grade 2	Oil, gasoline and fuel sources (diesel, petroleum) from mechanics, scrap metal
Area 4	Protected Parks	Storm water runoff, leaves, lawn clippings
Area 5	Manufacturing	Wood chips from the mill, industrial waste, chemicals, foam, scrap metal

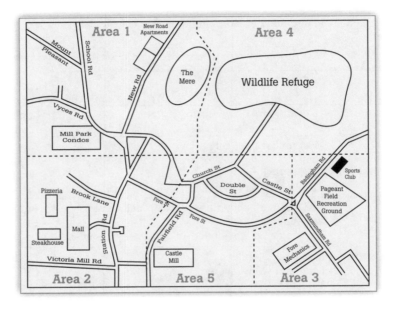

17. You are a sanitary engineer working at the city's sewage treatment plant. All of the city's sewage is processed at the plant. Based on the table and map above, what type of sewage comes from Fore Mechanics?

    A. toilets and garbage

    B. food packages and cleansers

    C. oil, gasoline, and fuel sources

    D. storm water runoff, leaves, and lawn clippings

    E. wood chips, industrial waste, and foam

18. Your supervisor asks you to identify types of sewage from the Vyces Road area. What is a conclusion you can draw about the sewage from this area?

    F. It contains materials that come from stores and restaurants.

    G. It contains material that is produced from homes.

    H. It is composed of hazardous material.

    J. It is composed of sewage that comes from nature.

    K. It contains food scraps and food packages.

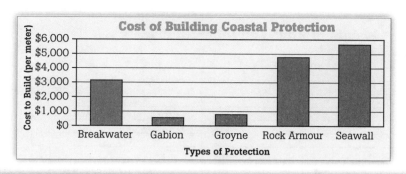

Coastal Protection

Protection	Description
Breakwater	• Built in deep water to protect a harbor or coastline by breaking waves farther offshore • Traditionally made from concrete blocks or natural stone sunk offshore, but can be made from different materials, such as oil drums and used tires • 15 years of useful life
Gabion	• Wall built to provide short-term protection from erosion • Stacked metal cages containing rocks; commonly, a cage is 1 meter × 1 meter • Easily damaged; replace in 5-10 years
Groyne	• Barriers or walls built 50-100 meters apart, perpendicular to the sea, to build up sand on the updrift side to absorb the waves' energy • Made from tropical hardwood, concrete, or rock • Should last 15-20 years
Rock Armour	• Barrier erected at the foot of dunes or cliffs to absorb the waves' energy; not effective in storm conditions • Large rocks placed with native stones • Limited lifespan
Seawall	• Sloped wall with a curved top that breaks the wave • Traditionally made from masonry, concrete, or rock • Should last 20-30 years

19. You are a civil engineer preparing a report for a series of coastal towns that want to protect their shorelines. Based on the graphics above, what is one conclusion you can draw about seawall?

   A. It is the most expensive type of protection because it has the longest lifespan.

   B. It is traditionally made from concrete blocks or natural stone and costs a little over $3,000.

   C. It is the most expensive type of protection because it is a mix of large rocks and native stones.

   D. It is made from tropical hardwood, concrete, or rock and lasts 20–30 years.

   E. It costs over $5,000 and has a 15–20 year lifespan.

20. Which of the following conclusions could you draw about a town that elects to build gabions?

   F. They want a type of protection that will last 15–20 years, and their budget is less than $1,000.

   G. They have oil drums and used tires they would like to use, and their budget is less than $1,000.

   H. They want a barrier to absorb the waves' energy, and their budget is less than $6,000.

   J. They want to provide short-term protection from erosion, and their budget is less than $1,000.

   K. They want a type of protection that will last 20–30 years, and their budget is less than $6,000.

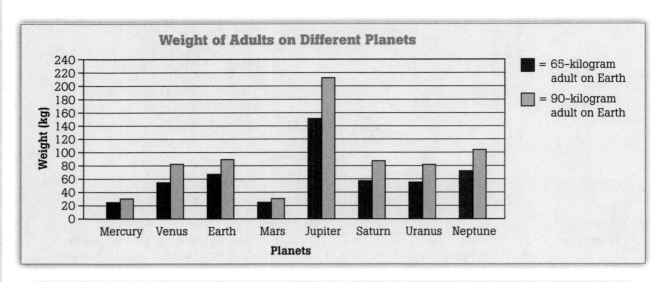

Planet	Surface Gravity	Surface Gravity Compared to Earth	How to Find Weight on Other Planets
Mercury	3.7 m/s²	0.38 times Earth's gravity	65 kg × 0.38 = 24.7 kg
Venus	8.87 m/s²	0.9 times Earth's gravity	65 kg × 0.9 = 58.5 kg
Earth	9.78 m/s²	1	65 kg × 1 = 65 kg
Mars	3.72 m/s²	0.38 times Earth's gravity	65 kg × 0.38 = 24.7 kg
Jupiter	24.79 m/s²	2.36 times Earth's gravity	65 kg × 2.36 = 153.4 kg
Saturn	8.96 m/s²	0.92 times Earth's gravity	65 kg × 0.92 = 59.8 kg
Uranus	8.69 m/s²	0.89 times Earth's gravity	65 kg × 0.89 = 57.85 kg
Neptune	11.15 m/s²	1.13 times Earth's gravity	65 kg × 1.13= 73.45 kg

21. You are an administrator at a natural history museum reviewing information to include in the new exhibit on gravity. According to the graphics above, if a man weighs 90 kilograms on Earth, on which planet would he weigh the most and why?

   A. Mars, because the gravity there is 38 times the gravity on Earth

   B. Jupiter, because the gravity there is 1.13 times the gravity on Earth

   C. Neptune, because a 90-kilogram adult would weigh over 100 kilograms there

   D. Jupiter, because the surface gravity there is greater than the surface gravity on any other planet

   E. Neptune, because the surface gravity there is greater than the surface gravity on Earth

22. Based on the graph and the table, what conclusion can you draw about gravity on the surface of Saturn?

   F. It is about the same as the gravity on the surface of Mercury.

   G. It is about the same as the gravity on the surface of Earth.

   H. It is about the same as the gravity on the surface of Mars.

   J. It is twice the gravity on the surface of Jupiter.

   K. It is about the same as the gravity on the surfaces of Venus and Uranus.

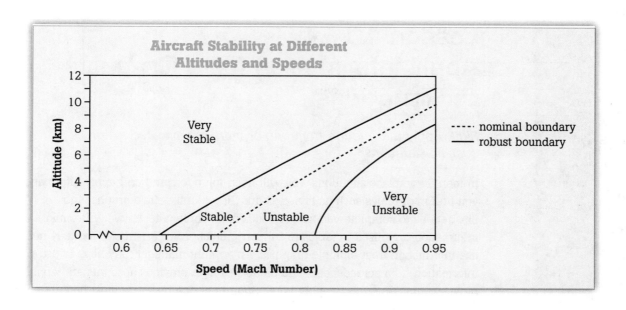

Aircraft Stability at Different Altitudes and Speeds

23. You are an aeronautics engineer testing an aircraft for stability. Based on the graph, at what Mach number can the aircraft be very stable from 1 up to 12 kilometers?

    A.   0.65

    B.   0.75

    C.   0.85

    D.   0.9

    E.   0.95

24. What conclusion can you draw about the relationship between altitude and speed (mach number) in the very stable section of the graphic?

    F.   The lower the altitude, the smaller the range of speed is in which an aircraft is very stable.

    G.   At high altitudes, an aircraft is very unstable at a wide range of speeds.

    H.   At every altitude, an aircraft is very stable regardless of the speed.

    J.   The lower the altitude, the larger the range of speed is in which an aircraft is very stable.

    K.   Aircrafts are always very unstable at low altitudes, regardless of the speed.

Answers are on page 258.

Lesson 13 ■ ■ ■
Apply Information from Graphics to Situations

Skill: Apply information from one or more complicated graphics to specific situations

In many workplace situations, you will need to understand and apply information you find in graphics such as tables, charts, line graphs, circle graphs, and illustrations to complete various projects. For example, a technical writer might use information organized in tables to support predictions in an article. You may need to use information from multiple graphics. An account manager may have to use information from spreadsheets and databases from previous accounts and apply it to new accounts. In order to apply information from graphics, you must first understand what information is shown and how it can be applied to workplace situations.

Skill Example

Paper Jam Directions

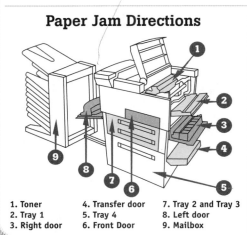

1. Toner
2. Tray 1
3. Right door
4. Transfer door
5. Tray 4
6. Front Door
7. Tray 2 and Tray 3
8. Left door
9. Mailbox

Understand information and identify location of information in a graphic.

Before applying information from graphics, first skim the graphic to understand what information is shown. For example, the graphic of the copy machine is labeled with numbers, and has a key to identify the name of each corresponding part. By skimming the graphic, you can familiarize yourself with the type and location of information in the graphic. This will help when applying information from the graphic to a specific situation.

Copy Quality Troubleshooting Chart

SYMPTOM	POSSIBLE CAUSES	REMEDY
Light Copy	Improper Exposure Adjustment	Adjust Light / Dark Setting
	Low Toner Concentration	Check Toner
Dark Copy	Improper Exposure Adjustment	Adjust Light / Dark Setting
	Improper Toner Concentration	Replace Developer
Blank Copy	Broken or Missing Corona Wire	Call Service Tech to Repair
	Faulty Corona Block Contacts	Call Service Tech to Repair
Black Copy	Blown Exposure Lamp	Call Service Tech to Replace
	Light Path/Optics Obstructed	Call Service Tech to Clear Obstruction

Skill Practice

Use the table to the left to answer the following questions.

1. Based on the table, which symptoms can be remedied without having to call the service technician?

   A. blank copy, black copy

   B. dark copy, black copy

   C. blank copy, light copy

   D. light copy, black copy

   E. light copy, dark copy

2. What supplies should you order to remedy the possible causes that can be fixed by office staff?

   F. developer and corona wire

   G. toner and developer

   H. toner only

   J. developer only

   K. obstruction and toner

Try It Out! ■ ■ ■

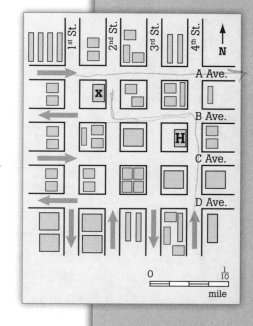

You are attending a conference out of town next week. You know that the city where the conference is being held has several one-way streets, which can make it difficult to drive from one place to another. The parking garage for the hotel (H) exits onto 4th St., and the garage for the convention center (X) is located on 2nd St. between A Ave. and B Ave. Based on the map, which route will you use to get from your hotel to the convention center's parking garage?

A. Turn south on 4th St. Turn west on D Ave. Turn north on 2nd St.

B. Turn south on 4th St. Turn west on C Ave. Turn north on 2nd St.

C. Turn north on 4th St. Turn west on B Ave. Turn north on 1st St.

D. Turn north on 4th St. Turn west on B Ave. Turn north on 2nd St.

E. Turn north on 4th St. Turn east on A Ave. Turn south on 1st St.

 Step 1 ## Understand the Problem ■ ■ ■

Complete the *Plan for Successful Solving.*

Plan for Successful Solving				
What am I asked to do?	**What are the facts?**	**How do I find the answer?**	**Is there any unnecessary information?**	**What prior knowledge will help me?**
Select a route from the hotel (H) to the convention center (X).	The streets allow only one-way traffic.	Test the possible routes on the map.	The conference is out of town.	Understanding of traffic laws. Arrows on maps indicate the direction of traffic.

 Step 2 ## Find and Check Your Answer ■ ■ ■

- Confirm your understanding of the question and revise your plan as needed.

- Based on your plan, determine your solution approach: *Using the map, I will trace the routes provided. By following the routes provided, I see that options A, B, and C do not obey the traffic laws and that option E does not lead to the convention center. Only option D follows the traffic laws and leads to the correct location. I will choose option D as my answer.*

- Check your answer. Review all the answers to determine if the answer you have selected is the correct answer.

- **Select the correct answer:**   D. Turn north on 4th St. Turn west on B Ave. Turn north on 2nd St.
  By examining the map closely and using the map symbols, you see that D leads to the correct destination and follows all traffic laws.

Problem Solving Tip

Maps often contain a scale that is a ratio you can use to convert a distance on the map to the actual distance. For example, the scale on the map in the *Try It Out!* example shows what $\frac{1}{10}$ mile of actual distance is equivalent to on the map.

Remember!

Symbols on maps and other graphics provide important clues to understand the graphic. Common symbols include a scale like the one shown on this map and arrows to identify the direction traffic travels.
- Maps can also include
- symbols that identify
- highways, rest areas, and
- terrain such as rivers and forest areas.

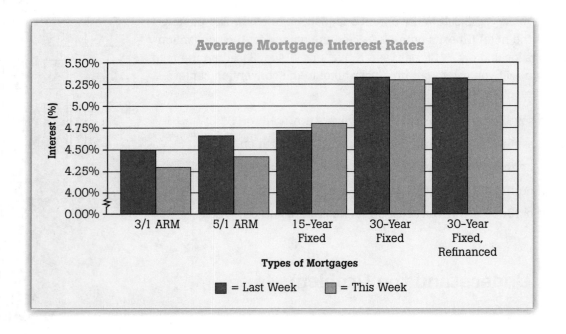

1. You are a mortgage loan officer who must keep track of the differences in mortgage interest rates. A client asks you to identify the mortgage that now offers the lowest interest rate. According to the bar graph shown, what mortgage now offers the lowest interest rate?

    A. a 3/1 ARM

    B. a 5/1 ARM

    C. a 15-year fixed

    D. a 30-year fixed

    E. a 30-year fixed, refinanced

2. As a loan officer, you have been asked by your supervisor to research mortgages with interest rates that are decreasing. You should research all of the mortgage types on the graph except

    F. a 3/1 ARM.

    G. a 5/1 ARM.

    H. a 15-year fixed.

    J. a 30-year fixed.

    K. a 30-year fixed, refinanced.

Troubleshooting Guide for Your MP3 Player

Symptom	Troubleshooting	Tips
Player shuts down	Check the battery symbol to be sure that your MP3 player has energy.	When the battery is more than half full, the battery symbol will appear green. If the battery is less than half full, recharge until it is at least half full.
Screen freezes	Use the on/off switch. Slide the switch back and forth.	None
	Hold the center, circular button for 10 seconds until the screen goes gray.	Place your MP3 player on a flat surface before pressing the center, circular button.
Won't sync with computer	Check that you have the most up-to-date software on your computer. If you do not, get the latest software updates.	To update the MP3 player's software, visit the company's Web site. Click the *Support* button. On the Support page, click the *Get Update* button.
	If you do have the most up-to-date software, install it again.	Follow prompts to delete all copies of the original software before installing it again.

If you continue to have a malfunctioning MP3 player, bring it back to the store. Bring your receipt.

From: Stuart Nuñez, Technology Development Department
To: Customer Service Department
Subject: Changes in the MP3 Player

Date: July 7

Please read through these changes and update your materials accordingly.

1. Change first tip to "When the battery is more than half full, the battery symbol will appear green. When the battery is less than half full, the battery symbol will appear red. If the battery is less than half full, recharge until it is at least half full."

2. Change third troubleshooting item to "Press the center, circular button for 10 seconds until the screen goes white."

3. Change fourth tip to "Notification of available downloads of software updates are automatically e-mailed to all registered users."

4. The new MP3 model also includes the following changes:
   · The width of the On/Off switch has been increased.
   · The size of the center, circular button has been increased.

---

3. You work as a customer service representative, helping customers when they encounter problems with the MP3 player manufactured by your company. A customer asks why an e-mail was sent "with a link to an update." How do you respond?

   A. The customer needs to download her user documentation.

   B. There is an update available for the MP3 player's software.

   C. The customer is eligible for an MP3 player upgrade.

   D. The customer needs to complete her registration.

   E. There is a new battery available for the MP3 player.

4. You need to help a customer recharge the battery in his MP3 player. Based on the memo and guide shown, how can the customer tell if the battery is at least half full?

   F. The battery symbol will appear red.

   G. The screen will go white.

   H. The battery symbol will appear gray.

   J. The screen will go green.

   K. The battery symbol will appear green.

Automobile Safety Features

Feature	Description
Adaptive cruise control	Sensors and radar enable cruise control to maintain a safe distance from the other vehicles. If the system senses a potential collision, it will brake hard and tighten the seatbelts. Your car will return to cruising speed when the lane is clear. The system can be overridden, or turned off, by simply tapping the brake.
Blind spot detection	Alerts the driver to cars or objects in the driver's blind spot.
Lane-departure warning	Evaluates the speed and distance of an approaching vehicle and warns the driver of potential danger when changing lanes. It can also warn the driver if the car is wandering out of its lane, which could be useful if the driver becomes distracted or drowsy.
Rollover prevention	Brakes and modulates the throttle to prevent potential rollover.
Adaptive headlights	The headlights follow the vehicle's direction, even bending the light when the vehicle turns. The headlights can change the beam's length or height.

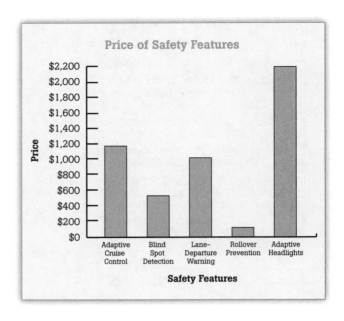

5. You own a car service that picks up and drops off clients at the airport early in the morning and late at night. When you purchase new vehicles, which safety feature would be the most helpful to your drivers while fitting your budget of $1,500?

　　A.　adaptive cruise control

　　B.　rollover prevention

　　C.　blind spot detection

　　D.　lane-departure warning

　　E.　adaptive headlights

6. Automated safety features that directly control the vehicle's movement without the driver taking any additional action can keep your company's safety record high. Which automated safety features would you purchase with a budget of $1,600?

　　F.　blind spot detection and adaptive headlights

　　G.　lane-departure warning and rollover prevention

　　H.　adaptive cruise control and rollover prevention

　　J.　adaptive headlights and lane-departure warning

　　K.　adaptive cruise control and blind spot detection

Lindy's Sandwich Shop Schedule

	Monday 4/10	Tuesday 4/11	Wednesday 4/12	Thursday 4/13	Friday 4/14	Saturday 4/15	Sunday 4/16
9 A.M.–1 P.M.	Colin S.	Cyndi K.	Colin S.	Colin S.	Danielle C.	Carlyle C.	Colin S.
1 P.M.–5 P.M.	Jay F.		Cyndi K.	Cyndi K.			Carlyle C.
5 P.M.–9 P.M.	Mark O.		Mark O.	Jay F.	Jay F.	Mark O.	

Employee Availability

Name	Maximum Hours	Notes
Carlyle C.	12	Sat. & Sun. only
Cyndi K.	24	Tues., Wed., Thurs. only
Colin S.	20	Mornings only
Mark O.	16	Evenings only, no Thurs.
Jay F.	16	No Tues., no weekends
Danielle C.	10	No Monday

Reminder: It is a violation of store policy for any part-time employee to work more than 8 continuous hours.

7. As the manager of Lindy's Sandwich Shop, you are creating the schedule. You have almost completed the schedule for your part-time employees, but still have the Tuesday evening shift to fill. Who is available to work the open shift on Tuesday?

- **A.** Cyndi K.
- **B.** Mark O.
- **C.** Colin S.
- **D.** Jay F.
- **E.** Danielle C.

8. Last night Danielle C. called to tell you she won't be able to work her Friday shift. You can fill her shift by scheduling

- **F.** Carlyle C. to work the entire shift.
- **G.** Cyndi K. to work the entire shift.
- **H.** Colin S. to work from 9 A.M.–1 P.M. and Jay F. to work from 1 P.M.–5 P.M.
- **J.** Colin S. to work from 9 A.M.–1 P.M. and Cyndi K. to work from 1 P.M.–5 P.M.
- **K.** Carlyle C. to work from 9 A.M.–1 P.M. and Jay F. to work from 1 P.M.–5 P.M.

Charter Aircrafts

Aircraft	Features	Passengers	Cost per Hour
Turboprop	• Can use runways that are too short for jets. • Most have a pressurized passenger cabin. • Limited baggage capacity and luggage storage.	4–8	$1,200
Light jet	• Small enough to use airports not accessible by many major airlines. • Most have a pressurized passenger cabin. • Limited baggage capacity and luggage storage.	4–8	$1,900
Midsize jet	• Small enough to use airports not accessible by many major airlines. • Have a pressurized passenger cabin. • Most have external baggage storage but might have limited baggage capacity if it has only internal storage.	5–9	$3,100
Heavy jet	• Small enough to use airports not accessible by many major airlines. • Features might include external baggage compartments, satellite phone, a full galley, and flight attendants.	10–19	$4,500
Turboprop airliner	• Can use runways that are too short for jets. • Most have a pressurized passenger cabin. • Some provide luxury services and seat configurations.	19–65	$2,500

Planes in Your Charter Company Fleet

Aircraft Type	Aircraft	Cruising Speed	Range (Miles)
Cheyenne III	Turboprop	more than 300 mph	1,000
Falcon 20	Midsize jet	500 mph	2,100
Gulfstream V	Heavy jet	530 mph	4,000
Jetstream 3100	Turboprop airliner	280 mph	500
Learjet 35	Light jet	440 mph	1,500

9. You are a scheduler for an airline charter company. A caller asks for a plane from Springfield, MO, to Aspen, CO (749 miles). She will bring 10 family members, each with one piece of luggage. Which plane do you recommend?

   A. Cheyenne III

   B. Falcon 20

   C. Gulfstream V

   D. Jetstream 3100

   E. Learjet 35

10. The owner of a small software development company wants to charter a plane for himself to a town 900 miles away. The town has a small airport with a short runway. Which plane do you recommend?

   F. Cheyenne III

   G. Falcon 20

   H. Gulfstream V

   J. Jetstream 3100

   K. Learjet 35

Silver Spring to Downtown Monday through Friday Morning

♿	ZONE	STATIONS	2102 AM	2104 AM	2106 AM	2108 AM	2110 AM	2112 AM	2114 AM	2116 AM	2118 AM	2120 AM	2122 AM	2124 AM	2126 AM	2128 AM	2130 AM	2132 AM	2134 AM
	J	Silver Spring LV:	4:46	5:13	5:35	6:08	6:14	6:30	6:38	6:53	6:58	—	7:16	7:28	—	8:45	—	10:45	—
♿	J	River Road	4:49	5:16	5:37	↓	6:18	↓	6:42	↓	7:01	—	7:19	7:31	—	8:48	—	10:48	—
	I	North Station	4:56	5:23	5:45		6:25		6:49		7:08	—	7:26	7:38	—	8:54	—	10:54	—
	I	People's Park	5:00	5:27	5:51		6:30		6:54		7:12	—	7:31	7:43	—	9:00	9:58	11:00	11:58
	H	Lace Ave	5:04	5:31	5:55	↓	6:34	↓	6:58	7:06	—		7:35	7:47	—	9:04	10:04	11:04	12:04
	H	Piper's Plaza	5:10	5:37	6:01	6:26	6:41	6:48	7:05	7:12	7:22	—	7:42	7:54	—	9:10	10:10	11:10	12:10
	F	Mapleton	5:20	5:48	6:12	6:37	—	6:59	—	7:23	7:33	—	7:53	8:05	—	9:20	10:20	11:20	12:20
	E	Wharf	5:29	5:57	6:22	—	6:57	—	7:21	—	7:42	—	8:02	—	8:29	9:29	10:29	11:29	12:29
♿	E	Gold Line	5:33	6:01	6:26	6:50	—	7:12	—	7:36	—	7:54	—	8:16	8:33	9:33	10:32	11:32	12:32
	D	Westborough	5:37	6:05	6:31	—	7:05	—	7:29	—	7:50	—	8:09	—	8:37	9:37	10:36	11:36	12:36
	D	Blue Field	5:40	6:08	6:34	6:57	↓	7:19	↓	7:43	↓	8:01	↓	8:22	8:40	9:40	10:39	11:39	12:39
	D	Gulf	5:43	6:11	6:37	7:00	↓	7:22	↓	7:46	↓	8:04	↓	8:25	8:43	9:43	10:42	11:42	12:42
	C	Neville Heights	5:46	6:14	6:41	7:04	7:12	7:26	7:36	7:50	↓	8:08	8:15	8:29	8:46	9:46	10:45	11:45	12:45
♿	C	Brookstone	5:50	6:19	6:46	↓	7:17	↓	7:41	↓	7:59	↓	8:19	↓	8:51	9:51	10:50	11:50	12:50
	C	Wonderland	5:53	6:22	6:49		7:20		7:44		8:03		8:22		8:54	9:54	10:53	11:53	12:53
	B	Cranston Ave.	5:57	6:26	6:52	↓	7:24	↓	7:48	↓	8:06	↓	8:25	↓	8:57	9:57	10:56	11:56	12:56
♿	A	Downtown	6:00	6:29	6:55	7:15	7:27	7:37	7:51	8:01	8:09	8:19	8:28	8:40	9:00	10:00	10:59	11:59	12:59

11. As a sales manager who lives in Silver Spring, you need to take the train from Silver Spring and arrive at Wonderland by 8:00 A.M. on Monday for a meeting. The sales representative who will accompany you to the meeting boards the train at the River Road station. Because she uses a wheelchair, both of you will need to exit the train at the wheelchair accessible station that is closest to your meeting. Which station do you use to exit the train?

    A.   Brookstone

    B.   Neville Heights

    C.   Cranston Ave

    D.   Wonderland

    E.   Gulf

12. You need to meet a sales associate at 8:30 A.M. Tuesday at the Piper's Plaza station. From your home in Silver Spring, what is the latest train you can take to meet the sales associate?

    F.   2120

    G.   2122

    H.   2124

    J.   2126

    K.   2128

Inspection of Hydroelectric Dam

Inspector Registration Number: OXf-cb1-2242	Approval Code: 998d	Date of Inspection: 8/11

Valve	Flow			
	8:00 A.M.	Noon	8:00 P.M.	Midnight
East #1	1,230 gal/sec	1,286 gal/sec	1,615 gal/sec	1,845 gal/sec
East #2	1,680 gal/sec	1,692 gal/sec	2,340 gal/sec	2,616 gal/sec
West #1	1,704 gal/sec	1,699 gal/sec	2,180 gal/sec	2,580 gal/sec
West #2	1,208 gal/sec	1,213 gal/sec	1,689 gal/sec	1,913 gal/sec

Accuracy of all measurements is ±25 gal/sec

Work Schedule

Day	Time	Inspector
8/10	7:00 A.M.–3:00 P.M.	J. Rayburn
8/10	3:00 P.M–11:00 P.M.	M. Mitchell
8/10	11:00 P.M–7:00 A.M.	C. Thomas
8/11	7:00 A.M.–3:00 P.M.	S. Lobowski
8/11	3:00 P.M–11:00 P.M.	E. Anderson
8/11	11:00 P.M.–7:00 A.M.	C. Thomas
8/12	7:00 A.M.–3:00 P.M.	J. Rayburn
8/12	3:00 P.M–11:00 P.M.	M. Mitchell
8/12	11:00 P.M–7:00 A.M.	C. Thomas

13. As a hydroelectric dam inspector, you must check the valve flow against the planned rates and identify any valve that does not have an increasing flow at each scheduled inspection. If any valve does not meet the planned rate, a maintenance team investigates. Based on yesterday's inspection, which valve must be investigated?

    A. West #2

    B. East #2

    C. East #1

    D. West #1

    E. West #1 and #2

14. The next morning, you notice that another dip in the flow rate occurred at noon on 8/12. You decide to discuss the situation with the inspector that recorded the flow rate. Which inspector do you ask to meet you?

    F. C. Thomas

    G. S. Lobowski

    H. J. Rayburn

    J. M. Mitchell

    K. E. Anderson

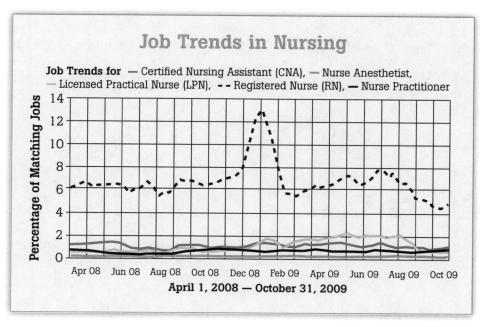

Job Trends in Nursing

Job Trends for — Certified Nursing Assistant (CNA), — Nurse Anesthetist, — Licensed Practical Nurse (LPN), - - Registered Nurse (RN), — Nurse Practitioner

Percentage of Matching Jobs

April 1, 2008 — October 31, 2009

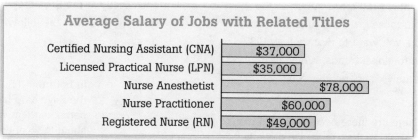

Average Salary of Jobs with Related Titles

Certified Nursing Assistant (CNA)	$37,000
Licensed Practical Nurse (LPN)	$35,000
Nurse Anesthetist	$78,000
Nurse Practitioner	$60,000
Registered Nurse (RN)	$49,000

15. Tracking employment trends is an important part of staying informed as a high school guidance counselor. The line graph above is from an employment Web site. It shows what percentage of the total jobs listed are in each of the five nursing jobs that are graphed. When one of your students asks you for information about the nursing career field, which type of certification would you recommend based on hiring trends?

    A. Registered nurse (RN)

    B. Licensed practical nurse (LPN)

    C. Certified nursing assistant (CNA)

    D. Nurse practitioner

    E. Nurse anesthetist

16. A nursing student explains that he is interested in becoming a nurse anesthetist. Based on the graphics, what guidance can you give him about pursuing this job?

    F. The salary is high, and there are a lot of jobs available compared to other nursing positions.

    G. The salary is low, and there are not a lot of jobs available compared to other nursing positions.

    H. Although the salary is high, there are not as many jobs available compared to other nursing positions.

    J. The salary is mid-range, and there are a lot of jobs available compared to other nursing positions.

    K. Although the salary is low, there are a lot of jobs available compared to other nursing positions.

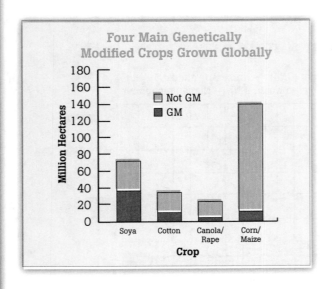

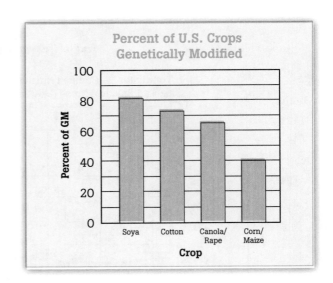

17. As a food scientist you are researching genetically modified (GM) crops grown in the U.S. compared to those grown around the world. In your research, you want to discuss how U.S. trends compare to global trends. Which of the following accurately compares the two?

    A.   There are more hectares of GM crops in the U.S. than there are globally.

    B.   There is a smaller percentage of GM crops in the U.S. than there is globally.

    C.   There are fewer hectares of GM crops in the U.S. than there are globally.

    D.   There is a higher percentage of GM crops in the U.S. than there is globally.

    E.   There is an identical percentage of GM crops in the U.S. as there is globally.

18. The head researcher wants you to look specifically at the Soya crop in the U.S. and globally. Which of the following accurately describes Soya?

    F.   In both the U.S. and globally, the Soya crop has the highest percentage grown genetically; about 80% of the U.S. crop and about 50% of the global crop is GM.

    G.   Only the U.S. Soya crop has the highest percentage grown genetically; about 80% of the U.S. crop is GM.

    H.   In both the U.S. and globally, the Soya crop has the highest percentage grown genetically; about 75% of the U.S. crop and about 20% of the global crop is GM.

    J.   Only the global Soya crop has the highest percentage grown genetically; about 50% of the global crop is GM.

    K.   The Soya crop has more hectares that are GM in the U.S. (about 80) than it does globally (about 37).

Pollutants Table		
Pollutant	**Emission Factor Rating**	
	Natural Gas Turbines	Oil Turbines
CO_2	A	A
Methane	C	NA
N_2O	E	NA
SO_2	B	B
TOC	B	C
VOC	D	E
PM-1 (Condensable)	C	C
PM-2 (Filterable)	C	C
PM-Total (Total of PM-1 and PM-2)		

Emission Factor Ratings	
Rating	**Description**
A	Excellent
B	Above average
C	Average
D	Below average
E	Poor

19. As an engineer for a global fuel company, you research pollutants. You have a pollutant with an above average emission rating in a natural gas turbine. You learn that this pollutant has an average emission rating in an oil turbine. Based on the pollutants table and emission factor rating chart, what is this pollutant?

    A. CO_2

    B. Methane

    C. SO_2

    D. TOC

    E. VOC

20. You are working as a fuel company engineer compiling a study on emission factors of various pollutants and greenhouse gases. Your supervisor asks you to add a row to the Pollutants Table that shows the total emissions ratings for all particulate matter (PM). Based on the pollutants table and rating chart, what emission factor rating should you enter in for PM-Total both for natural gas and oil turbines?

    F. A

    G. B

    H. C

    J. D

    K. E

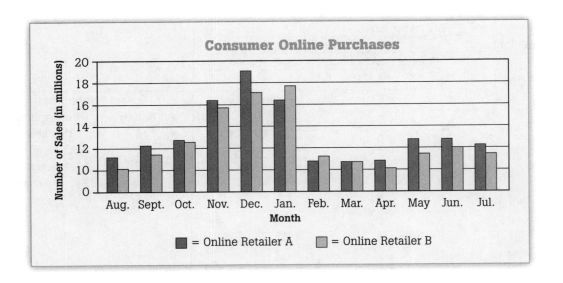

Consumer Online Purchases

21. As the owner of a gift basket company, you sell your products through two different online retailers. In planning for the upcoming year, you are trying to determine which months will be the most profitable. Based on the bar graph, in which month do you have the most sales potential by selling through Retailer B?

    A. November

    B. December

    C. January

    D. February

    E. March

22. Before you plan a 2-week vacation, you want to determine the period during which sales will be the lowest. During which month is it best to take the trip?

    F. August

    G. December

    H. January

    J. April

    K. June

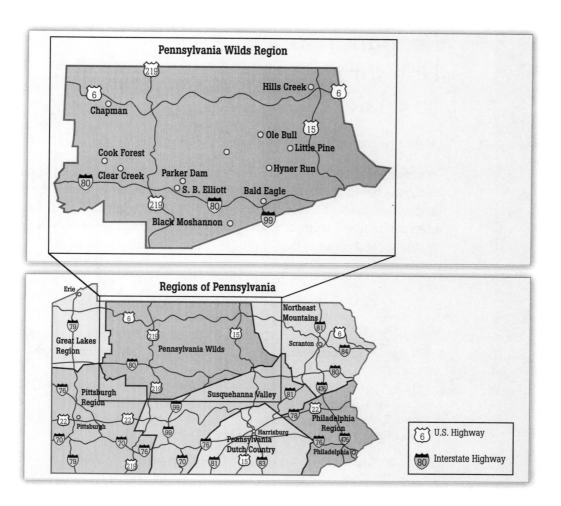

Pennsylvania Wilds Region

Regions of Pennsylvania

6 U.S. Highway

80 Interstate Highway

23. You are a shipping coordinator who regularly chooses routes from Pittsburgh to deliver heavy equipment to customers throughout Pennsylvania. You are scheduling an equipment delivery from your warehouse in Pittsburgh. Including the Pittsburgh region, what is the fewest number of regions the shipment will travel through to make deliveries in both Philadelphia and Scranton in the same trip?

A. 2

B. 3

C. 4

D. 5

E. 6

24. Your company has decided to rent cabins at the Hills Creek State Park for a weeklong retreat that will encourage the department managers to improve their communication skills. According to the maps, which set of directions is the most direct route (least number of routes possible) from the home office in Pittsburgh to Hills Creek State Park?

F. U.S. 22 to U.S. 219 to I-80 to U.S. 15

G. I-76 to I-99 to U.S. 15

H. I-79 to U.S. 6

J. U.S. 22 to U.S. 219

K. I-80 to U.S. 15

Answers are on page 258.

Lesson 14 ■ ■ ■
Use Information from Graphics to Make Decisions

Skill: Use the information to make decisions

In different jobs and for different careers, you will frequently need to make decisions based on specific information. Often, the information will be organized in graphics, such as tables, charts, line graphs, circle graphs, and illustrations. For example, in many workplace and personal purchasing scenarios, you may need to decide what product to buy based on tables of product features and prices.

Skill Examples

DESIGN SOFTWARE OPTIONS			
Software Version	**Released**	**Operating System**	**Cost**
Pro X	Last Year	Magna or Piper	$410.00
Pro Z	This Year	Magna or Piper	$450.00
Pro Z (must already own Pro X)	This Year	Magna or Piper	$160.00
Pro Z Extra	This Year	Piper	$670.00
Pro Z Extra (must already own Pro X)	This Year	Piper	$250.00

Example 1
Use a table to determine what information is displayed.

By looking at the column headings, you can compare options based on version, release year, operating system, and cost.

Example 2
Apply information from graphics to help you make a decision.

If you use only the Magna operating system, look at the column titled "Operating System" and eliminate any software that is not Magna-based.

Skill Practice

Use the table above to answer the following questions.

1. A start-up company needs the software version that is newest, works with Magna, and is the cheapest. Their computers are new and do not have a previous software version. Based on the table, what software meets the company's needs?

   A. Pro X

   B. Pro Z

   C. Pro Z (Upgrade Version)

   D. Pro Z Extra

   E. Pro Z Extra (Upgrade Version)

2. Your company uses Piper-based computers that do not have a previous software version. What is the cheapest way to get Pro Z Extra?

   F. Purchase Pro Z (Upgrade Version)

   G. Purchase Pro Z and Pro Z (Upgrade Version)

   H. Purchase Pro Z Extra

   J. Purchase Pro X and Pro Z Extra (Upgrade Version)

   K. Purchase Pro Z Extra (Upgrade Version)

Try It Out! ■ ■ ■

As a sanitary engineer, you must report high triclosan levels detected in Area 1 to the correct regional manager. Which regional manager should you report this to?

A. Gil Vern

B. Theresa Linth

C. Viv McGuire

D. Lou Burlowski

E. Sylvia Frank

	Regional Manager	Sewage	Pollutants
Area 1	Gil Vern	Residential (toilets, baths, showers, sinks)	NO_3^- $C_{12}H_7Cl_3O_2$
	Theresa Linth	Small business (plastic, cardboard, appliances)	PVC
Area 2	Viv McGuire	Manufacturing (industrial waste, chemical runoff)	Diesel
Area 3	Lou Burlowski	Parks (storm water runoff, leaves, clippings)	Soil
	Sylvia Frank	Small business (food scraps, food packages)	BHA PO_4^{3-}

Pollutant Abbreviations

NO_3^- = Nitrates

$C_{12}H_7Cl_3O_2$ = Triclosan

PVC = Polyvinyl chloride

BHA = food preservative

PO_4^{3-} = Phosphates

Step 1 — Understand the Problem ■ ■ ■

Complete the *Plan for Successful Solving*.

Plan for Successful Solving				
What am I asked to do?	**What are the facts?**	**How do I find the answer?**	**Is there any unnecessary information?**	**What prior knowledge will help me?**
Identify the regional manager to contact.	There are high levels of triclosan in Area 1. Each manager deals with specific pollutants.	Identify the abbreviation for triclosan. Then, locate it within the Area 1 listings.	I do not need to look for the abbreviations for any pollutants besides triclosan.	When using tables to make decisions, I should first try to eliminate options so that I can narrow my focus.

Step 2 — Find and Check Your Answer ■ ■ ■

■ Confirm your understanding of the question and revise your plan as needed.

■ Based on your plan, determine your solution approach: *First, I will skim the "Pollutant Abbreviations" table to identify the abbreviation for triclosan* $(C_{12}H_7Cl_3O_2)$. *Then, I will limit my search by first identifying which managers are in charge of Area 1. Based on the two remaining options, I will look to the "Pollutants" column to determine which manager should be contacted for high levels of* $C_{12}H_7Cl_3O_2$.

■ Check your answer. Review all options to determine if the answer you have selected is the correct one.

■ **Select the correct answer:** A. Gil Vern
By first limiting the search to Area 1, Gil Vern can easily be identified as the regional manager who handles situations in which high levels of triclosan are detected in Area 1.

Problem Solving Tip

Be sure to consider what information you need before reading every piece of information within a table. By doing so, you can eliminate answer options and save time.

Remember!

Graphs, tables, and charts often include abbreviations as well as acronyms. Being familiar with common abbreviations for things such as chemical elements and units of measurement can help you more easily understand the information and the meaning of the content presented in graphics.

Livingston Conference Center

	Small Meeting Rooms		Auditoriums		Seminar Room	Large Meeting Room	Ballroom	Computer Labs		Common Areas	
Room Number	4	7	22	25	15	13	29	5	6	10	20
Capacity	50	50	100	100	75	100	125	50	50	N/A	N/A
Dimensions	22 × 34	20 × 30	45 × 55	40 × 50	30 × 40	35 × 40	110 × 55	20 × 35	20 × 35	101 × 15	101 × 15
Features											
32″ Monitors	X	X									
Teleconferencing	X		X	X	X						
Ethernet Hookup	X							X	X		
Audio Reinforcement			X	X	X	X					
LCD Projector			X	X	X				X		

Design Seminar Schedule of Events

	Event	Speaker	Location	Enrollment
Thursday				
8:00 A.M.–12:30 P.M.	Registration	N/A	10	N/A
9:00–9:15 A.M.	Welcome	Sharon McAdams	29	125
9:30 A.M.–12:00 P.M.	Design Software	Juan Lopez	6	30
1:00–2:50 P.M.	New Computers	Elizabeth Henderson	25	53
3:00–3:30 P.M.	Career Growth	Jason Liang	29	115
3:45–5:00 P.M.	Tomorrow's Technology Today	Maria Santiago	22	75
Friday				
8:00–10:00 A.M.	Sign-In	N/A	20	N/A
9:00–9:50 A.M.	Design History and Practice	Maria Santiago	7	50
10:00 A.M.–12:00 P.M.	Innovative Design	Jason Liang	5	30
1:00–2:50 P.M.	CAD Seminar	Juan Lopez	6	30
3:00–3:30 P.M.	Furthering Your Education	Elizabeth Henderson	29	65
3:45–5:00 P.M.	Seminar Wrap-up	Sharon McAdams	13	90
7:00–11:00 P.M.	Networking Dinner	N/A	29	250

1. You are the event coordinator for a design seminar to be held Thursday morning through Friday evening. The chairperson has requested a room equipped with an LCD projector for an hour-long presentation to 94 attendees at 1:30 P.M. on both days. Which room meets these requirements?

   A. Room 4

   B. Room 6

   C. Room 15

   D. Room 22

   E. Room 25

2. A presenter e-mailed you earlier today. She requested two rooms with Ethernet hookup from 10 A.M. to 11 A.M. on Thursday. There will be 40 attendees in each room. Which two rooms are available?

   F. Rooms 4 and 5

   G. Rooms 4 and 6

   H. Rooms 5 and 6

   J. Rooms 13 and 29

   K. Rooms 22 and 25

Engineering Publishing Catalog

Textbook Code	Full Color	Full Chapter(s) on Special Content					Cost (Per 100)	Reviewed by ABET
		Molecular Engineering	Nanotechnology	Systems Biology	GM Crops	Robotics		
ENG-51Y	Y	✔	✔			✔	$4,800	✔
ENG-76P	N	✔		✔	✔	✔	$4,090	✔
ENG-46L	N		✔			✔	$10,000	✔
ENG-81T	Y	✔	✔	✔	✔	✔	$5,800	✔
ENG-44R	N			✔			$6,000	

Call 1-800-OUR-TEXT for assistance with ordering.
To receive the textbooks by September 1,
you must place your order by July 31.

3. As an engineering instructor, you must choose the textbook you will use to teach your classes. You need a textbook that includes a chapter on nanotechnology and prefer one that costs less than $50 per book. According to the textbook catalog shown, what textbook should you pick?

A. ENG-51Y

B. ENG-76P

C. ENG-46L

D. ENG-81T

E. ENG-44R

4. This semester you are also teaching an advanced engineering class. For this class, you need a textbook that contains chapters on molecular engineering, robotics, and systems biology. You also prefer that the textbook be in full color. According to the textbook catalog shown, what textbook should you pick?

F. ENG-51Y

G. ENG-76P

H. ENG-46L

J. ENG-81T

K. ENG-44R

Northfield Health Clinic Schedule

Doctor	Specialty	Availability This Week		Availability Next Week	
Dr. Chaudhary	Cardiology (heart)	Mon.	9–9:15 A.M. 3–3:15 P.M. 5–5:15 P.M.	Mon.	10:30–10:45 A.M. 5:15–5:30 P.M.
		Tues.	After 4 P.M.	Tues.	N/A
		Wed.	N/A	Wed.	N/A
		Thurs.	2:45–3 P.M.	Thurs.	1:15–1:30 P.M.
		Fri.	N/A	Fri.	Before noon
Dr. Huntington	Otolaryngology (ear, nose & throat)	Mon.	8:45–9 A.M. 4:45–5 P.M.	Mon.	N/A
		Tues.	8:45–9 A.M.	Tues.	N/A
		Wed.	N/A	Wed.	5:15–5:30 P.M.
		Thurs.	N/A	Thurs.	8:45–9 A.M.
		Fri.	8:45–9 A.M.	Fri.	8:45–9 A.M. 4:45–5 P.M.
Dr. Sung	Gastroenterology (stomach and intestines)	Mon.	After 4 P.M.	Mon.	N/A
		Tues.	11:45–12 P.M.	Tues.	N/A
		Wed.	N/A	Wed.	N/A
		Thurs.	3:15–3:30 P.M. 5:15–5:30 P.M.	Thurs.	N/A
		Fri.	8:45–9 A.M.	Fri.	N/A

Patient Messages

Name	Time Called	Day Called	Medical Issue	Time Available	Phone Number
Warren Johnson	6:15 P.M.	Sunday	Abdominal pain; previous intestinal infection	Any Tues. after noon	555-8379
Nina Gomez	7:00 P.M.	Saturday	Minor chest pain	Next Tues. only after 4 P.M.	555-1022
Jacob Evans	9:45 P.M.	Sunday	Chronic pain in nose	Thurs. mornings before 10 A.M.	555-4349
Dorothy McCormick	5:15 A.M.	Sunday	Ear infection	Any day before noon	555-0656
Jessica Sweet	7:00 A.M.	Monday	Heart palpitations	Tuesday before noon or any time on Wednesday	555-8968
Russell Miller	6:45 A.M.	Monday	Chronic high blood pressure	Wednesday afternoon	555-1503

5. You are in charge of scheduling appointments at a health clinic. When you arrive at work at 7:00 A.M. on Monday morning, you have messages from several patients. At what time and with which doctor do you schedule an appointment for Dorothy McCormick?

    A.   Dr. Huntington; next Wed.; 5:15 P.M.

    B.   Dr. Chaudhary; next Fri.; before noon

    C.   Dr. Huntington; this Mon.; 8:45 A.M.

    D.   Dr. Sung; this Fri.; 8:45 A.M.

    E.   Dr. Chaudhary; this Mon.; 9 A.M.

6. Dr. Chaudhary had a cancellation and is available next Tuesday at 4:30 P.M. Which patient should you schedule to take this appointment and why?

    F.   Warren Johnson; has abdominal pain and is available any Tuesday after noon

    G.   Nina Gomez; has minor chest pain and is available next Tuesday after 4:00 P.M.

    H.   Jacob Evans; has chronic pain in his nose and is available Thursday mornings before 10:00 A.M.

    J.   Jessica Sweet; has heart palpitations and is available Tuesday before noon and any time on Wednesday

    K.   Russell Miller; has chronic high blood pressure and is available any Wednesday afternoon

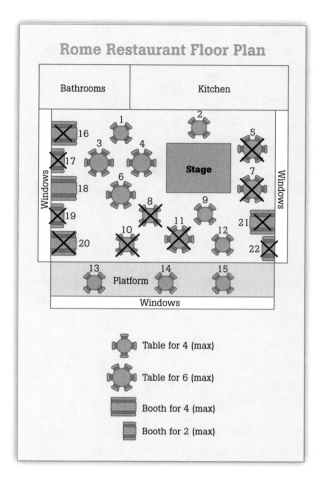

Rome Restaurant Floor Plan

Bathrooms

Kitchen

Stage

Platform

Windows

Table for 4 (max)

Table for 6 (max)

Booth for 4 (max)

Booth for 2 (max)

Reservation List

Saturday 6/4

6:30			8:00		
Irving (4)	O	#8	Slavin (4)	E	#16
Ewing (6) W	E	#5	Caldo (2)		
Costa (2) B	O	#17	Sing (4)	E	#21
Wu (5) W	E	#7			
7:00			**8:30**		
McDonald (2) W B	E	#22	Martinez (2)		
Connors (3)	O	#10	Carter (4) B, W		
Del Rosario (4) B W	O	#20			
Lark (2) W	E	#19			
7:30			**9:00**		
Stewart (5) W	O	#11			
Ortiz (4) W B					

Notes
- Number in parentheses = People in party
- Number after number sign (#) = Table or booth number
- B = Requests booth   O = Arrived on time
- W = Requests window seat   E = Arrived early
- P = Requests platform section   L = Arrived late

7. As a hostess at a restaurant, you keep track of reservations and seat people when they arrive. The Ortiz party arrives fifteen minutes late and asks that you do not seat them near the bathroom. Where do you seat them?

  A. Table 15

  B. Table 16

  C. Table 18

  D. Table 19

  E. Table 2

8. You generally allow 90 minutes for a party to eat and for the server to clear and set the table. A party of two without a reservation comes in at 7:50. They ask if they can be seated in a booth. You want to seat them as quickly as possible, but must be sure that customers who have made reservations are not impacted. What should you tell the party?

  F. Yes, they can sit at table 17.

  G. No, but they can wait about 30 minutes and sit at table 20.

  H. Yes, they can sit at table 21.

  J. Yes, they can sit at table 19.

  K. No, but they can wait about 30 minutes and sit at either table 19 or 22.

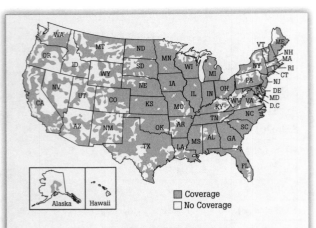

National Mobile 1

Monthly Minutes	Price	Per-Minute Rate After Allowance
450	$39.99	$0.45
900	$59.99	$0.40
1,350	$79.99	$0.35
Unlimited National Minutes	$99.99	N/A

INTERNATIONAL RATES*	
Location	Price
North America	
Canada	$0.09
Europe	
France	$0.17
Germany	$0.27
Italy	$0.36
Netherlands	$0.28
Spain	$0.32
United Kingdom	$0.26
South America	
Argentina	$0.36
Chile	$0.35
Venezuela	$0.36
Asia	
China	$0.14
India	$0.30
Japan	$0.19
Korea	$0.23

*With an International Calling Plan.

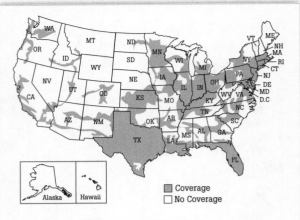

Flitter Wireless

Monthly Minutes	Price	Per-Minute Rate After Allowance
200	$25.99	$0.50
450	$35.99	$0.50
900	$55.99	$0.45
Unlimited National Minutes	$115.99	N/A

INTERNATIONAL RATES*	
Location	Price
North America	
Canada	$0.99
Europe	
France	$0.09
Germany	$0.17
Italy	$0.23
Netherlands	$0.20
Spain	$0.25
United Kingdom	$0.09
South America	
Argentina	$0.40
Chile	$0.38
Venezuela	$0.37
Asia	
China	$0.18
India	$0.50
Japan	$0.23
Korea	$0.45

*With an International Calling Plan.

9. You are an administrative assistant for a company that has salespeople all across the country. You need to set up salespeople with either National Mobile 1 or Flitter Wireless based on their location, their minute usage, and their international calling. What is one reason you might decide to assign a salesperson to Flitter Wireless?

   A. He is located in Wyoming, needs unlimited minutes, and makes no international calls.

   B. He is located in northern Texas, needs unlimited minutes, and frequently calls Canada.

   C. He is located in Florida, needs 450 minutes and rarely goes over his limit, and frequently calls Europe.

   D. He is located in Maine, needs unlimited minutes, and frequently calls Asia.

   E. He is located in South Dakota, needs 450 minutes, and frequently calls India.

10. The Regional Sales Manager is based in Texas and travels all over the Midwest. The most important thing is for her phone to work where she lives and travels, but she also needs unlimited monthly minutes. She makes frequent calls to Europe. Which cell phone provider do you sign her up for and why?

   F. Flitter Wireless; because they have the best rates on calls to Europe

   G. National Mobile 1; because they have the best rates on calls to Europe

   H. Flitter Wireless; because they have the best coverage in Texas.

   J. Flitter Wireless; because they have a lower priced 900-minute plan

   K. National Mobile 1; because they have the most coverage in the Midwest and a lower monthly price for unlimited calls

11. One of the sales associates who lives in Canada needs 200 minutes a month and frequently calls Asia. Which provider do you give him and why?

   A. Flitter Wireless; because they have low rates to Asia

   B. National Mobile 1; because they have low rates to Canada

   C. Flitter Wireless; because they have a 200-minute plan

   D. National Mobile 1; because they have low rates to Asia

   E. There is not enough information to make a decision.

12. A new sales associate lives in Maine, uses 1,300 minutes a month at most, and frequently calls Canada. Which provider and plan do you give her and why?

   F. Flitter Wireless; Unlimited minutes; this plan has the most minutes for the least amount and low prices to Canada

   G. National Mobile 1; 450 minutes; this plan is inexpensive and has low prices to Canada

   H. National Mobile 1; 1,350 minutes; this plan has coverage in Maine and low prices to Canada

   J. Flitter Wireless; 200 minutes; this plan is inexpensive and has coverage in Maine

   K. Flitter Wireless; 1,350 minutes; this plan has low prices to Canada and coverage in Maine

Light Southwestern-Style Vegetable

Ingredients: Chicken Broth, Celery, Tomatoes, Carrots, Green Sweet Peppers, Corn, Black Beans, Red Bell Peppers, Salt, Sugar, Onion Powder, Garlic, Chili Pepper.

Nutrition Facts

Serving Size 1 cup
Servings per Container about 2

Amount Per Serving	
Calories 60	Calories from Fat 5
	% Daily Value
Total Fat .5g	1%
Saturated Fat 0g	0%
Trans Fat 0g	
Polyunsaturated Fat 0g	
Monounsaturated Fat 0g	
Cholesterol 0g	0%
Sodium 690mg	29%
Total Carbohydrate 12g	4%
Dietary Fibers 4g	16%
Sugars 3g	
Protein 3g	
Vitamin A 20%	Vitamin C 0%
Calcium 4%	Iron 6%

Creamy Chicken Wild Rice

Ingredients: Chicken Broth, Cooked White Chicken Meat, Wild Rice, Celery, Rice, Onions, Modified Food Starch, Soybean Oil, Water, Salt, Sugar, Soy Protein Concentrate, Butter, Dried Egg Yolk.

NOTE: Contains egg, soy, and milk ingredients

Nutrition Facts

Serving Size 1 cup
Servings per Container about 2

Amount Per Serving	
Calories 140	Calories from Fat 45
	% Daily Value
Total Fat 5g	8%
Saturated Fat 1g	6%
Trans Fat 0g	
Polyunsaturated Fat 2g	
Monounsaturated Fat 1.5g	
Cholesterol 15mg	4%
Sodium 860mg	36%
Total Carbohydrate 18g	6%
Dietary Fibers 1g	4%
Sugars 1g	
Protein 6g	
Vitamin A 0%	Vitamin C 0%
Calcium 0%	Iron 2%

Italian-Style Wedding

Ingredients: Chicken Broth, Carrots, Cooked Meatballs (Beef, Water, Eggs, Textured Soy Protein Concentrate, Romano Cheese, Bread Crumbs, Corn Syrup, Sugar, Hydrogenated Soybean Oil, Salt, Yeast, Whey, Soy Flour, Onions, Natural Flavor, Garlic Powder, and Parsley), Enriched Tubetti Pasta (Egg Whites, Riboflavin, Folic Acid), Spinach, Onions, Modified Corn Starch, Carrot Puree, Hydrolyzed Vegetable Protein (Corn, Soy).

NOTE: Contains wheat, egg, soy, and milk ingredients

Nutrition Facts

Serving Size 1 cup
Servings per Container about 2

Amount Per Serving	
Calories 90	Calories from Fat 20
	% Daily Value
Total Fat 2g	3%
Saturated Fat 1g	4%
Trans Fat 0g	
Polyunsaturated Fat	1g
Monounsaturated Fat	0g
Cholesterol 10mg	3%
Sodium 480mg	20%
Total Carbohydrate 11g	4%
Dietary Fibers 1g	4%
Sugars 2g	
Protein 5g	
Vitamin A 30%	Vitamin C 0%
Calcium 2%	Iron 4%

13. As a nutritionist, you help your clients choose the meals that best fit their dietary needs. You are working with a patient who is on a reduced sodium diet because he has high blood pressure. Which soup do you recommend for him and why?

    A. Creamy Chicken Wild Rice; because it contains 4% of the daily value of sodium

    B. Italian-Style Wedding; because it contains spinach

    C. Creamy Chicken Wild Rice; because it contains milk ingredients

    D. Light Southwestern-Style Vegetable; because it has the fewest calories

    E. Italian-Style Wedding; because it has only 480mg of sodium

14. Another patient needs a soup that is high in vitamin A, has no trans fat, and does not contain any soy products because she is allergic to soy. Which soup do you recommend and why?

    F. Italian-Style Wedding; because it contains no trans fat

    G. Creamy Chicken Wild Rice; because it contains milk ingredients

    H. Light Southwestern-Style Vegetable; because it contains no soy

    J. Creamy Chicken Wild Rice; because it contains no trans fat

    K. Italian-Style Wedding; because it is high in vitamin A

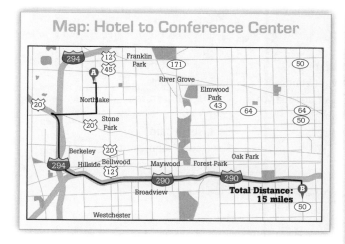

Map: Hotel to Conference Center

Franklin Park
River Grove
Elmwood Park
Northlake
Stone Park
Berkeley
Hillside Bellwood
Maywood Forest Park
Oak Park
Broadview
Westchester

Total Distance: 15 miles

Transportation Costs

Yellow Cab	
Flag Pull (price for first mile)	$3.00
Additional Mile	$1.50
Every 6 Minutes of Waiting Time	$2.00
Additional Passenger	$1.00
Airport Fee	Flat $25.00 fee, includes tolls and tip. Additional $5.00 charge per passenger.
Tip	15% of total (for regular service) Tipping is considered a standard courtesy.
Royalty Hotel Shuttle	
Fee Up to 10 Miles	$15.50
Fee Up to 20 Miles	$25.00
Fee Up to 30 Miles	$35.50
Includes	Tip, no extra fee for wait time, price is per passenger

15. You work as an administrative assistant and must book trips for employees. The assistant to the vice president is going on a business trip for a conference. You need to instruct her on how to get from the Royalty Hotel at Point A on East Wagner Drive to the conference center at Point B on Rte. 50. The total distance there is 15 miles and the meeting is an hour long. You should choose the transportation that makes the most sense and is the least expensive. Which type of transportation should she take to the conference center, and what is the cost?

    A.   Royalty Hotel Shuttle; $15.50

    B.   Royalty Hotel Shuttle; $25.00

    C.   Yellow Cab; $22.50

    D.   Yellow Cab; $24.00

    E.   Yellow Cab; $27.60

16. The vice president is also going to the conference and staying at the Royalty Hotel. You need to plan how she will get from the hotel to the airport. The airport is a 20-minute drive and 13 miles away. She will be taking her assistant with her to the airport and would like to take whichever transportation makes the most sense and is the least expensive. Which type of transportation should they take and why?

    F.   Royalty Hotel Shuttle; it is only $25.00 for the pair

    G.   Yellow Cab; it is only $30.00 for the pair

    H.   Royalty Hotel Shuttle; it is only $30.00 for the pair

    J.   Yellow Cab; it is paid by the mile, which is the lowest price

    K.   Royal Shuttle; it is only $50.00 for the pair

Flooring Material Options

Type	Maintenance	Durability	Comfort
Marble	Low	Seal to prevent stains	Cold, hard, slick
Terra cotta tile	Average	Seal to protect against wear	Cold, hard, textured
Concrete	Average	Extremely durable	Cold, hard
Wood parquet	Low	Extremely durable	Cool, semi-hard
Laminate	Low	Durable	Semi-cool, semi-hard

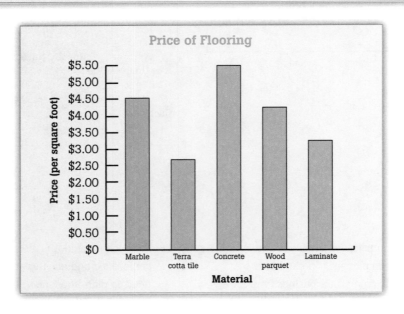

Price of Flooring

17. You are decorating your office to impress the potential clients who want your architecture firm to design a new building. You have limited your options to five different materials. Your office suite is approximately 900 square feet, your budget is $3,000, and you prefer whatever option has the lowest maintenance. Which material do you select?

   A. Marble

   B. Terra cotta tile

   C. Concrete

   D. Wood parquet

   E. Laminate

18. You signed a contract with a new client, increasing the amount you can spend on flooring to $4,000. Based on your new budget, which type of flooring do you select?

   F. Marble

   G. Terra cotta tile

   H. Concrete

   J. Wood parquet

   K. Laminate

Flight Options

	Airport	Departure (local time)	Arrival (local time)	Details	Price (Roundtrip)
Option 1	JFK	9:15 P.M.	11:32 P.M.	Direct flight; 3 hrs 17 min	$220
	Chicago O'Hare International	1:11 P.M.	4:44 P.M.	Direct flight; 2 hrs 33 min	
Option 2	JFK	5:27 P.M.	7:03 P.M.	Direct flight; 2 hrs 36 min	$250
	Chicago O'Hare International	9:15 A.M.	12:27 P.M.	Direct flight; 2 hrs 12 min	
Option 3	JFK	7:55 P.M.	9:20 P.M.	Direct flight; 2 hrs 25 min	$195
	Chicago Midway International	9:15 A.M.	12:27 P.M.	Direct flight; 2 hrs 12 min	
Option 4	JFK	6:34 P.M.	10:20 P.M.	1 layover; 4 hrs 46 min	$160
	Chicago Midway International	7:00 P.M.	1:24 A.M.	1 layover; 5 hrs 24 min	

19. You are an administrative assistant booking flights for New York employees to visit the Chicago office. The morning that the managing editor returns, she must attend a breakfast meeting from 8:00 A.M. to 9:30 A.M. at the Chicago office. That evening, she must also attend a dinner meeting with authors in New York at 7:30 P.M. She prefers direct flights if possible. Per company cost-saving measures, you should select the least expensive flight that fits the editor's schedule. Which airport and flight should you book for her and why?

    A.   Option 2; it is a direct flight.

    B.   Option 3; it is a direct flight and it costs $195.

    C.   Option 4; it costs $160.

    D.   Option 3; it allows her to attend both meetings.

    E.   Option 1; it allows her to attend both meetings.

20. In which of the following situations would you make the decision to book Option 4 for the managing editor's flight out of Chicago?

    F.   if she has to arrive in Chicago for a meeting that starts at noon

    G.   if she wants to take a direct flight to the airport closest to the hotel

    H.   if her budget is less than $200.00 and she can reschedule her dinner meeting

    J.   if she has to be in New York by the early afternoon

    K.   if her budget is less than $250 and she wants to be close to the hotel

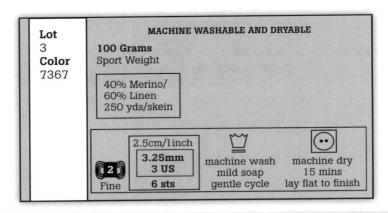

Common Yarn Weights

Yarn Weight	Number ID and Symbol	U.S. Needle Size	Common Uses
Lace	0	000-1	Lace knitting
Super fine, fingering, or baby-weight	1	1-3	Light layettes, socks
Fine or sports-weight	2	3-6	Light sweaters, baby blankets, accessories
Light worsted or DK (double-knitting)	3	5-7	Sweaters and other garmets, lightweight scarves
Medium- or worsted-weight, afghan, Aran	4	7-9	Sweaters, blankets, outdoor wear (hats, scarves, mittens, etc.)
Bulky or chunky	5	10-11	Rugs, jackets, blankets
Super bulky	6	13-15	Heavy blankets and rugs, sweaters

21. You own and operate a craft store that focuses on knitting. Over time, you have lost customers to larger retail chains. To attract younger customers, you are starting a class for beginning knitters. As part of your first class, you ask the students to study a yarn label. Which information on the yarn label determines what students can make with the yarn?

   A. number ID and symbol

   B. lot number

   C. color

   D. care instructions

   E. dye number

22. Based on the yarn label and the table, what would you use the yarn to make?

   F. lace

   G. scarves

   H. blankets

   J. rugs

   K. baby blankets

Credit Card Offers

Credit Card	Interest Rate (APR)	Annual Fee	Balance Transfer	Cash Back	Frequent-Flyer Miles	Credit Score Needed	Notes
CashIn	14.9	--	Yes	2% at gas stations; 1% other purchases	--	760-850	--
SpendIt	13.24	--	Yes	--	--	660-850	E-mail and text alerts
Stuff	14.99	--	--	5% in specific categories	--	None	Building credit
Teller	11.99	--	Yes	--	--	660-850	$0 liability on unauthorized purchases
Glint	18.23	$39	4% of each transaction (Min $10)	--	--	None	Building credit

23. You are in the process of starting a catering business. You carefully track every penny spent, and you decide you need to use a credit card rather than cash to purchase some supplies. You need a credit card that has a low interest rate and takes advantage of your 780 credit score. Based on the information presented, which credit card would you choose?

    A.   CashIn

    B.   SpendIt

    C.   Stuff

    D.   Teller

    E.   Glint

24. You make deliveries in a company van and are frequently filling the gas tank. Your credit score is 780. Which card do you qualify for that provides rewards that could help your business?

    F.   CashIn

    G.   SpendIt

    H.   Stuff

    J.   Teller

    K.   Glint

Answers are on page 258.

Level 6 Performance Assessment

The following problems will test your ability to answer questions at a Level 6 rating of difficulty. These problems are similar to those that appear on a Career Readiness Certificate test. For each question, you can refer to the answer key for answer justifications. The answer justifications provide an explanation of why each answer option is either correct or incorrect and indicate the skill lesson that should be referred to if further review of a particular skill is needed.

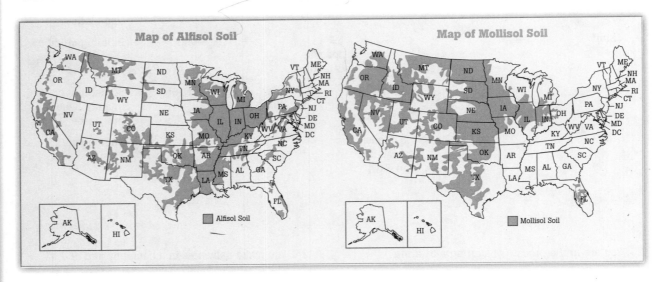

1. You are a writer for a scientific agricultural journal, working on an article about the different soils in the United States. According to soil maps shown, what state has both alfisol soil and mollisol soil?

  A. New York

  B. Arkansas

  C. Illinois

  D. Pennsylvania

  E. Nebraska

2. Alfisol soil is good for growing crops. The principal agricultural crops grown on afisol soil are corn, wheat, and wine grapes. Mollisol soil is also highly farmable soil. It is used principally for growing grain and cereal crops. In the United States, the region that produces much of the country's grain crop is called the Grain Belt. Given this information and using the maps above, what is one conclusion you can draw?

  F. Iowa is part of the Grain Belt.

  G. Nevada grows lots of wine grapes.

  H. Florida produces the most corn.

  J. The East Coast is part of the Grain Belt.

  K. Georgia produces the most grain.

Hair Color Guide

Type of Hair Color	Price	Stylists	Does Not Contain	Contains	Good For	Lasts
Semi-Permanent Hair Color	$45	Soledad, Michelle, Sean, & Gabby	Ammonia, Peroxide	Aloe Vera, Vitamins	Gray-blending; Subtle color enhancement; Use after relaxing or perming; Darkening hair one or two levels	6–12 Shampoos
Demi-Permanent Hair Color	$75	Sean, Michelle, & Gabby	Ammonia	Botanic-derived ingredients; (low levels of Peroxide)	Intense color enhancement; Cover and blend gray hair; Use after relaxing or perming; Darkening hair more than 3 levels	12–24 Shampoos
Permanent Hair Color	$120	Sean & Gabby	Ammonia	Peroxide	Darker or lighter change; Gray Coverage (Do not use after relaxing or perming)	Permanent

3. As a receptionist in a hair salon, you are in charge of scheduling appointments. A customer comes in and wants a demi-permanent hair coloring. What is one conclusion you could draw about your client?

A. She is sensitive to dyes that contain peroxide.

B. She wants a color that will wash out in 6–12 shampoos.

C. She wants to spend less than $50 on her hair color.

D. Soledad is her preferred stylist.

E. She wants temporary color that will cover and blend gray hair.

4. Based on the chart above, what conclusion can you draw about the use of peroxide in hair dyes?

F. Peroxide is an ingredient that helps to lighten or darken hair.

G. Peroxide is used only to darken hair.

H. If hair dye contains peroxide, it cannot be used after perming or relaxing.

J. Peroxide is an ingredient that must be used in all hair dyes.

K. Peroxide is used only when the hair dye is permanent.

Train Options

	Departure Station	Departure Time (local time)	Arrival Time (local time)	Details	Price
Option 1	Boston–South Station	11:00 A.M.	6:50 P.M.	Standard Train; Coach; 7 hrs. 50 min	$130
	Washington, DC–Union Station	12:00 P.M.	7:50 P.M.	Standard Train; Coach; 7 hrs. 50 min.	
Option 2	Boston–South Station	8:15 A.M.	3:01 P.M.	Express Train; Business Class; 6 hrs. 46 min.	$372
	Washington, DC–Union Station	12:15 P.M.	6:45 P.M.	Express Train; Business Class; 6 hrs. 30 min.	

Flight Options

	Departure Airport	Departure Time (local time)	Arrival Time (local time)	Details	Price
Option 1	Boston–Logan International	4:00 P.M.	9:32 P.M.	Coach; 1 stop; 5 hrs. 32 min.	$120
	Washington–Dulles International	3:00 P.M.	7:15 P.M.	Coach; 1 stop; 4 hrs. 15 min.	
Option 2	Boston–Logan International	2:15 P.M.	3:46 P.M.	Coach; Non-stop; 1 hr. 31 min.	$162
	Washington–Dulles International	9:35 A.M.	10:54 P.M.	Coach; Non-stop; 1 hr. 19 min.	
Option 3	Boston–Logan International	4:47 P.M.	10:01 P.M.	First Class; 1 stop; 5 hrs. 14 min.	$440
	Washington–Dulles International	8:10 A.M.	12:56 P.M.	First Class; 1 stop; 4 hrs. 46 min.	
Option 4	Boston–Logan International	9:15 A.M.	10:38 A.M.	First Class; Non-stop; 1 hr. 23 min.	$1,381
	Washington–Dulles International	10:45 A.M.	12:05 P.M.	First Class; Non-stop; 1 hr. 20 min.	

5. As an administrative assistant, you are responsible for booking trips for the sales team. You are booking a round-trip business trip for one of your sales representatives to go from Boston to Washington, DC. The total round-trip budget for her trip is $200. She has requested that you book the quickest possible trip. According to the information shown, what is the best travel option for her trip?

A. Flight option 1

B. Train option 1

C. Flight option 2

D. Train option 2

E. Flight option 4

6. The vice president of sales is also going to Washington, DC, from Boston. He has requested that you book him on the express train (Train option 2). Which of the following is not a reasonable conclusion?

F. He wants to arrive in Washington, DC by 3:30 P.M.

G. He has a higher travel budget than the sales representative.

H. He is not concerned about how long it takes him to reach his destination.

J. He needs to get there in the quickest possible way.

K. He prefers to travel on trains instead of airplanes.

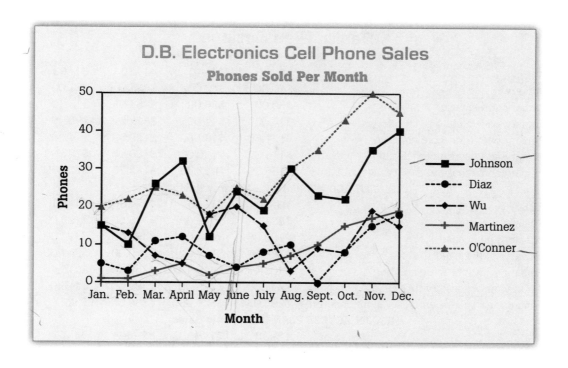

D.B. Electronics Cell Phone Sales

Phones Sold Per Month

7. You are an assistant manager at an electronics store that sells cell phones. You are reviewing the yearly report of the number of cell phones your sales associates sold each month. Based only on the sales report, which sales associate should be considered for a bonus?

    A.   Johnson

    B.   Diaz

    C.   Wu

    D.   Martinez

    E.   O'Conner

8. What is one conclusion you can draw by looking at the graph?

    F.   Wu is the least successful at selling cell phones.

    G.   O'Conner sold the most cell phones each month.

    H.   Halfway through the year, Martinez's cell phone sales began to consistently increase.

    J.   Halfway through the year, Wu's cell phone sales began to consistently decrease.

    K.   Every sales associate sold more phones in November than in December.

Health Plan Options

HEALTH ACCESS PLAN A—Monthly Rates

AGE	18–30	31–40	41–50	51–63
Primary	$40.00	$43.00	$48.00	$61.00
Primary and spouse	$80.00	$86.00	$96.00	$122.00
Primary with 1 child	$74.00	$77.00	$82.00	$95.00
Primary with 2 or more children	$121.60	$124.60	$129.60	$142.60
Primary and spouse with 1 child	$114.00	$120.00	$130.00	$156.00
Primary and spouse with 2 or more children	$166.70	$172.70	$182.70	$208.70

HEALTH ACCESS PLAN B—Monthly Rates

AGE	18–30	31–40	41–50	51–63
Primary	$83.00	$97.00	$128.00	$196.00
Primary and spouse	$166.00	$194.00	$256.00	$392.00
Primary with 1 child	$134.00	$148.00	$179.00	$247.00
Primary with 2 or more children	$205.40	$219.40	$250.40	$318.40
Primary and spouse with 1 child	$217.00	$245.00	$307.00	$443.00
Primary and spouse with 2 or more children	$296.05	$324.05	$386.05	$522.05

HEALTH ACCESS PLAN C—Monthly Rates

AGE	18–30	31–40	41–50	51–63
Primary	$104.00	$118.00	$154.00	$234.00
Primary and spouse	$205.00	$236.00	$308.00	$465.00
Primary with 1 child	$169.00	$183.00	$219.00	$299.00
Primary with 2 or more children	$260.00	$274.00	$310.00	$390.00
Primary and spouse with 1 child	$273.00	$301.00	$373.00	$533.00
Primary and spouse with 2 or more children	$373.75	$401.75	$473.75	$633.75

9. You work in human resources helping new employees choose one of three health plans. A new employee makes an appointment with you for help in choosing a plan. Which of the following questions might you ask him to help figure out which is the right plan for him?

A. Are you a smoker?

B. Do you have children?

C. Do you need dental care?

D. Are you the primary insurance provider for the family?

E. Can you afford $700 a month?

10. An employee would like to add her spouse to her health plan. If the spouse meets eligibility requirements, what is the difference in the cost?

F. $40

G. $83

H. Not enough information. You need to know her age and if she is the primary insurance provider for her family.

J. Not enough information. You need to know which plan she has.

K. Not enough information. You need to know the spouse's age and which plan the employee has.

Carmichael Civic Center Room Specifications

	Luxury Suite	Super Suite	Priority Suite	Clubhouse Lounge	Atrium	Ballroom	Field House*	Outdoor BBQ Space*	Parking Lots
Room Dimension									
Square Footage	1,850	3,800	4,100	13,000	47,000	60,000	80,000	25,000	9,000,000 (over 200 acres)
Ceiling (max ft.)	8	9	8	8-40	8-40	8-40	70	—	—
Capacity by Function Type									
Theater	24	80	120	200	1,200	1,200	2,500	2,000	—
Classroom	12	20	105	100	200	200	2,000	—	—
Cocktail Reception	30	70	150	300	1,200	2,000	2,500	2,000	—
Banquet (sit-down)	20	60	12	200	900	1,400	2,500	1,100	—

* Not attached to Civic Center. Shuttle available; departs from center entrance and north end of parking lot.

11. As an event planner for a computer supply company, you are planning a cocktail reception followed by a sit-down banquet for 1,100 people at the Carmichael Civic Center. Which two rooms should you use?

    A. Atrium for cocktails; Ballroom for the banquet

    B. Theater for cocktails; Atrium for the banquet

    C. Field House for cocktails; Ballroom for the banquet

    D. Ballroom for cocktails; Field House for the banquet

    E. Clubhouse Lounge for cocktails; Atrium for the banquet

12. You are also planning a special rewards ceremony cocktail reception for the company's top 25 sales representatives and their dates. Which room should you use?

    F. Priority Suite

    G. Super Suite

    H. Luxury Suite

    J. Atrium

    K. Clubhouse Lounge

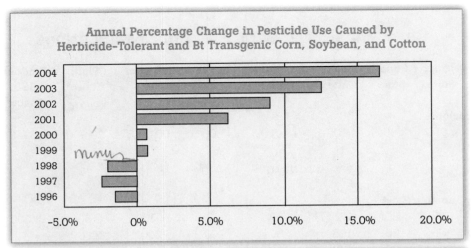

Annual Percentage Change in Pesticide Use Caused by Herbicide-Tolerant and Bt Transgenic Corn, Soybean, and Cotton

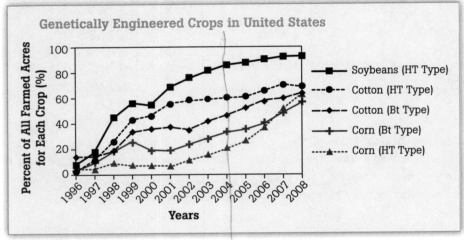

Genetically Engineered Crops in United States

13. You work as a scientific consultant to a government agency studying the effect of genetically engineered crops. What can you determine from the two graphs?

    A. Growing genetically engineered crops has no negative effects.

    B. After an initial decrease when genetically engineered crops were introduced, pesticide use has increased every year.

    C. Since 1996, the use of pesticides has decreased.

    D. The yield of genetically engineered crops has increased more than 15 percent.

    E. Less pesticide is needed to grow genetically engineered crops.

14. According to the graph, what was the overall pattern of growth of the percentage of farmed acres growing soybeans (HT type) from 2000 to 2008?

    F. It decreased and then increased.

    G. It increased and then decreased.

    H. It remained the same.

    J. It steadily decreased.

    K. It steadily increased.

Pembroke Fruit Orchard Ripening Times

Fruit	Ripening Time
Apples	
Early Gold	Late August
McIntosh	Early September to Mid-October
Golden Delicious	October
Red Delicious	Late September to October
Empire	October
Idared	Mid- to Late October
Peaches	
White Peaches	Mid-July to Mid-August
Yellow Peaches	Mid-July to Mid-August
Berries	
Cherries	Late June to Mid-July
Blueberries	Early July to Early August
Blackberries	Late July to Late August

Pembroke Fruit Orchard Map

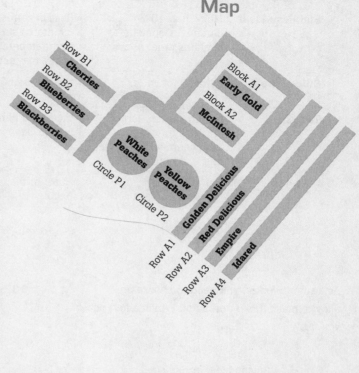

Row B1 Cherries
Row B2 Blueberries
Row B3 Blackberries
Circle P1 White Peaches
Circle P2 Yellow Peaches
Block A1 Early Gold
Block A2 McIntosh
Row A1 Golden Delicious
Row A2 Red Delicious
Row A3 Empire
Row A4 Idared

15. As an orchard worker at a fruit farm, you harvest fruit and answer customers' questions. In late August, a customer is looking for ripe berries to make a pie. Where on the farm do you send her?

   A. Block A1

   B. Row B3

   C. Row B1

   D. Circle P2

   E. Row A3

16. A teacher and her students arrive at the orchard on a field trip, and she takes her class to the rows of apple trees. She asks you to help teach the students about ripening times. Which of the apples in the rows ripens the earliest?

   F. Early Gold

   G. McIntosh

   H. Golden Delicious

   J. Empire

   K. Red Delicious

Some Iron Alloys

Alloy	Contains	Properties	Uses
Stainless Steel	More than 10% chromium, sometimes contains other alloys	Resists corrosion, maintains strength at high temperatures, easily maintained	Automotive and food processing products, medical and health equipment, decorative applications
Silicon Steel	Silicon	Has magnetic properties	Transformers, power generators, electric motors
Tool Steel	Strong carbide forms (such as tungsten, molybdenum, vanadium, and chromium)	Increased hardness and resistance to heat	Tools (axes, metal cutters, and others)
Cast Iron	Carbon	Hard, brittle, easily fusible	Pots and pans, bridges

17. As an iron worker, you need to choose an alloy to make a blender motor. Which alloys could you use?

    A. Silicon steel or tool steel

    B. Stainless steel or cast iron

    C. Stainless steel or silicon steel

    D. Cast iron or silicon steel

    E. Tool steel or cast iron

18. You are a civil engineer building an electric motor. According to the table, which iron alloy should you use?

    F. Stainless steel

    G. Silicon steel

    H. Tool steel

    J. Cast iron

    K. Any of the alloys will work.

Metropolitan Daily Newspaper Ad Rates

		1 X	5 X	13 X	26 X	29 X	52 X
Full Page	4/color	$11,990	$9,592	$8,753	$8,393	$7,794	$7,194
	B&W	$10,900	$8,720	$7,957	$7,630	$7,085	$6,540
Half Page	4/color	$6,710	$5,368	$4,898	$4,697	$4,362	$4,026
	B&W	$6,100	$4,880	$4,453	$4,270	$3,965	$3,660
Third Page	4/color	$4,620	$3,696	$3,373	$3,234	$3,003	$2,772
	B&W	$4,200	$3,360	$3,066	$2,940	$2,730	$2,520
Quarter Page	4/color	$3,630	$2,904	$2,650	$2,541	$2,360	$2,178
	B&W	$3,300	$2,640	$2,409	$2,310	$2,145	$1,980
Sixth Page	4/color	$1,650	$1,320	$1,205	$1,155	$1,073	$990
	B&W	$1,500	$1,200	$1,095	$1,050	$975	$900
Eighth Page	4/color	$1,078	$862	$787	$755	$701	$647
	B&W	$980	$784	$715	$686	$637	$588
Twelfth Page	4/color	$715	$572	$522	$501	$465	$429
	B&W	$650	$520	$475	$455	$423	$390
Business Card	4/color	$330	$264	$241	$231	$215	$198
	B&W	$300	$240	$219	$210	$195	$180

19. You are a marketing assistant for a high-end clothing boutique. The marketing manager asks you to schedule an ad to run in the *Metropolitan Daily* at least 29 times. She also told you that your budget is $2,500 per ad if you run the ad 29 times and $1,400 per ad if you run the ad 52 times. The two most important things for the ad are that it should appear as big as possible and in color. Which ad do you run?

    A. Twelfth Page; 4/color; 52 times

    B. Third Page; 4/color; 29 times

    C. Quarter Page; 4/color; 52 times

    D. Quarter Page; 4/color; 29 times

    E. Full Page; 4/color; 52 times

20. Because of a drop in sales, the same marketing manager has decided that the ad must run as many times as possible, but it is now acceptable for the ad to be in black and white. Your budget remains the same, $2,500 per ad for 29 times and $1,400 per ad for 52 times. Which ad do you run?

    F. Quarter Page; B&W; 29 times

    G. Sixth Page; B&W; 52 times

    H. Quarter Page; 4/color; 29 times

    J. Quarter Page; 4/color; 52 times

    K. Sixth Page; 4/color; 52 times

Fast Food Nutritional Information

	Hamburger (ketchup, mustard, pickles, and onions)	Chicken Sandwich (mayo dressing and lettuce)	Fish Sandwich (tartar sauce and cheese)
Serving Size	3.5 oz. (100 g)	5 oz. (143 g)	5 oz. (142 g)
Calories	250	360	380
Calories from Fat	80	150	170
Total Fat (g)	9	16	18
Saturated Fat (g)	3.5	3	3.5
Trans Fat (g)	0.5	0	0
Cholesterol (mg)	25	35	40
Sodium (mg)	520	830	640
Carbohydrates	31	40	38
Dietary Fiber (g)	2	2	2
Sugars (g)	6	5	5
Protein (g)	12	14	15
Vitamin A (% daily value)	0	0	2
Vitamin C (% daily value)	2	2	5
Calcium (% daily value)	10	10	15
Iron (% daily value)	15	15	2

21. You are a nutritionist reviewing nutrition information at a fast-food restaurant to help your clients make informed decisions when they go out to eat. What is one reason you might decide to recommend that your client does not order a chicken sandwich?

    A. It has the most total fat.

    B. It has the most sodium.

    C. It has the most calories.

    D. It has the least amount of iron.

    E. It has the least amount of saturated fat.

22. Why might you decide to recommend the hamburger to your clients?

    F. It has the least calories from fat.

    G. It is the largest sandwich.

    H. It has the most calcium.

    J. It has the least sugars.

    K. It has the most dietary fiber.

Answers are on pages 258.

Answer Key ■ ■ ■

Level 3

Lesson 1 (pp. 2–15)
Skill Practice:

1. A   2. J

On Your Own:

1. E	7. A	13. D	19. C
2. K	8. G	14. F	20. H
3. E	9. A	15. A	21. C
4. F	10. F	16. J	22. G
5. D	11. E	17. B	23. D
6. K	12. F	18. J	24. K

Lesson 2 (pp. 16–29)
Skill Practice:

1. C   2. F

On Your Own:

1. C	7. B	13. E	19. D
2. J	8. F	14. F	20. K
3. A	9. D	15. D	21. A
4. K	10. G	16. G	22. J
5. C	11. B	17. B	23. D
6. K	12. K	18. G	24. F

Level 3 Performance Assessment (pp. 30–40)

Item Number 1 (Lesson 1)

A. Incorrect: $6\frac{1}{4}$. This is the entry for Sunday, 3/31.

B. Incorrect: $7\frac{1}{2}$. This is the entry for Tuesday, 3/26.

C. Incorrect: 8. This is the entry for Monday, 3/25.

D. Incorrect: $8\frac{1}{4}$. This is the entry for Thursday, 3/28.

E. **Correct:** 9. This is the entry for Wednesday, 3/27.

Item Number 2 (Lesson 1)

F. Incorrect: Monday and Tuesday. There are hours worked for both of these days.

G. Incorrect: Wednesday and Thursday. There are hours worked for both of these days.

H. Incorrect: Thursday and Friday. While there are no hours worked recorded for Friday, there are for Thursday.

J. **Correct:** Friday and Saturday. There are no hours worked recorded for either of these days.

K. Incorrect: Saturday and Sunday. While there are no hours worked recorded for Saturday, there are for Sunday.

Item Number 3 (Lesson 1)

A. Incorrect: Field A. Field A is one of the largest two fields.

B. Incorrect: Field B. Field B is 160 acres, which is smaller than the largest fields, but it is not the smallest.

C. **Correct:** Field C. Field C is the smallest field, at 80 acres.

D. Incorrect: Field D. Field D is one of the largest two fields.

E. Incorrect: the pasture. The pasture is not a field to be plowed.

Item Number 4 (Lesson 1)

F. Incorrect: Fields A and B. Field A is 240 acres, but Field B is only 160 acres.

G. Incorrect: Fields A and C. Field A is 240 acres, but Field C is only 80 acres.

H. **Correct:** Fields A and D. Fields A and D are both 240 acres, so these are the fields you should plant.

J. Incorrect: Fields C and D. Field D is 240 acres, but Field C is only 80 acres.

K. Incorrect: Fields B and C. Field B is only 160 acres, and Field C is only 80 acres.

Item Number 5 (Lesson 1)

A. Incorrect: 40″ × 42″. These are the dimensions of one of the living room windows.

B. Incorrect: 42″ × 80″. The dimensions of the window in the bedroom have been reversed. It should be 80″ × 42″.

C. **Correct:** 80″ × 42″. The dimensions of the bedroom window are 80″ × 42″.

D. Incorrect: 11′ 1″ × 13′ 9″. These are the dimensions of the bedroom itself.

E. Incorrect: 18′ 1″ × 14′ 10″. These are the dimensions of the living room.

Item Number 6 (Lesson 1)

F. Incorrect: 0. There are several windows in the unit. They are located along the living room and bedroom walls and marked with the word window.

G. Incorrect: 1. There is one window in the bedroom, and two additional windows in the living room.

H. Incorrect: 2. There are two windows in the living room, and one additional window in the bedroom.

J. Correct: *3.* There are two windows in the living room and one in the bedroom.

K. Incorrect: *4.* There are only three windows in the unit. Although there are additional labels along the bedroom wall leading to the foyer, these are closets, not windows.

Item Number 7 *(Lesson 1)*

A. Incorrect: *Take temperature orally.* Item 4a on the chart is marked to show that this is permissible.

B. Incorrect: *Take blood pressure using the arm.* Item 3a on the chart is marked to show that you can use the arm to take blood pressure.

C. Incorrect: *Move the patient so you can take the vital signs.* Item 2 on the chart is marked to show that you are allowed to "position patient for task."

D. Correct: *Take blood pressure using sites other than the arm.* Item 3b on the graphic is marked to show that this activity is not permissible.

E. Incorrect: *Throw away supplies you use to take the vital signs.* Item 7 on the chart is marked to show that you are allowed to "dispose of used supplies."

Item Number 8 *(Lesson 1)*

F. Incorrect: *Count breaths.* Item 6 on the graphic is marked to show that you are allowed to "count respirations" (breaths).

G. Incorrect: *Take the pulse radially.* Item 5a is marked to show that you can take the pulse radially.

H. Correct: *Take the pulse apically.* This is marked as permissible under special circumstances under item 5b.

J. Incorrect: *Take the axillary temperature.* Item 4b is marked to show that you are allowed to take the axiallary temperature.

K. Incorrect: *Assemble the equipment you need.* Item 1 is marked to show this is permissible.

Item Number 9 *(Lesson 1)*

A. Incorrect: *thumb pointing upward.* This signal indicates you should raise the boom.

B. Incorrect: *index finger pointing toward the boom.* This signal indicates you should swing the boom.

C. Incorrect: *hands closed, thumbs pointing at each other.* This is a two-hand signal that means you should retract the boom.

D. Correct: *index finger pointing downward, making circles.* This signal indicates that you should lower the load.

E. Incorrect: *thumb pointing downward, hand moving from right to left.* This signal indicates you should lower the boom and raise the load.

Item Number 10 *(Lesson 1)*

F. Incorrect: *Raise the boom.* The signalman will point his thumb up to tell you to raise the boom.

G. Incorrect: *Lower the boom.* The signalman will point his thumb down to tell you to lower the boom.

H. Incorrect: *Swing the boom.* The signalman will point to tell you the direction you should swing the boom.

J. Correct: *Retract the boom.* The signalman will hold out both fists, closed, with thumbs pointing at each other to tell you to retract the boom.

K. Incorrect: *Extend the boom.* The signalman will hold out both fists, closed, with thumbs pointing away from each other to tell you to extend the boom.

Item Number 11 *(Lesson 2)*

A. Incorrect: *Rate: $0, Days: 3.* Neither of the saws are free.

B. Incorrect: *Rate: $17.50, Days: 2.* The rate is correct, but you need the small saws for 3 days.

C. Correct: *Rate: $17.50, Days: 3.* Small saws are $17.50 per day and you need all the saws for 3 days.

D. Incorrect: *Rate: $17.50, Days: 5.* The rate is correct, but you need the saws for 3 days.

E. Incorrect: *Rate: $35.00, Days: 3.* This is the rate for the large saws. Line 3 is the line for small saws.

Item Number 12 *(Lesson 2)*

F. Incorrect: *lines 1 and 2.* This is partly correct. You will make a change in line 1 but not in line 2, which is for the tool bucket without hand cutter.

G. Correct: *lines 1 and 4.* You will add 1 to the number of tool buckets with hand cutters on line 1 and to the number of large wet saws on line 4.

H. Incorrect: *lines 2 and 3.* Neither of these is correct. They are the lines for the tool bucket without hand cutters and the small saws.

J. Incorrect: *lines 2 and 4.* This is partly correct. You will change line 4, but not line 2.

K. Incorrect: *lines 3 and 4.* This is partly correct. You will change line 4, but not line 3.

Item Number 13 *(Lesson 1)*

A. Incorrect: *$0.08.* This is the price per copy.

B. Incorrect: *$0.30.* This is the tax.

C. Incorrect: *$3.76.* This is the amount for the job before the tax.

D. **Correct:** *$4.06.* This is the entire cost of the job. The amount is located at the bottom, under the tax and total amount before the tax.

E. Incorrect: *$47.00.* Forty-seven is the number of copies made (quantity), not the total cost.

Item Number 14 *(Lesson 1)*

F. Incorrect: *Unit Price.* The amount listed for this item is $.08 per page.

G. Incorrect: *Tax.* This amount is listed as $.30.

H. **Correct:** *Number of Copies.* This amount is listed as 47, and matches the amount listed under "Quantity."

J. Incorrect: *Total.* This amount is listed as $4.06.

K. Incorrect: *Subtotal.* There is no amount listed in this space.

Item Number 15 *(Lesson 2)*

A. Incorrect: *9 A.M. and 4 P.M.* 9 A.M. is correct for Monday. You did not work on Thursday.

B. Incorrect: *6 P.M. and 4 P.M.* 6 P.M. is your time out for Monday, not your time in. You did not work on Thursday.

C. Incorrect: *nothing and 6 P.M.* You worked on Monday, so nothing is not correct. You did not work on Thursday.

D. **Correct:** *9 A.M. and nothing.* 9 A.M. is correct for Monday. You did not work on Thursday.

E. Incorrect: *6 P.M. and nothing.* 6 P.M. was the time you left on Monday. Nothing is correct for Thursday because you did not work that day.

Item Number 16 *(Lesson 2)*

F. Incorrect: *bath.* You bathed the patient on Monday, Wednesday, and Friday, but not Saturday.

G. Incorrect: *meal preparation.* You did more than prepare a meal on Saturday.

H. Incorrect: *bath, housekeeping.* This is partly correct. You did not bathe the patient on Saturday and you did more than housekeeping.

J. **Correct:** *meal preparation, housekeeping.* These are the two tasks you completed on Saturday, 9/17.

K. Incorrect: *meal preparation, bath, housekeeping.* You did not bathe the patient on Saturday.

Item Number 17 *(Lesson 2)*

A. Incorrect: *50°C.* This is a temperature. It has nothing to do with the hardness of the water, which is the information that should be recorded on line 1.

B. Incorrect: *Aqua Dial.* This is the type of scale reducer that has been fitted. This information belongs on line 3, not line 1.

C. Incorrect: *220 ppm.* Line 1 asks a yes/no question in regards to this calcium hardness measurement.

D. Incorrect: *Check the "No" box.* The yes/no question on line 1 indicates a hard water area as being above 200 ppm. If the water hardness is 220 ppm, then it is a hard water area.

E. **Correct:** *Check the "Yes" box.* The information says that the hardness is 220 ppm. This is greater than 200 ppm, so the "Yes" box should be checked on line 1.

Item Number 18 *(Lesson 2)*

F. Incorrect: *Line 6, write* 50°C. Line 6 is for cold water inlet temperature, not hot water outlet temperature.

G. Incorrect: *Lines 2 and 3, check the "Yes" box and write* Aqua Dial. These lines do not refer to your inspection of the hot water outlet temperatures.

H. Incorrect: *Line 1, write* 220 ppm. This line refers to water hardness, not your inspection of the hot water outlet temperatures.

J. Incorrect: *Line 7, check the "No" box and write* 50°C. This is partly correct. The outlet temperature is 50°C.

K. **Correct:** *Line 7, check the "Yes" box and write* 50°C. This is correct. You checked the hot water at all outlets and the temperature is 50°C.

Item Number 19 *(Lesson 2)*

A. Incorrect: *"Proposal Form" and "Receipt of Addendum."* This is partly correct. You can't mark the receipt of addendum as complete because it has not yet been received.

B. Incorrect: *"Identical Tie Bids Statement" and "Proposal Form."* You need to sign and notarize the identical tie bids statement. However, the proposal form can be marked as complete.

C. Incorrect: *"Identical Tie Bids Statement" and "Florida Occupational License."* You can mark the Florida occupational license as complete, but you need to sign and notarize the identical tie bids statement before you can mark this item as complete.

D. Incorrect: *"Florida Occupational License"* and *"Receipt of Addendum."* You can mark the Florida occupational license, but you need to receive and then complete, sign, and notarize the addendum form before you can mark it as complete.

E. **Correct:** *"Proposal Form"* and *"Florida Occupational License."* You have completed, signed, and notarized the proposal form and you have a copy of your occupational license. Both of these items can be checked off.

Item Number 20 *(Lesson 2)*

F. Incorrect: *Sign it.* You have already signed the form.

G. **Correct:** *Notarize it.* You have done everything but notarize the form. Once this is done, you can mark this step as complete.

H. Incorrect: *Complete it.* You have already completed the form. You need to do two more things, according to the checklist.

J. Incorrect: *Make a copy of it.* The checklist does not say you need to make a copy of the form.

K. Incorrect: *Complete and sign it.* You have already completed and signed the form. According to the checklist, the form must now be notarized.

Item Number 21 *(Lesson 2)*

A. Incorrect: *2nd day.* This service will not guarantee delivery for the following day.

B. Incorrect: *international.* The package is being shipped from Texas to Michigan. This does not require international delivery.

C. **Correct:** *overnight.* The package will be delivered the next day with overnight delivery service.

D. Incorrect: *courier.* Courier service would not be the appropriate delivery method for a package going to another state.

E. Incorrect: *certified mail.* Certified mail does not address delivery time, so it does not answer the question.

Item Number 22 *(Lesson 2)*

F. Incorrect: *20 pounds, 7 ounces.* This is the package weight, which should be entered on the line 2A.

G. Incorrect: *25-687-6341.* This is the account number, which should be written on line 3.

H. Incorrect: *281-857-5000.* This is your phone number. Since you are the sender, this should be written on line 5.

J. Incorrect: *313-686-2200.* This is the recipient's fax number, not his phone number.

K. **Correct:** *313-686-2255.* This is the recipient's phone number.

Level 4

Lesson 3 (pp. 42–55)
Skill Practice:

1. C   2. G

On Your Own:

1. B	7. D	13. A	19. B
2. H	8. G	14. K	20. J
3. B	9. A	15. A	21. B
4. G	10. G	16. K	22. J
5. E	11. B	17. B	23. B
6. G	12. H	18. K	24. J

Lesson 4 (pp. 56–69)
Skill Practice:

1. B   2. G

On Your Own:

1. C	7. E	13. E	19. B
2. G	8. J	14. G	20. F
3. D	9. D	15. B	21. D
4. G	10. G	16. K	22. G
5. D	11. C	17. E	23. A
6. J	12. G	18. G	24. F

Lesson 5 (pp. 70–83)
Skill Practice:

1. E   2. J

On Your Own:

1. D	7. C	13. E	19. E
2. K	8. H	14. F	20. F
3. C	9. A	15. A	21. D
4. F	10. J	16. F	22. G
5. A	11. D	17. C	23. D
6. K	12. H	18. F	24. G

Lesson 6 (pp. 84–97)
Skill Practice:

1. B   2. G

On Your Own:

1. A	7. D	13. B	19. E
2. K	8. J	14. G	20. G
3. D	9. D	15. B	21. B
4. G	10. K	16. K	22. K
5. B	11. D	17. E	23. C
6. J	12. H	18. G	24. F

Lesson 7 (pp. 98–111)

Skill Practice:

    1. B   **2.** J

On Your Own:

1. B	**7.** B	**13.** E	**19.** D
2. J	**8.** F	**14.** J	**20.** G
3. E	**9.** C	**15.** B	**21.** B
4. F	**10.** K	**16.** F	**22.** K
5. E	**11.** E	**17.** D	**23.** E
6. K	**12.** H	**18.** K	**24.** J

Level 4 Performance Assessment (pp. 112–122)

Item Number 1 *(Lesson 6)*

  A. Incorrect: *The chart does not display enough information to draw any conclusions.* Enough information is provided to identify a downward trend in the number of employed manufacturing workers.

  B. **Correct:** *Every year, fewer manufacturing workers have full-time jobs.* The number of full-time manufacturing workers decreases every year.

  C. Incorrect: *Fewer manufacturing workers are hired every year.* Having fewer employees does not mean that fewer workers were hired.

  D. Incorrect: *Salaries for manufacturing workers have decreased every year.* This answer is not related to the data in the chart.

  E. Incorrect: *Fewer items are manufactured every year.* A reduction in the workforce does not mean that fewer items are manufactured. For example, improved equipment could manufacture more items and require fewer workers.

Item Number 2 *(Lesson 6)*

  F. **Correct:** *The chart does not display enough information to draw any conclusions.* The chart does not identify the types of manufactured goods that are affected. It only identifies the employment levels.

  G. Incorrect: *Durable goods are affected.* The chart does not identify the types of manufactured goods that are affected.

  H. Incorrect: *Vehicles are affected.* The chart does not identify the types of manufactured goods that are affected.

  J. Incorrect: *Machinery is affected.* The chart does not identify the types of manufactured goods that are affected.

  K. Incorrect: *All types of manufactured goods are equally affected.* The chart does not identify the types of manufactured goods that are affected.

Item Number 3 *(Lesson 3)*

  A. Incorrect: *4'6".* This is the measurement of the width, the shorter side.

  B. **Correct:** *5'6".* This is the measurement of the length, the longer side.

  C. Incorrect: *6'4".* This measurement does not appear in the graphic.

  D. Incorrect: *6'5".* This measurement does not appear in the graphic.

  E. Incorrect: *45°.* This is the angle of the corner joint.

Item Number 4 *(Lesson 3)*

  F. Incorrect: *one 3" wood screw, one 1" × 4" piece of high quality pine, and one 4" × $\frac{3}{4}$" right angle corner brace.* There are not enough of any of the materials needed to build the frame.

  G. Incorrect: *one 3" wood screw, four 1" × 4" pieces of high quality pine, and four $\frac{3}{4}$" right angle corner braces.* There are not enough screws, and the dimensions for the corner braces are incomplete.

  H. Incorrect: *four 3" wood screws, four 1" × 4" pieces of high quality pine, and four 4'6" right angle corner braces.* There are enough screws and pieces of pine, but the dimensions of the right angle corner braces are incorrect.

  J. **Correct:** *four 3" wood screws, four 1" × 4" pieces of high quality pine, and four 4" × $\frac{3}{4}$" right angle corner braces.* Four of each of the materials shown in the graphic are needed in order to construct the frame.

  K. Incorrect: *three 3" wood screws, four 1" × 4" piece of high quality pine, and four $\frac{3}{4}$" right angle corner braces.* There are not enough screws, and the dimensions for the corner braces are incomplete.

Item Number 5 *(Lesson 5)*

  A. Incorrect: *The High Definition Starter Deal costs more and has free high definition.* While this is true, it is not the best summary because there are additional differences.

  B. Incorrect: *The High Definition Starter Deal has more digital cable channels, free high definition, unlimited local calling, and it costs more.* The High Definition Starter Deal does not have more digital cable channels, and both deals have unlimited local calling.

  C. Incorrect: *The High Definition Starter Deal has Security Assistance, unlimited national long-distance calling, and it costs more.* While this is true, it is not the best summary because there are additional differences.

D. Correct: *The High Definition Starter Deal has free high definition, Security Assistance, unlimited national long-distance calling, voice mail, and it costs more.* This summarizes all the differences between the two packages.

E. Incorrect: *The High Definition Starter Deal costs more, has* Rocket *Internet, Security Assistance,* Demand It! *movies and shows, and it costs less.* The High Definition Starter Deal does not have *Rocket* Internet, both packages have *Demand It!* Movies and shows, and it does not cost less.

Item Number 6 *(Lesson 5)*

F. Incorrect: *As the package gets better, the difference between the price for the first 12 months and the price thereafter decreases.* This is the opposite of what happens; the price actually increases.

G. Correct: *As the package gets better, the difference between the price for the first 12 months and the price thereafter increases.* The difference in cost increases ($10 more for Digital Cable Value Deal, $15 more for High Definition Starter Deal, and $20 more for High Definition Super Deal), as the package gets better.

H. Incorrect: *As the package gets better, the difference between the price for the first 12 months and the price thereafter is $15.* There is a $15 difference only for the High Definition Starter Deal, not for all of the packages.

J. Incorrect: *As the package gets better, the difference between the price for the first 12 months and the price thereafter is $20.* There is a $20 difference only for the High Definition Super Deal, not for all of the packages.

K. Incorrect: *As the package gets better, the difference between the price for the first 12 months and the price thereafter is $40.* This is the difference in the price between the High Definition Super Deal for the first 12 months and the Digital Cable Value deal for the first 12 months.

Item Number 7 *(Lesson 7)*

A. Incorrect: *The amount of aluminum cans wasted has decreased between years 1 and 21, and the recycling rate is lower in year 21 than it was in year 1.* There was actually an increase in the amount of aluminum cans wasted, not a decrease. The recycling rate is lower.

B. Incorrect: *The amount of PET bottles wasted has increased between years 1 and 21, and the recycling rate has decreased between*

these years. While the amount of PET bottles has significantly increased between years 1 and 21, the recycling rate has also increased.

C. Incorrect: *The amount of aluminum cans and PET bottles wasted has increased between years 1 and 21, and the recycling rate has consistently decreased.* Although the amount of aluminum cans and PET bottles has increased, the recycling rate has not consistently decreased.

D. Correct: *The amount of aluminum cans wasted has increased between years 1 and 21, and the recycling rate is lower in year 21 than it was in year 1.* The number of tons of aluminum cans wasted has increased between years 1 and 21, and the recycling rate is lower in year 21 (about 45%) than it was in year 1 (about 50%).

E. Incorrect: *The amount of aluminum cans and PET bottles wasted has decreased between years 1 and 21, and the recycling rate has consistently increased.* The amount of aluminum cans and PET bottles wasted has increased, not decreased. The recycling rate has not consistently increased; it has gone up and down throughout the years.

Item Number 8 *(Lesson 7)*

F. Incorrect: *Fewer people are recycling in year 21 than were in year 1.* If fewer people were recycling, there would be a lower recycling rate, not a higher one.

G. Incorrect: *Fewer people are wasting PET bottles in year 21 than in year 1.* The amount wasted is higher, suggesting that more people are wasting PET bottles.

H. Incorrect: *The PET bottles in year 21 weigh more than the ones in year 1.* The amount wasted in tons is about 7 times higher; it is unlikely that PET bottles weigh that much more.

J. Incorrect: *There are fewer PET bottles being sold in year 21 than there were in year 1.* If there were fewer PET bottles being sold, there would likely be fewer wasted.

K. Correct: *There are more PET bottles being sold in year 21 than there were in year 1.* An increase in the number sold would explain an increase in amount wasted despite an increase in recycling rates.

Item Number 9 *(Lesson 4)*

A. Incorrect: *Install cable, 580 Elk Rd.* The work listed on Invoice RG–368 should be for SB Cable, and based on the Daily Appointments notes, this is correct.

B. Incorrect: *Adjust customer equipment, 55 Jackson Ave.* The work listed on Invoice RG–368 should be for SB Cable, and based on the Daily Appointments notes, this is correct.

C. Incorrect: *Measure signal strength, 815 Marilyn St.* The work listed on Invoice RG–368 should be for SB Cable, and based on the Daily Appointments notes, this is correct.

D. **Correct:** *Equipment repair, 858 5th Blvd.* The work listed on Invoice RG–368 should be for SB Cable, but based on the Daily Appointments notes, this work was done for ViewCast Cable. You would not write it on this invoice.

E. Incorrect: *Install cable, 12 Emerson Ln.* The work listed on Invoice RG–368 should be for SB Cable, and based on the Daily Appointments notes, this is correct.

Item Number 10 *(Lesson 4)*

F. Incorrect: *0.5 hour.* This was not the total hours worked for ViewCast Cable based on the hours listed in the Daily Appointments notes section.

G. **Correct:** *1.5 hours.* Based on the the Daily Appointments notes section, you worked 1 hour for one job and 0.5 hour for another for ViewCast Cable.

H. Incorrect: *3.5 hours.* This was not the total hours worked for ViewCast Cable based on the hours listed in the Daily Appointments notes section.

J. Incorrect: *4 hours.* This was not the total hours worked for ViewCast Cable based on the hours listed in the Daily Appointments notes section.

K. Incorrect: *7 hours.* This was the total hours worked for SB Cable, not for ViewCast Cable.

Item Number 11 *(Lesson 6)*

A. Incorrect: *The number of persons per household steadily increased between 1971 and 2001.* The graph indicates that the number of persons per household decreased between 1971 and 2001, from between 3.1 and 3.2 in 1971, to nearly 2.6 in 2001.

B. Incorrect: *The number of persons per household was the same in 1971 as it was in 2001.* The graph indicates that the number of persons per household was between 3.1 and 3.2 in 1971 and nearly 2.6 in 2001.

C. Incorrect: *The number of persons per household increased between 1971 and 1989 and then decreased between 1989 and 2001.* The graph indicates that numbers decreased consistently between 1971 and 1989, rose between 1989 and 1995, and then decreased again between 1995 and 2001.

D. Incorrect: *The number of persons per household was less in 1971 than it was in 2001.* The number of persons was actually higher in 1971 than it was in 2001.

E. **Correct:** *The number of persons per household generally decreased between 1971 and 2001.* The graph indicates that, despite an increase between 1989 and 1995, the number of persons per household generally decreased between 1971 and 2001.

Item Number 12 *(Lesson 6)*

F. Incorrect: *While the number of persons per household remained the same, the number of vehicles per household decreased.* The graphic does not support this trend.

G. Incorrect: *While the number of persons per household decreased, the number of vehicles per household decreased.* The graphic does not support this trend.

H. Incorrect: *While the number of persons per household increased, the number of vehicles per household increased.* The graphic does not support this trend.

J. Incorrect: *While the number of persons per household increased, the number of vehicles per household decreased.* The graphic does not support this trend.

K. **Correct:** *While the number of persons per household decreased, the number of vehicles per household increased.* Despite a decrease in the number of persons per household, the number of vehicles per household has not been impacted; the number of vehicles per household has actually increased.

Item Number 13 *(Lesson 3)*

A. **Correct:** *Bromine.* The symbol for the element with an atomic number of 35 is "Br," and the Chemical Element Symbols chart indicates that "Br" is the symbol for Bromine.

B. Incorrect: *Copper.* The atomic number for Copper is 29.

C. Incorrect: *Helium.* The atomic number for Helium is 2.

D. Incorrect: *Iodine.* The atomic number for Iodine is 53.

E. Incorrect: *Nickel.* The atomic number for Nickel is 28.

Item Number 14 *(Lesson 3)*

F. Incorrect: *2.* 2 is the atomic number for Helium.

G. Incorrect: *13.* 13 is the atomic number for Aluminum.

H. Correct: *18.* The Chemical Element Symbols chart indicates that "Ar" is the symbol for Argon, and the Periodic Table of Elements shows that 18 is the corresponding atomic number.

J. Incorrect: *28.* 28 is the atomic number for Nickel.

K. Incorrect: *29.* 29 is the atomic number for Copper.

Item Number 15 *(Lesson 5)*

A. Incorrect: *From September 2008 to September 2009, ownership of Ringtell phones increased by 15%, while ownership of ClearestEdge phones slightly decreased.* This trend is not supported by the graphs, as ClearestEdge's market share increased by 15% during this time.

B. Incorrect: *From September 2008 to September 2009, ownership of ClearestEdge phones decreased by 15%, while ownership of Ringtell phones slightly increased.* This trend is not supported by the graphs, as ClearestEdge's market share increased by 15% during this time, while Ringtell's slightly decreased.

C. Correct: *From September 2008 to September 2009, ownership of ClearestEdge phones increased by 15%, while ownership of Ringtell phones slightly decreased.* This is the trend supported by the graphs.

D. Incorrect: *From September 2008 to September 2009, ownership of both ClearestEdge and Ringtell phones increased by 15%.* This trend is not supprted by the graphs, as only ClearestEdge's market share increased by 15% during this time.

E. Incorrect: *From September 2008 to September 2009, ownership of both ClearestEdge and Ringtell phones decreased by 15%.* This trend is not supported by the graphs, as neither ClearestEdge nor Ringtell saw their market share decrease by 15% during this time.

Item Number 16 *(Lesson 5)*

F. Incorrect: *ClearestEdge lost market share while Ringtell slowly gained market share.* Since ClearestEdge introduced its new phone in July 2007, it has not lost market share, and Ringtell has not slowly gained market share.

G. Correct: *ClearestEdge gained significant market share while Ringtell slowly lost market share.* Since ClearestEdge introduced its new phone in July 2007, its market share has increased from 3% to over 30%. Ringtell began losing market share in 2008.

H. Incorrect: *While ClearestEdge's market share remained the same, Ringtell slowly lost market*

share. Since ClearestEdge introduced its new phone in July 2007, its market share has steadily increased.

J. Incorrect: *ClearestEdge and Ringtell both slowly lost market share.* Since ClearestEdge introduced its new phone in July 2007, it has not lost market share.

K. Incorrect: *ClearestEdge gained market share while Ringtell slowly gained market share as well.* Since ClearestEdge introduced its new phone in July 2007, it has gained market share, but Ringtell began losing market share in 2008.

Item Number 17 *(Lesson 7)*

A. Incorrect: *Printer A.* This printer does not offer the fastest turnaround time.

B. Incorrect: *Printer B or Printer C.* While printer C does offer the fastest turnaround time, Printer B does not.

C. Correct: *Printer C.* Printer C offers a turn around time of 1 day for one hundred copies, which is the fastest turnaround time of all the printers listed.

D. Incorrect: *Printer D.* This printer does not offer the fastest turnaround time.

E. Incorrect: *Printer B or Printer D.* Neither of these printers offers the fastest turnaround times.

Item Number 18 *(Lesson 7)*

F. Correct: *Printer A.* Printer A fits the time constraints and offers 4-color both sides for the cheapest price.

G. Incorrect: *Printer A or Printer B.* While Printer A offers the best deal, Printer B does not accommodate the time table of five days needed for the job.

H. Incorrect: *Printer C.* While Printer C is the fastest, it is also the most expensive.

J. Incorrect: *Printer D.* Printer D does not offer the cheapest deal and will only print on one side.

K. Incorrect: *Printer C or Printer D.* Neither Printer C nor Printer D offers an economical package for the library's needs.

Item Number 19 *(Lesson 5)*

A. Incorrect: *The programs with the most expensive 30-second ad spots in both 2008 and 2009 were* All Sports Spotlight, Sophie's House, *and* The Station. *All Sports Spotlight* and *Sophie's House* were the top two programs with the most expensive 30-second ad spots in 2008 and 2009, but there was a third program whose ad spots cost more than *The Station.*

B. Incorrect: *The programs with the most expensive 30-second ad spots in both 2008 and 2009 were* All Sports Spotlight, Sophie's House, *and* Forever Free. *All Sports Spotlight and Sophie's House were the top two programs with the most expensive 30-second ad spots in 2008 and 2009, but there was a third program whose ad spots cost more than Forever Free.*

C. Incorrect: *The programs with the most expensive 30-second ad spots in both 2008 and 2009 were* All Sports Spotlight, Sophie's House, *and* Milky Way Diaries. *All Sports Spotlight and Sophie's House were the top two programs with the most expensive 30-second ad spots in 2008 and 2009, but there was a third program whose ad spots cost more than Milky Way Diaries.*

D. Incorrect: *The programs with the most expensive 30-second ad spots in both 2008 and 2009 were* All Sports Spotlight, Forever Free, *and* The Station. *All Sports Spotlight was one of the programs with the most expensive 30-second ad spots in 2008 and 2009, but there were two other programs whose ad spots cost more than Forever Free and The Station.*

E. **Correct:** *The programs with the most expensive 30-second ad spots in both 2008 and 2009 were* All Sports Spotlight, Sophie's House, *and* Two Trails. *These three shows had the most expensive ad spots in both years.*

Item Number 20 *(Lesson 5)*

F. Incorrect: Milky Way Diaries; *Weekly viewership increased in 2008.* Viewership of *Milky Way Diaries* decreased in 2008.

G. **Correct:** Milky Way Diaries; *Weekly viewership decreased in 2008.* The price of ad spots for *Milky Way Diaries* decreased, which does not match the other shows. The likely reason for this is the decrease in viewership (from 10.5 million in 2007 to 9.6 million in 2008).

H. Incorrect: Two Trails; *Weekly viewership decreased in 2008.* The price of ad spots for *Two Trails* increased, as it did for most of the shows. Viewership also increased for *Two Trails*.

J. Incorrect: The Station; *Weekly viewership stayed the same in 2009.* The price of ad spots for *The Station* increased, as it did for most of the shows. Viewership did not stay the same; it increased.

K. Incorrect: Forever Free; *Weekly viewership increased in 2008.* The price of ad spots for *Forever Free* increased, as it did for most of the shows. Viewership did increase.

Item Number 21 *(Lesson 7)*

A. **Correct:** *Sub-Saharan Africa.* Sub-Saharan Africa spent the least of all regions on its military.

B. Incorrect: *Russia.* Russia spent $70 billion on its military, but this is not the smallest amount spent by a country.

C. Incorrect: *Latin America.* Latin America spent $39 billion on its military, but this is not the smallest amount spent by a region.

D. Incorrect: *China.* China spent $122 billion on its military, which is one of the highest amounts spent by a country or region.

E. Incorrect: *Central/South Asia.* Central/South Asia spent $30 billion on its military, but this is not the smallest amount spent by a region.

Item Number 22 *(Lesson 7)*

F. Incorrect: *The United States spent more on the military than any other country or region.* This assumption is confirmed by the information presented in the graph.

G. **Correct:** *Russia and China's combined military spending totaled more than half that of the United States.* The information in the graph indicates that the combined spending of Russia and China is less than half that of the United States, so this assumption can be eliminated as false.

H. Incorrect: *The budget for nuclear weapons falls under the U.S. Department of Energy.* The information shown in the graph has nothing to do with this assumption. Therefore, the assumption cannot be confirmed or eliminated.

J. Incorrect: *The European countries reduce military spending every year.* The information shown in the graph has nothing to do with this assumption. Therefore, the assumption cannot be confirmed or eliminated.

K. Incorrect: *China spent less on its military than Europe spent.* This assumption is confirmed by the information presented in the graph.

Level 5

Lesson 8 (pp. 124–137)
Skill Practice:

1. D   2. H

On Your Own:

1. D	7. B	13. C	19. B
2. F	8. K	14. F	20. K
3. C	9. D	15. B	21. C
4. F	10. G	16. J	22. K
5. C	11. A	17. E	23. A
6. J	12. K	18. G	24. J

Lesson 9 (pp. 138–151)
Skill Practice:

1. B   2. F

On Your Own:

1. A	7. C	13. D	19. B
2. J	8. G	14. G	20. K
3. E	9. D	15. D	21. B
4. J	10. F	16. G	22. J
5. E	11. D	17. B	23. B
6. F	12. J	18. F	24. G

Lesson 10 (pp. 152–165)
Skill Practice:

1. C   2. J

On Your Own:

1. E	7. A	13. C	19. E
2. H	8. F	14. G	20. F
3. D	9. C	15. A	21. C
4. G	10. J	16. J	22. J
5. B	11. E	17. C	23. B
6. F	12. F	18. J	24. J

Lesson 11 (pp. 166–179)
Skill Practice:

1. B   2. F

On Your Own:

1. E	7. D	13. C	19. C
2. H	8. G	14. H	20. G
3. D	9. C	15. E	21. E
4. J	10. J	16. F	22. K
5. D	11. C	17. C	23. D
6. H	12. F	18. F	24. K

Level 5 Performance Assessment (pp. 180–190)

Item Number 1 *(Lesson 8)*

A. Incorrect: *2.* The 54″ table and 60″ table each hold a minimum of six people. However, there is one more table that holds a minimum of at least six.

B. Incorrect: *3.* Three tables hold six people or more, but the table that measures 48″ can also seat up to six people.

C. **Correct:** *4.* The table that measures 48″ can hold up to six people, and the tables that measure 54″, 60″, and 72″ all hold at least six people.

D. Incorrect: *5.* This number is too large. Look at the diagram to help you find number of people that can be seated at each table.

E. Incorrect: *6.* This number is much too large. Look at the diagram to help you find the number of people that can be seated at each table.

Item Number 2 *(Lesson 8)*

F. Incorrect: *1.* There is more than one square table that seats four people.

G. **Correct:** *2.* There are only two square tables that seat four people. They measure 30″ x 30″ and 36″ x 36″.

H. Incorrect: *3.* There are three round tables that have four people as a maximum. However, only two of them are square.

J. Incorrect: *4.* There are four round tables that have four people as a maximum or minimum. You need square tables.

K. Incorrect: *6.* This is the total number of tables that can seat four. You need square tables.

Item Number 3 *(Lesson 8)*

A. Incorrect: *a.* According to the "Glasses" section, this is the water glass.

B. **Correct:** *b.* According to the "Glasses" section, the champagne flute is to the right of the water glass, which is above the knives.

C. Incorrect: *c.* According to the "Glasses" section, this is the wine glass.

D. Incorrect: *d.* According to the "Glasses" section, this is the sherry glass.

E. Incorrect: *e.* This is the butter plate. Champagne is a beverage.

Item Number 4 *(Lesson 8)*

F. Incorrect: *white wine glass.* This is placed beside the champagne flute.

G. Incorrect: *sherry glass.* This is placed at the far right in the line of glasses.

H. Incorrect: *butter plate.* This is placed above the forks.

J. **Correct:** *napkin.* The text states that, "the napkin is placed on top of the charger."

K. Incorrect: *server plate.* This is another name for the charger.

Item Number 5 *(Lesson 10)*

- **A.** Incorrect: *Attendance was highest in the fall.* Attendance was high during the fall, but it was not the highest for the year.

- **B.** Incorrect: *Attendance was highest in the spring.* Attendance rose during the spring, but it did not reach its peak.

- **C.** Incorrect: *Attendance was highest in the winter.* December, January, and February had the lowest attendance.

- **D.** **Correct:** *Attendance was highest in the summer.* General museum admissions during the months of June, July, and August were the highest for the year.

- **E.** Incorrect: *There were no patterns in attendance.* The admissions numbers increased and decreased during the year. Use these trends to answer the question.

Item Number 6 *(Lesson 10)*

- **F.** Incorrect: *Mummies.* This special exhibit did not have the largest overall attendance.

- **G.** Incorrect: *Inspiring Fashion.* This special exhibit did not have the largest overall attendance.

- **H.** **Correct:** *American Presidents.* This special exhibit had the largest overall attendance.

- **J.** Incorrect: *Pirates!* This special exhibit did not have the largest overall attendance.

- **K.** Incorrect: *The Ancient Americas.* This special exhibit did not have the largest overall attendance.

Item Number 7 *(Lesson 10)*

- **A.** Incorrect: *The level of dehydration is not important.* Percentage of dehydration is listed on the chart along with weight, so this factor is important.

- **B.** **Correct:** *The amount of fluid needed increases as dehydration levels increase.* The chart shows that as the percentage of dehydration increases, more fluid is needed.

- **C.** Incorrect: *The amount of fluid needed increases as dehydration levels decrease.* The chart shows that the opposite is true.

- **D.** Incorrect: *The amount of fluid needed decreases as dehydration levels increase.* The chart shows that the opposite is true.

- **E.** Incorrect: *The amount of fluid needed increases and then decreases as dehydration levels decrease.* As the percentage of dehydration increases, more fluid is needed.

Item Number 8 *(Lesson 10)*

- **F.** Incorrect: *Body weight is not important.* As body weight increases, more fluid is needed.

- **G.** Incorrect: *The amount of fluid needed decreases as body weight increases.* The chart shows that the opposite is true.

- **H.** Incorrect: *The amount of fluid needed increases as body weight decreases.* The chart shows that the opposite is true.

- **J.** **Correct:** *The amount of fluid needed decreases as body weight decreases.* The amount of fluid needed is relative to the body weight, so as the body weight increases or decreases, so too does the amount of fluid needed.

- **K.** Incorrect: *The amount of fluid needed increases and then decreases as body weight increases.* The amount of fluid needed is relative to the body weight.

Item Number 9 *(Lesson 10)*

- **A.** **Correct:** *Most of the time when there is a drop in occupancy, there is a drop in total revenue.* This trend is correct based on the graphs.

- **B.** Incorrect: *Every time there is a rise in occupancy, there is a rise in total revenue.* There were two instances in these graphs where occupancy rose, and in one of those cases (1960–1961) there was a drop in revenue.

- **C.** Incorrect: *A drop or rise in occupancy has no related effect to a drop or rise in the change in total revenue.* The graphs do show a trend in the relationship between a change in occupancy and a change in total revenue.

- **D.** Incorrect: *Every time there is a rise in occupancy, there is a drop in total revenue.* There were two instances in these graphs where occupancy rose, and in only one of those cases (1960–1961) was there a drop in revenue.

- **E.** Incorrect: *When there is a drop in occupancy, there is never a drop in revenue.* When there is a drop in occupancy, there is often a drop in total revenue.

Item Number 10 *(Lesson 10)*

- **F.** Incorrect: *1944–1945.* An increase, not a decline, took place during this range of years.

- **G.** Incorrect: *1969–1970.* While total revenue and operating income declined during this range of years, expenses increased.

- **H.** Incorrect: *1990–1991.* A decline took place during this range of years, but it was not the most significant decline that took place.

J. Correct: *2000–2003.* The most significant decline took place during this range of years.

K. Incorrect: *2007–2009.* A decline took place during this range of years, but it was not the most significant decline that took place.

Item Number 11 *(Lesson 11)*

A. Correct: *Delivery goes up in the winter and down in the summer.* The graph and table show that natural gas delivery is highest during the winter months.

B. Incorrect: *Delivery goes up in the summer and down in the winter.* According to the graph and the table, the opposite is true.

C. Incorrect: *Delivery is about the same throughout the year.* The graph and table show a wide range of delivery amounts throughout the year.

D. Incorrect: *Delivery was most consistent from 2001 to 2003.* Each year varies in a similar way; one year is not more consistent than another.

E. Incorrect: *Delivery varies a lot from year to year.* Each year has similar trends in data. There is not much variety from year to year.

Item Number 12 *(Lesson 11)*

F. Correct: *December, January, February, March.* Each of these months has twice had the highest delivery totals for the year.

G. Incorrect: *January, February, March, April.* All of these months except April have had the highest monthly delivery totals for the various years shown.

H. Incorrect: *September, October, November, December.* Of these months, only December has had the highest monthly delivery totals for the year. This occurred in 2002 and 2003.

J. Incorrect: *June, July, August, September.* The summer months have the lowest delivery totals.

K. Incorrect: *March, April, May, June.* Of these months, only March has had the highest monthly delivery totals for the year. This occurred in 2005 and 2006.

Item Number 13 *(Lesson 10)*

A. Correct: *Clean weeding allows for plants to grow more.* The graph shows that with clean weeding the monthly girth rises faster, then maintains a consistently higher level than circle weeding.

B. Incorrect: *Circle weeding allows for plants to grow more.* The graph shows that with circle weeding, the monthly girth is consistently less than with clean weeding.

C. Incorrect: *Both weeding patterns allow for identical rates of plant growth.* The monthly growth levels are not similar.

D. Incorrect: *Plants that are clean weeded grow more quickly in the winter months.* The graph does not show that clean-weeded plants grow more quickly in the winter.

E. Incorrect: *Plants that are circle weeded grow more quickly in the winter months.* The graph does not show that circle-weeded plants grow more quickly in the winter.

Item Number 14 *(Lesson 10)*

F. Incorrect: *The growth of both kinds of plants slowed.* The graph shows that the opposite is true.

G. Correct: *The growth of both kinds of plants increased.* From November to December of the second year, the growth increased for both circle-weeded and clean-weeded plants.

H. Incorrect: *Clean-weeded plants grew at a much slower rate than circle-weeded plants.* Clean-weeded plants did not grow less during this time.

J. Incorrect: *The growth for both kinds of plants was almost the same as the earlier months.* The chart does not show that the growth for both is the same as previous months.

K. Incorrect: *Clean-weeded plants grew at a much greater rate than circle-weeded plants.* Clean-weeded plants did not grow at a much greater rate during this time.

Item Number 15 *(Lesson 11)*

A. Correct: *increased imports and consumption.* The data shows that imports and consumption have increased for all three.

B. Incorrect: *decreased imports and consumption.* Imports and consumption have not decreased for all three.

C. Incorrect: *increased imports and decreased consumption.* Imports and consumption have increased for all three.

D. Incorrect: *no change in consumption; decreased imports.* There has been a change in consumption.

E. Incorrect: *decreased consumption; no change in imports.* There has been increased consumption and increased imports for all three.

Item Number 16 *(Lesson 11)*

F. Incorrect: *Exports have increased consistently every year.* There are several years where exports decreased.

G. Incorrect: *Exports have decreased consistently ever year.* Although exports have decreased, they have not decreased every year.

H. Incorrect: *Exports have increased every other year.* There are a few years where exports have increased, but it does not follow the trend of every other year.

J. Incorrect: *Exports have decreased every other year.* There are several years in a row where exports have decreased.

K. **Correct:** *There is no consistent trend in export data.* Exports for vegetables, melons, potatoes, and beef have varied throughout the years with no obvious pattern.

Item Number 17 *(Lesson 10)*

A. Incorrect: *Unemployment was low in 2000, and it has been steadily increasing since 2001.* The graphics show unemployment rising and then dropping, before rising significantly starting in 2007.

B. Incorrect: *Unemployment was low in 2000, it rose from 2001 to 2003, and it began to decline in 2007.* While it is correct that unemployment was low in 2000 and rose from 2001 to 2003, it did not begin to decline in 2007.

C. Incorrect: *Unemployment was high in 2000, it rose from 2001 to 2003, it began to decline in 2004, and it began to rise sharply in 2005.* Unemployment was low in 2000 compared to later years, and it did rise from 2001 to 2003. However, while it began to decline in 2004, it did not rise sharply in 2005.

D. **Correct:** *Unemployment was low in 2000, it rose from 2001 to 2003, it began to decline in 2004, and it began to rise sharply in 2007.* This accurately describes the trend shown in the graphs.

E. Incorrect: *Unemployment was high in 2000, and it has declined and risen in predictable sharp peaks and valleys since then.* Unemployment was low in 2000 compared to later years, but the peaks and valleys are varied and not predictable based on what is shown in the graphs.

Item Number 18 *(Lesson 10)*

F. Incorrect: *The unemployment rate in both California and the rest of the United States reached its lowest point at the end of the decade.* At the end of the decade, the unemployment rate reached a peak for both California and the rest of the United States.

G. Incorrect: *While the unemployment rate in California rose dramatically toward the end of the decade, it decreased significantly for the rest of the Untied States.* The unemployment rate in both California and the rest of the United States rose dramatically toward the end of the decade.

H. Incorrect: *Whenever the unemployment rate in the United States increased, it generally decreased in California.* The unemployment rate in California had a trend that was similar to the trend in the rest of the United States.

J. Incorrect: *Whenever the unemployment rate in the California increased, it generally decreased in the rest of the United States.* The unemployment rate in California had a trend that was similar to the trend in the rest of the United States.

K. **Correct:** *While the unemployment rates in California and the United States have followed similar patterns, the rate has been consistently higher in California.* The graphs show that the unemployment percentage has been consistenty higher in California.

Item Number 19 *(Lesson 11)*

A. Incorrect: *Accidental Death & Dismemberment.* This is an accidental death plan, but it does not offer a premium waiver.

B. Incorrect: *Term Life Option 2.* This plan offers neither a premium waiver nor an accidental death benefit.

C. Incorrect: *Individual & Family.* This plan offers a premium waiver but not an accidental death benefit.

D. Incorrect: *Term Life Option 1.* This plan offers neither a premium waiver nor an accidental death benefit.

E. **Correct:** *Life Insurance.* This plan offers both a premium waiver and an accidental death benefit.

Item Number 20 *(Lesson 11)*

F. Incorrect: *Life Insurance; Term Life Option 2; Individual & Family.* This is partly correct. Life Insurance and Individual & Family offer dependent coverage until age 25. Term Life Option 2 does not.

G. Incorrect: *Term Life Option 2; Term Life Option 1; Individual & Family.* This is partly correct. Individual & Family offers dependent coverage until age 25. Term Life Option 2 and Term Life Option 1 do not.

H. **Correct:** *Life Insurance; Individual & Family; Accidental Death & Dismemberment.* These three plans offer dependent coverage until age 25.

J. Incorrect: *Term Life Option 2; Term Life Option 1; Accidental Death & Dismemberment.* This is partly correct. Accidental Death & Dismemberment offers dependent coverage until age 25. Term Life Option 2 and Term Life Option 1 do not.

K. Incorrect: *Life Insurance; Term Life Option 1; Accidental Death & Dismemberment.* This is partly correct. Life Insurance and Accidental Death & Dismemberment offer dependent coverage until age 25. Term Life Option 1 does not.

Item Number 21 *(Lesson 9)*

A. Incorrect: *a deal for a multi-night, household, leisure trip.* Multi-night, household, leisure trips are the least popular deal according to the table, so this is not a good choice.

B. Incorrect: *a deal for an overnight, individual trip.* Overnight, individual trips are popular, but there is another kind of trip that is more popular.

C. Incorrect: *a deal for a multi-night, individual, business trip.* Trends indicate that this kind of trip is one of the least popular kinds of domestic travel.

D. Incorrect: *a deal for an overnight, household trip.* According to the table, overnight household trips are not very popular.

E. **Correct:** *a deal for a multi-night, individual, leisure trip.* According to the table, the most popular trips taken in the United States are multi-night, individual, leisure trips. This would most likely be the best-selling deal.

Item Number 22 *(Lesson 9)*

F. Incorrect: *U.S. domestic travel went down from 1999 to 2005.* Travel went up several times from 1999 to year 2005.

G. Incorrect: *U.S. domestic travel was higher in 2001 than it was in 2005.* The overall figures for 2001 are lower than they are for 2005.

H. Incorrect: *U.S. domestic travel was higher in 1999 than it was in 2005.* The overall figures for 1999 are lower than they are for 2005.

J. Incorrect: *U.S. domestic travel consistently increased every year.* Travel goes up and down; there is no consistent pattern.

K. **Correct:** *U.S. domestic travel has gone up and down, but was higher in 2005 than it was in 1999.* The travel patterns change from year to year, but overall the figures are generally higher for 2005 than they are for 1999.

Level 6

Lesson 12 (pp. 192–205)
Skill Practice:

1. A   2. H

On Your Own:

1. E	7. C	13. B	19. A
2. J	8. J	14. F	20. J
3. C	9. C	15. D	21. D
4. H	10. F	16. G	22. K
5. B	11. B	17. C	23. A
6. F	12. K	18. G	24. F

Lesson 13 (pp. 206–219)
Skill Practice:

1. E   2. G

On Your Own:

1. A	7. B	13. D	19. D
2. H	8. H	14. H	20. H
3. B	9. C	15. A	21. C
4. K	10. F	16. H	22. J
5. D	11. A	17. D	23. D
6. H	12. H	18. F	24. H

Lesson 14 (pp. 220–233)
Skill Practice:

1. B   2. J

On Your Own:

1. D	7. C	13. E	19. E
2. F	8. K	14. H	20. H
3. A	9. C	15. B	21. A
4. J	10. K	16. G	22. K
5. C	11. E	17. E	23. D
6. G	12. H	18. J	24. F

Level 6 Performance Assessment (pp. 234–244)

Item Number 1 *(Lesson 12)*

A. Incorrect: *New York.* Based on the maps, New York has alfisol soil but does not have mollisol soil.

B. Incorrect: *Arkansas.* Based on the maps, Arkansas has alfisol soil Arkansas but does not have mollisol soil.

C. **Correct:** *Illinois.* Based on the maps, Illinois has both alfisol soil and molisol soil.

D. Incorrect: *Pennsylvania.* Based on the maps, Pennsylvania has alfisol soil but does not have mollisol soil.

E. Incorrect: *Nebraska.* Based on the maps, Nebraska has mollisol soil but does not have alfisol soil.

Item Number 2 *(Lesson 12)*

F. **Correct:** *Iowa is part of the Grain Belt.* The Grain Belt is described as a region that produces much of the country's grain crop. Mollisol soil is used principally for growing grain and on the Map of Mollisol Soil, Iowa is almost entirely shaded.

G. Incorrect: *Nevada grows lots of wine grapes.* Wine grapes are grown on alfisol soil. According the Map of Alfisol Soil, Nevada has very little of this type of soil. This is not a reasonable conclusion.

H. Incorrect: *Florida produces the most corn.* Although Florida does contain alfisol soil according to the map, and this soil is used for producing corn, there is nothing in the map or question that indicates that Florida does produce corn or that it produces the most corn.

J. Incorrect: *The East Cost is part of the Grain Belt.* The Grain Belt is described as a region that produces much of the country's grain crop. Mollisol soil is used principally for growing grain, and on the Map of Mollisol Soil, the East Coast does not have a lot of shading.

K. Incorrect: *Georgia produces the most grain.* Mollisol soil is used for growing grain, and according to the map, Georgia does not have any of this soil.

Item Number 3 *(Lesson 12)*

A. Incorrect: *She is sensitive to dyes that contain peroxide.* Demi-permanent hair color does contain low levels of peroxide.

B. Incorrect: *She wants a color that will wash out in 6–12 shampoos.* While semi-permanent colors wash out in 6–12 shampoos, demi-permanent colors last 12–24 shampoos.

C. Incorrect: *She wants to spend less than $50 on her hair color.* A demi-permanent color costs $75.00.

D. Incorrect: *Soledad is her preferred stylist.* While Soledad is a stylist for semi-permanent color, she is not for demi-permanent color.

E. **Correct:** *She wants temporary color that will cover and blend gray hair.* According to the chart, demi-permanent color, lasts "12–24 shampoos" and works to "cover and blend gray hair."

Item Number 4 *(Lesson 12)*

F. **Correct:** *Peroxide is an ingredient that helps to lighten or darken hair.* According to the table, peroxide is used in hair dyes for lightening and darkening hair color.

G. Incorrect: *Peroxide is used only to darken hair.* While peroxide is used for darkening hair color, it is also used in permanent hair coloring, which is used for lightening hair as well.

H. Incorrect: *If hair dye contains peroxide, it cannot be used after perming or relaxing.* Demi-permanent color, which contains low levels of peroxide, is suitable for use after perming or relaxing.

J. Incorrect: *Peroxide is an ingredient that must be used in all hair dyes.* Semi-permanent hair dye does not contain any peroxide.

K. Incorrect: *Peroxide is used only when the hair dye is permanent.* Low levels of peroxide are used in demi-permanent dyes, which are not permanent.

Item Number 5 *(Lesson 12)*

A. Incorrect: *Flight option 1.* Although this is within the budget, it is not the quickest way possible within the budget.

B. Incorrect: *Train option 1.* Although this is within the budget, there is another option also within the budget that is much quicker.

C. **Correct:** *Flight option 2.* This answer is both within the budget ($162) and timely (1 hour 31 minutes to Washington, DC).

D. Incorrect: *Train option 2.* While this is the quickest of the two train options, it is not within budget. There is another option that is both less expensive and more time efficient.

E. Incorrect: *Flight option 4.* Although this is the quickest time to Boston, it is well over the budget.

Item Number 6 *(Lesson 12)*

F. Incorrect: *He wants to arrive in Washington, DC by 3:30.* The express train arrives in Washington, DC at 3:01 P.M., so this is a reasonable conclusion. The only other option is flight option 4, which is far more expensive.

G. Incorrect: *He has a higher travel budget than the sales representative.* The total cost of a round trip train for a trip to Washington, DC is $172 over the sales representative's travel budget of $200. This is a reasonable conclusion.

H. Incorrect: *He is not concerned about how long it takes him to reach his destination.* Four other travel options would get him to Washington, DC quicker. If he were concerned with time, he would likely choose to fly.

J. **Correct:** *He needs to get there in the quickest possible way.* This is not a reasonable conclusion because if he wanted to get there the quickest way possible, he would choose to fly rather than take a train.

K. Incorrect: *He prefers to travel on trains instead of airplanes.* Cost and time are two common factors when booking a trip. Two of the flights are less expensive and all are quicker. Therefore, it is reasonable to conclude that the reason for his choice is that he prefers to travel by train.

Item Number 7 *(Lesson 12)*

A. Incorrect: *Johnson.* Johnson's sales increased at times, but he was not the best salesman.

B. Incorrect: *Diaz.* Diaz increased sales near the end of the year, but his overall performance was not the best.

C. Incorrect: *Wu.* Wu's performance is about average compared to the other associates.

D. Incorrect: *Martinez.* Martinez drastically underperformed compared to the other associates.

E. **Correct:** *O'Conner.* O'Conner consistently outsold most of the other sales associates.

Item Number 8 *(Lesson 12)*

F. Incorrect: *Wu is the least successful at selling cell phones.* In general, Wu's line is in the middle of the chart. This does not make her the least successful.

G. Incorrect: *O'Conner sold the most cell phones each month.* Although O'Conner often had the most number of cell phone sales, there were a few months when Johnson sold the same number of phones or more. Be aware of answers that use absolute terms like "always."

H. **Correct:** *Halfway through the year, Martinez's cell phone sales began to consistently increase.* Beginning in June, Martinez's cell phone sales consistently increased.

J. Incorrect: *Halfway through the year, Wu's cell phone sales began to consistently decrease.* Although Wu's cell phone sales dropped from June into August, after that they began to increase rather than consistently decrease.

K. Incorrect: *Every sales associate sold more phones in November than in December.* While O'Conner and Wu sold more phones in November than in December, Johnson, Diaz, and Martinez sold more phones in December.

Item Number 9 *(Lesson 13)*

A. Incorrect: *Are you a smoker?* There is nothing in the table that indicates health questions, such as if the employee is a smoker, are part of choosing among the three health plans.

B. **Correct:** *Do you have children?* The costs of the health plans vary based on certain criteria such as the number of children.

C. Incorrect: *Do you need dental care?* There is nothing in the table that indicates that any of these plans include or do not include dental care.

D. Incorrect: *Are you the primary insurance provider for the family?* All of the plans assume that the employee is the primary insurance provider. If the employee was on his or her spouse's insurance and was not the primary, he or she would not ask you for help picking a plan.

E. Incorrect: *Can you afford $700 a month?* There are a variety of prices for the health plans, but not even the most expensive one is $700 a month.

Item Number 10 *(Lesson 13)*

F. Incorrect: *$40.* While $40 is the difference for an 18–30 year old Plan A subscriber with a spouse versus without a spouse, there is not enough information in the question to determine that this is correct.

G. Incorrect: *$83.* While $83 is the difference for an 18–30 year old Plan B subscriber with a spouse versus without a spouse, there is not enough information in the question to determine that this is correct.

H. Incorrect: *Not enough information. You need to know her age and if she is the primary insurance provider for the family.* You already know that she is the primary. There is also another piece of missing information you need to find the answer.

J. Incorrect: *Not enough information. You need to know which plan she has.* While you do need to know which plan she has to figure out the answer, there is another piece of information you need as well.

K. **Correct:** *Not enough information. You need to know the spouse's age and which plan the employee has.* To figure out the difference between the costs, you need to know both the spouse's age and which of the three plans she has.

Item Number 11 *(Lesson 13)*

A. **Correct:** *Atrium for cocktails; Ballroom for the banquet.* The Atrium, which fits 1,200 people for a cocktail reception, will fit all the people without being too big. The Ballroom, which fits 1,400 people for a sit-down banquet, will also fit all of the people without being too big.

B. Incorrect: *Theater for cocktails; Atrium for the banquet.* Theater is a style of sitting people, not a room in the Carmichael Civic Center. While the Atrium would fit enough people for the cocktail reception, it seats only 900 people for a sit-down banquet.

C. Incorrect: *Field House for cocktails; Ballroom for the banquet.* Although the Field House fits up to 2,500 people for a cocktail reception, you have less than half that amount and it is not attached to the center, and therefore it would not be a good choice. The Ballroom, which fits 1,400 people for a sit-down banquet, will work for the sit-down banquet.

D. Incorrect: *Ballroom for cocktails; Field House for the banquet.* The Ballroom fits nearly twice as many people as you need for a cocktail reception; a better choice would be a smaller room. The Field House seats 2,500 people for a sit-down banquet, much more than what you need, and it is not attached to the center.

E. Incorrect: *Clubhouse Lounge for cocktails; Atrium for the banquet.* The Clubhouse Lounge does not fit enough people for your cocktail reception. While the Atrium would be enough room for the cocktail reception, it only seats 900 for a sit-down banquet.

Item Number 12 *(Lesson 13)*

F. Incorrect: *Priority Suite.* The Priority Suite fits up to 150 people for a cocktail reception. The maximum number of guests will be only 50 people, so you do not need that much room.

G. **Correct:** *Super Suite.* The Super Suite fits up to 70 people for a cocktail reception. If all of the sales representative's bring a guest, there would be a total of 50 people. The Super Suite is a good size for 50 people.

H. Incorrect: *Luxury Suite.* The Luxury Suite fits up to 30 people for a cocktail reception. If it was just the sales representatives, this would be big enough. However, since the representatives are invited to bring a date, you need to choose a room that will fit up to 50 people.

J. Incorrect: *Atrium.* The Atrium fits up to 1,200 people for a cocktail reception. This is much more room than you need.

K. Incorrect: *Clubhouse Lounge.* The Clubhouse Lounge fits up to 300 people for a cocktail reception. This is more room than you need.

Item Number 13 *(Lesson 13)*

A. Incorrect: *Growing genetically engineered crops have no negative effects.* The increased use of pesticide could be linked to genetically engineered crops.

B. **Correct:** *After an initial decrease when genetically engineered crops were introduced, pesticide use has increased every year.* The data from the graphs confirm there may be a

relationship between genetically engineered crops and pesticide use.

C. Incorrect: *Since 1996, the use of pesticides has decreased.* Pesticide use has increased since 1999.

D. Incorrect: *The yield of genetically engineered crops has increased more than 15 percent.* The graphs do not indicate any change in yield occurred, though this may be assumed based on the line graph.

E. Incorrect: *Less pesticide is needed to grow genetically engineered crops.* Pesticide use has increased while genetically engineered crops have also become more prevalent, suggesting that the opposite is true.

Item Number 14 *(Lesson 13)*

F. Incorrect: *It decreased and then increased.* According to the graph although the percentage did decrease in 2000, this was after three years of increase.

G. Incorrect: *It increased and then decreased.* According to the graph, the percentage only decreased once during the time period shown.

H. Incorrect: *It remained the same.* According to the graph, the percentage did not remain the same from 2000 to 2008.

J. Incorrect: *It steadily decreased.* According to the graph, the opposite is true.

K. **Correct:** *It steadily increased.* According to the graph, the percentage steadily increased from 2000 to 2008.

Item Number 15 *(Lesson 13)*

A. Incorrect: *Block A1.* Block A1 contains Early Gold apples. While these do ripen in late August, the customer is looking for berries, not apples.

B. **Correct:** *Row B3.* Blackberries, which ripen from Late July to Late August, are located in row B3.

C. Incorrect: *Row B1.* Row B1 contains Cherries, which ripen from Late June to Mid July. The customer is looking for berries that are ripe later, in late August.

D. Incorrect: *Circle P2.* Circle P2 contains yellow peaches, which are not berries and do not ripen in late August.

E. Incorrect: *Row A3.* Row A3 contains Empire apples, which are not berries and do not ripen until October.

Item Number 16 *(Lesson 13)*

F. Incorrect: *Early Gold.* While Early Gold apples are the apples that ripen the earliest, they are located in the blocks of apples. The teacher is only concerned with the apples in the rows.

G. Incorrect: *McIntosh.* Although McIntosh apples are one of the earliest apples to ripen, they are located in the blocks, not in the rows.

H. Incorrect: *Golden Delicious.* Golden Delicious apples ripen in October, but there is another type of apple that ripens earlier.

J. Incorrect: *Empire.* Empire apples ripen in October, but there is another type of apple that ripens earlier.

K. **Correct:** *Red Delicious.* Red Delicious apples ripen from late September to October, and are located in the rows of apples.

Item Number 17 *(Lesson 14)*

A. Incorrect: *Silicon steel or tool steel.* Silicon steel is used for "electric motors," which would include a blender motor. However, nothing under the uses for tool steel indicates it could be used for a blender motor.

B. Incorrect: *Stainless steel or cast iron.* Stainless steel is used for "food processing products," which would include a blender motor. However, nothing under the uses for cast iron indicates it could be used for a blender motor.

C. **Correct:** *Stainless steel or silicon steel.* Stainless steel is used for "food processing products," which would include a blender motor. Silicon steel is used for "electric motors," which would also include a blender motor.

D. Incorrect: *Cast iron or silicon steel.* Nothing under the uses for cast iron indicates it could be used for a blender motor. Silicon steel is used for "electric motors," which would include a blender motor.

E. Incorrect: *Tool steel or cast iron.* Nothing under the uses for tool steel or cast iron indicates that these alloys could be used for a blender motor.

Item Number 18 *(Lesson 14)*

F. Incorrect: *Stainless steel.* The fourth column in the chart lists how the different alloys are commonly used. Stainless steel is not commonly used in electric motors.

G. **Correct:** *Silicon steel.* Silicon steel is used in transformers and electric motors, so this would be an iron alloy that is used for building an electric motor.

H. Incorrect: *Tool steel.* Tool steel is used to create tools, not electric motors.

J. Incorrect: *Cast iron.* Cast iron is used to create pots, pans, and bridges, not to create electric motors.

K. Incorrect: *Any of the alloys will work.* Electric motors only appear in the silicon steel row as a use. The others alloys do not list electric motors.

Item Number 19 *(Lesson 14)*

A. Incorrect: *Twelfth Page; 4/color; 52 times.* This ad fits within the budget and it is in color, but it is not the largest size ad possible within the budget.

B. Incorrect: *Third Page; 4/color; 29 times.* This ad does not fit within the $2,500 budget you were given to work with.

C. Incorrect: *Quarter Page; 4/color; 52 times.* This ad does not fit within the $1,400 budget for an ad that is run 52 times.

D. **Correct:** *Quarter Page; 4/color; 29 times.* This ad is within budget constraints, in color, and is the largest size you can run and still meet the other requirements.

E. Incorrect: *Full Page; 4/color; 52 times.* While this ad is the biggest size of all of the answer options and is in color, it does not fit the budget guidelines.

Item Number 20 *(Lesson 14)*

F. Incorrect: *Quarter Page; B&W; 29 times.* Although this is within budget, you want to run the ad as many times as possible, which would be 52 times, not 29.

G. Incorrect: *Sixth Page; B&W; 52 times.* This is the correct size and the correct number of times, but you can also run the ad in 4 color and stay in your budget for 52 times. Although the directions say it is "acceptable for the ad to be in black and white," it is not necessary. Since the color is within your budget, you should choose the ad that runs 52 times at a sixth page in color.

H. Incorrect: *Quarter Page; 4/color; 29 times.* This ad is within your budget, but you want to run it 52 times, not 29.

J. Incorrect: *Quarter Page; 4/color; 52 times.* This is not within your $1,400 budget for 52 times.

K. **Correct:** *Sixth Page; 4/color; 52 times.* The sixth page ad is the largest ad that fits within your budget for 52 times. The black and white is within the budget and while black and white is acceptable, it is not required. For only $90 more (and still $410 under budget) you can have the ad appear in color.

Item Number 21 *(Lesson 14)*

A. Incorrect: *It has the most fat.* At 18 grams of fat, the fish sandwich has more total fat than the chicken sandwich.

B. **Correct:** *It has the most sodium.* The chicken sandwich has the most sodium of the three sandwiches with 830 grams.

C. Incorrect: *It has the most calories.* The fish sandwich has 380 calories, which is more than the 360 calories in the chicken sandwich.

D. Incorrect: *It has the least amount of iron.* The fish sandwich, not the chicken sandwich, has the least amount of iron.

E. Incorrect: *It has the least amount of saturated fat.* While it is true that the chicken sandwich has the least amount of saturated fat, this is a good nutritional quality of the chicken sandwich. This would be a reason to recommend the chicken sandwich rather than a reason to not recommend it.

Item Number 22 *(Lesson 14)*

F. **Correct:** *It has the least calories from fat.* Of the three sandwiches, the hamburger has the least amount of calories from fat with only 80.

G. Incorrect: *It is the largest sandwich.* At 3.5 ounces, the hamburger is actually the smallest sandwich.

H. Incorrect: *It has the most calcium.* The fish sandwich, not the hamburger, has the most calcium.

J. Incorrect: *It has the least sugars.* The hamburger has one gram more of sugar than both the chicken sandwich and fish sandwich.

K. Incorrect: *It has the most dietary fiber.* All of the sandwiches have the same amount of dietary fiber.